C000172883

THE BOOK OF
MINEHEAD
WITH ALCOMBE

The Book of Minehead *with Alcombe*

Hilary Binding
& Douglas Stevens

HALSGROVE

First published in Great Britain in 2000
Revised and reprinted 2012

British Library Cataloguing-in-Publication Data
A CIP record for this title is available from the British Library

ISBN 978 0 85704 177 7

HALSGROVE
Halsgrove House,
Ryelands Business Park,
Bagley Road, Wellington, Somerset TA21 9PZ
Tel: 01823 653777 Fax: 01823 216796
email: sales@halsgrove.com

Part of the Halsgrove group of companies
Information on all Halsgrove titles is available at: www.halsgrove.com

Printed and bound in China by Everbest Printing Ltd

Image on title page: *A girl in Tithings Court, 1890s(?)* (Harold Lomas)

Preface to 1977 Edition

How does one commemorate one hundred years of business, of service to the community, of the many, many, friends made? We felt that sponsoring this new history of Minehead would be a way. My grandfather, Isaac Floyd, started his own business in Minehead and used to travel the countryside on his pony serving the country folk and farmers from 1877 onwards. Then, helped by his wife, a shop was established. The family grew up, three sons and two daughters entering the business. The shop was enlarged and being a corner site it became a landmark and a focal point in the life of the town, eventually turning into a department store.

In writing these few words I would like to pay tribute to the very loyal staff, past and present, who have served the firm over the years. What must remain unwritten is a whole book of anecdotes about life at Floyds! I would also like to thank our two historians, Hilary Binding and Douglas Stevens, for the hours of painstaking research and toil they have devoted to the writing of this book; and to thank also all those mentioned in the acknowledgements.

Bernard Culverwell
March 1977
Managing Director and grandson of the founder of Floyds of Minehead

Maypole team (taught by Mrs Howard) in the Mentone field in the Parks, c.1925. Left to right, back: Elsie Slade, Dora Hatch, Hilda Upham, Dora Cornish, Kathleen Jones, ? Price, Phyllis Steer, Dorothy Court, Joyce Webber, Eirene Beer, Doris Martin, Winifred Morris, Viola Seaward, Joan Plenty; front: Iris Symons, Doris Coles, Marjorie Plenty, Edna Tarr, Gwen Jones, Lily Cornish, Vera Plenty, Betty Long, Vera Uppington, Dorothy Farmer, Margaret Hill.

Model yacht club outside the Pier Hotel, early 1900s.

Greenaleigh Farm: popular Victorian and Edwardian venue for cream teas and junket.

Contents

Preface to 1977 Edition 5
Acknowledgements 8
Introduction 11

Chapter 1: Minehead: 1066-1485 13
Chapter 2: The Manor of Minehead: 1485-1800 23
Chapter 3: The Port of Minehead: 1500-1800 29
Chapter 4: The Parliamentary Borough: 1559-1832 41
Chapter 5: War, Privateering and Smuggling 49
Chapter 6: Church and Chapel: 1485-1800 61
Chapter 7: Law and Order: 1500-1800 71
Chapter 8: The Town and People: 1500-1800 81
Chapter 9: Poverty and Agriculture: 1791-1851 91
Chapter 10: Holiday Resort: 1794-1901 103
Chapter 11: Education: 1767-1998 113
Chapter 12: Religion: 1800-1900 117
Chapter 13: Industry: 1750-1950 121
Chapter 14: Shopping, c.1900 125
Chapter 15: Alcombe: 1086-1953 129
Chapter 16: Search for Identity: The Twentieth Century 141
Chapter 17: After the Millennium 156

Acknowledgements to 1977 Edition

During the preparation and writing of this book we have been given generous help by very many people. It is not possible to mention each one by name but we are nonetheless grateful for their ready assistance and encouragement. Without the initiative and sponsorship of Mr Bernard Culverwell our work would never have begun. Prebendary Hancock's *History of Minehead* provided an invaluable starting point and a mine of information for our labours. Our thanks are due to Colonel Walter Luttrell for allowing us to photograph some of his family portraits and use the remarkable collection of Luttrell papers in the Somerset Record Office. The staff of the Somerset Record Office have patiently advised and assisted us in every way. The County Archivist, Mr Ivor Collis, and the Assistant Archivist, Mr Derek Shorrocks, have given valuable help. Dr R.W. Dunning and Mr Robin Bush have introduced us to material we might otherwise have overlooked and helped on many occasions with the interpretation of documents. Mr David Bromwich at the Local History Library in Taunton and Mrs K. Evans, the Minehead Librarian, and her staff, have given generous assistance.

Miss Carol Angus researched the section on Education and Mr Brian Murless that on the Minehead Brickworks. Mr D.J.S. Gardner provided information on Minehead Postal History. Minehead Local History Study Group did patient work on the tithe map, the 1851 census, the *West Somerset Free Press* and other documents. Their interest and support has been invaluable. Mr J.K. Ridler read parts of the script and offered useful advice as did Mr and Mrs R.J.S. Orwin. Mr W.M. Wigfield drew our attention to the papers deposited by the Society of Friends at the Somerset Record Office, and Mr John Gilman made us aware of two important petitions and of Captain Nathaniel Bullocke who wrote one of them.

We are grateful to Prebendary Ward and the churchwardens of St Michael's, Minehead, for permission to examine the large collection of parish papers and particularly to Mr E. Lewis for arranging access to them. Mr Frank Hawtin kindly organised an archaeological dig on a supposedly mass grave. Through no fault of his, eight days of hard work produced no evidence in support of this ancient tradition. Mr Michael Aston gave advice on archaeology, and Commander E.H.P. Williams helped in dating several old buildings. Dr R.F. Youell advised on local mineral deposits. Mr Tom Smith allowed us to use and quote freely from his unpublished thesis on the Luttrells and Minehead. Mr Jack Hurley gave ready access to back numbers of the *West Somerset Free Press* and much helpful advice. Mr Archie Galliford researched and prepared the initial copies of the maps and drew the 'Map of West Somerset Coast' and Surbey's Survey. The remainder were drawn by Mr Robert Winn of Taunton. Mr R.G. Larcombe and Mr Brian Murless enlivened the text with their drawings.

For permission to reproduce the pictures we wish particularly to thank the Ilfracombe Museum, Victoria and Albert Museum, Mr Ivor Lomas, Colonel Walter Luttrell, Mr J.R.A. Thorne, Mr R. Kingsley Tayler, Mr F.A. Bennett, Mr David Jessup and Castle Studios, Nether Stowey. We extend our thanks to many others, impossible to name individually. Mesdames Elizabeth Aldred, Catherine Babbage and Irene Crail all typed parts of the script, and Mrs Christine Stevens typed and revised a number of chapters. Mr Victor Bonham-Carter saw the book through the press.

H.B. and D.S.

Note: *Generally throughout the book quotations have been modernised in both spelling and punctuation, but occasionally the original form has been retained.*

Acknowledgements to 2012 Edition

I would like to thank the many people who have helped me compile this book, provided information and lent photographs. Besides those people credited opposite I would especially like to thank Alcombe Methodist Church, Leslie Axon, Ray Blackwell, Dorothy Bryant, Jackie Burge, Tony Calloway, the late Roy Chenappa, Margaret Chorley, Dennis and Cecily Corner, Oliver Davies, Ruby Edbrooke, Carol Ell, the late Lady Fisher of Lambeth, members of the Henson and Hagley families, Mike Hine, Violet Jones, Molly Kievill, Middleton Press (P. Conibeare), Minehead Library, Minehead and West Somerset Golf Club, Ken Portch, the Red Cross (West Somerset), Malcolm Scott, Somerset Archaeological and Natural History Society, Adam Stanley, the staff at Westerley, Margaret Williams and Vera Yeandle.

In preparing this volume for publication I have often thought of Douglas Stevens, co-author of the text, with affection, and have wished that he were still here to discuss knotty problems of fact and interpretation. I thank him for his inspiration.

In addition to the many people who over the years have helped and encouraged me in researching the story of Minehead, I would like to thank all those patient Minehead folk who have answered my persistent questions and frantic emails while I have been preparing the new edition of this book. Thanks too to everyone who has provided images - they are credited in the text.

Hilary Binding
2012

Blacksmiths at Court Green, c.1905.

The Parish Church from Lower Moor Farm.

Introduction

The seaside resort of Minehead is situated at the foot of North Hill, an outcrop of Exmoor which rises steeply from the shore and shelters the town from the prevailing winds. Some 1000 years or more ago Minehead nestled close to the hill with three separate settlements centred around the church, the mill and the harbour, but in the nineteenth century it expanded rapidly and shops and houses now occupy most of the lowland area within the parish boundaries. Many of the new houses are occupied by people who have retired to the town from other areas and who make up a high percentage of Minehead's population. In the summer the town caters for thousands of holiday visitors, many of whom stay at Butlins while others seek the traditional beauty and solitude of the surrounding countryside.

Booting the victim in the Parade on Hobby Horse Day c. 1890.

Minehead's name has often been thought to be connected with mining but this is not the case. The name is first found in written documents in 1046 in the form Mynheafdon. Other forms include Maneheve in the Domesday Book, Menehewed in 1225 and Menedun in the same year. The first element of the name is similar to the Welsh mynydd and is the Old English myned meaning a hill. The second element, dun, also means a hill, so Minehead is clearly named after the north hill behind which it shelters. The settlements of Myne, formerly on the hill itself, took their names similarly. Bratton, spelt earlier Bracton, comes from the word Braectun meaning a newly-cultivated settlement. This seems to indicate that Bratton was a secondary settlement, developed in Saxon times when the population of Minehead outgrew its original site and looked elsewhere for subsistence.

Prehistoric man preferred the higher land in the area to the valley mouth which must often have been liable to flooding. Numbers of microlithic flints have been found both on North Hill and at Higher Hopcott indicating that Mesolithic man roamed the area in search of food. Flint arrowheads of the Bronze Age have also been found and there is a group of fairly small round barrows near Selworthy Beacon. Unfortunately these have suffered from the ravages of the military occupation during the Second World War.

In the Iron Age settlers made an enclosure on the hill spur now known as Furzebury Brake near the ruins of East Myne Farm. A five-foot high rampart circles half an acre of land. A stream in Grexy Combe would have supplied water, and there are signs of a Celtic field system nearby where the land may have been cultivated during the Iron Age. Such a settlement, poised on the hill, a fine lookout place, may well have survived until the coming of the Saxons in the eighth and ninth centuries. It is unlikely that the Romans lingered in the area, preferring to reach the look-out station at Glenthome by sea, though they may have followed a coastal route from the seaward end of the Poldens through the region.

The Saxons probably settled in Minehead first for its fishing potential. There is no record of Viking attacks on Minehead at the time of those on Porlock and Watchet, which indicates that Minehead was still relatively unimportant. Gradually the place developed, Bratton was settled and at Myne Saxons eventually occupied the ancient farm. Land was cleared and cultivated; crops grown and stock kept, and fish supplemented the villagers' diet. This is how the people of Minehead lived at the time of the Norman Conquest.

Top and above: *The building commonly known as the Old Priory, c.1880. Built in the late-fifteenth century, it may have been owned by one of the groups of monastic landowners in Minehead; the same building as a restaurant, c.1910.*

Chapter 1
Minehead: 1066–1485

One of the earliest written references to Minehead is in the Domesday Book; the return made for taxation purposes in 1086 under the direction of King William I. It is there, then, that we will begin our detailed look at Minehead's history. However, the bare facts about a place taken from that survey can prove confusing and irrelevant to the ordinary reader, without some explanation of how land was held and worked during the early Norman period.

It is very easy to generalise on this matter and specialists will perhaps forgive the following simplification. In 1086 England was divided into manors; sizeable pieces of land each granted to their respective 'lord' by the king. Such manors were similar to small villages but did not necessarily correspond with a particular village or parish. In Minehead parish there were three manors.

Within these manors the land was divided between the lord himself, who might be resident or non-resident, and the people of the manor who were granted varying amounts of land in return for specific work and other duties on the lord's land. In this way all the arable land was worked and subsistence was provided for everyone without recourse to money. The lord's land was known as 'demesne' land. In many places, including Minehead, the arable land was in two or three huge, open fields divided into strips. Each man, including the lord, held a number of these strips scattered about the open fields. The fields were worked communally: in any one year one field was usually sown with wheat, another with barley and beans, and the third lay fallow and provided rough grazing so that the soil might regain some of its goodness. Besides the arable land, there was also pasture, meadow and woodland, some held in demesne and some being set aside for common use.

The men of the village each had a particular status. Villeins and bordars to a lesser and greater extent were tied to the land and their lord, while the life of the serf or slave was completely under the lord's control. The presence of individual farms apart from the main open fields in Minehead implies that some of the villeins held a status fairly near to that of freemen - those who are not mentioned in the Domesday entries for the town may in some cases have been free landowners in their own right. One question that is difficult to answer is what the terms 'hide' and 'virgate' mean in the Domesday record for the Minehead manors. The hide is a unit of land for taxation purposes and originally of an acreage that could support one family. The acreage would vary from place to place depending on the type of land in question. A virgate was a fourth part of a hide.

A five-hide manor was a common unit in West Somerset but the description was arbitrary and the acreage irrelevant. By the fourteenth century a virgate had become a stereotyped 48-acre unit and was the standard for land-holdings from the de Mohuns, the lords of Dunster and Minehead at that time. Clearly the information in the Domesday survey is not comprehensive. It was provided in answer to specific questions; given orally to clerks unaccustomed in some cases to the local dialect and needed for government administration and taxation purposes. We must not expect too much from the Domesday returns.

The Norman Settlement

Just before the Norman Conquest the area now covered by the ecclesiastical parish of Minehead consisted mainly of three small manors, Minehead, Bratton and Mene. Within these manors, but apart from the main groupings of population, there were, almost certainly, a number of small farmholdings. Minehead was the largest unit belonging to the Saxon lord Algar who also held Alcombe. Nearby lay the fertile lands of Bratton in the valley and on the hill the more austere moorland holding of Mene. Bratton belonged to Aelfric who also held Dunster while Mene was held by Leofwin. After the Norman settlement, the three manors were linked to the great estates of the Mohun family with their fortress at Dunster, built to maintain order in the west of Somerset. William de Mohun who came from Moyon, near St Lo in Normandy, fought with King William at Hastings and was his formidable representative in Somerset, holding at least seventy manors, most within the county, and filling the office of Sheriff of Somerset. His successors were also King's men, involved in national affairs, often at court, who would have left much of the administration of the estates to local officials who would have been responsible for their good management.

In 1086 the Domesday record tells us that Minehead was held directly by William de Mohun. The manor was taxed for five hides, a usual unit in the West Country for the provision of a knight to the royal host but not implying any particular acreage. Two and a half hides were held by the lord in demesne with ploughland enough for three ploughs and this was worked by twelve slaves. Twenty-seven villeins and twenty-two smallholders (bordars) worked the remaining two and a half hides having ploughland for ten ploughs together with twelve acres of meadow, twenty-four acres of woodland and pasture, four leagues by two leagues in extent. Stock held included one horse, sixteen beasts (oxen), ten swine and 300 sheep, the latter and the large amount of pasture implying the intensive use of rough grazing around the cultivated fields of the manor. There was also a mill.

Mene, to the north-east of Selworthy Beacon, was also held by William de Mohun, and was sub-let to Geoffrey. This manor was much smaller, only being taxed for half a hide. It seems to have been worked primarily as a sheep farm from Dunster, for there were 107 sheep and fifty she-goats run on the fifty acres of pasture. There was also one acre of meadow and four acres of wood. The ploughland for two ploughs was held in demesne and was worked by four slaves and also one bordar. The number of sheep, 407, running on these two manors, indicates that there may have been some central planning from Dunster which allocated sheep to these manors with so much moorland grazing. The wool was perhaps brought to a common weighing point before being put out for processing or sold out of the area. This would correspond with William de Mohun's use of the manor of Cutcombe as a centre for horse-rearing. We do not know when the manor of Mene was taken directly into the hands of the lord but it was probably fairly early since there is no reference to it as a separate manor in any later documents.

The de Mohun family continued to hold Minehead and Mene along with Dunster until, in 1375, Joan was left a widow by John de Mohun who appears to have been in financial difficulties. It seems that he deliberately left land to his wife in such a way that it could be sold after his death. Joan, whose three daughters all married well, preferred the high life in London to country life in West Somerset and willingly sold the reversion of the Dunster estates to Lady Elizabeth Luttrell for 10 000 marks. Elizabeth, daughter of the Earl of Devon and a great-granddaughter of Edward I, had married, perhaps beneath her but perhaps for love, Andrew Luttrell, a member of a younger branch of the family who held East Quantoxhead. Although she did not outlive Joan to enjoy her Dunster purchase, Elizabeth must have been content to know that her son Hugh would inherit the Dunster estates, although they were only finally secured for him after a lawsuit involving Joan de Mohun's daughters.

Throughout the 1400s the Luttrell men were involved in national affairs and the administration of the estates would have been left to the steward and bailiff. Although in later years Luttrells were to take an active interest in the running of the estate, at this stage they were content to leave it to the professionals to raise as much income from the manors as was possible. During the Wars of the Roses James Luttrell's involvement in the Lancastrian cause meant that, with the Yorkist success at the Battle of Wakefield, he was attainted with others of treason. His estates were seized by Edward IV in 1461 and granted to Sir William Herbert in 1463. James had been killed in the Battle of St Albans in 1461 so it was to his heirs that the estates were restored after the Battle of Bosworth in 1485.

Throughout much of the later-medieval period the de Mohuns and then the Luttrells held Minehead, along with Dunster and Kilton; Bratton, however, continued to be held as a separate manor although Mene was quickly absorbed into the de Mohun holding and lost its individuality. Bratton was given to William under the Norman Settlement and sub-let to Roger. It was a small valley manor of three virgates. Two virgates were held in demesne and these included enough land for two ploughs which was worked by one slave. Two villeins and four bordars worked the other virgate with two ploughs. There were twelve beasts and sixty she-goats, two acres of meadow and one hundred acres of pasture. This manor had been greatly improved since the Norman takeover and had increased in value from five shillings to thirty shillings, much more than the average.

By the early 1300s Bratton was held by a family who had taken their name from the manor. Robert de Bratton was granted land in Wydon during the reign of Edward I and was presumably well established in the area by the end of 1317. An oratory at Bratton was licensed by Bishop Drokensford for Robert de Bracton to be served by his own priest. There are no grounds for believing that Henry de Bracton, the great jurist, was a member of this particular family. The male de Bratton line died out during the reign of Henry VIII and the property was then held by two sisters, Alice, who married William Fry of Yarty, and Joan, wife of William Sedborough of Lynor Abbot in Devonshire. In 1565 the Sedborough part was sold to William Fry and the Fry family then

Top: *Bratton Court. The gatehouse looking inwards. Note the use of oak in the window frame.*

Above: *Bratton Court. The gatehouse from the courtyard. The louvred chimney was perhaps originally set in the roof of the hall.*

owned Bratton until 1726. In that year Robert Fry died leaving only his youngest daughter who married the second Lord King to whose family the property passed. The present owner, Lord Lytton, is a descendant of this family.

Bratton Court was the manor house and within the four-square protective courtyard the house retains the core of the medieval hall with the remains of the screen and entrance passage, at the north end. At the south end is a room which was probably the original parlour or private room for the lord and his family. At an angle to this main block stands a two-storey perpendicular-style building which once contained kitchens and storerooms on the ground floor and above is a room traditionally held to be the chapel of the manor house. Opposite is the gatehouse with substantial gates of oak. A feature of the house is the use of oak for many of the window frames, evidence that although stone was available, wood was a common building material. Another example of this use is the unusual wooden arch separating a side chapel from the chancel in St Michael's Church.

There is still a great deal of work, both on documents and on the ground, to be done on the early history of Minehead and so only the most tentative ideas can be put forward about the town during the Norman period. One thing that seems certain is that although there is no mention of a fishing industry in Minehead in the Domesday return, the port must by then have been established for fishing if not for trade. John Gilman sees the origin of Minehead in such a fishing settlement, and certainly a large number of people would have been involved primarily in making a living from the sea by the eleventh century. These would be over and above the agricultural tenants numbered in the survey and their simple huts would have been clustered at the foot of North Hill below the North Field.

To understand the topography of Minehead at Domesday, we have to rely to a certain extent on maps of a later date and on the continuity of place names. Maps of eighteenth- and nineteenth-century Minehead show clearly an earlier open-field system spreading to the north and south of the stream which now runs underground through the town from the Parks to the sea. If the twenty-seven villeins of the Domesday account are to be regarded as free farmers, some of them must have held a small acreage in the open fields, while others held larger consolidated units on the ancient sites around the church established on the hill and at Periton, Woodcombe, Hindon, Wydon, Lynch and Combeshead. All these farms seem likely to be of Saxon origin since their names incorporate Old English elements even though they are not mentioned by name until the 1200s. These smallholdings of the villeins would

North Hill in 1874. The medieval strip-farming pattern is still discernible in the lower fields, once part of the North Field. In the foreground are heaps of limestone imported from Aberthaw waiting to be processed in the limekiln that was sited at the bottom corner of the present Northfield Hotel garden. This scene was recorded by James Date on his photographic expedition to Minehead.

have consisted of simple wood-framed huts and barns surrounded by small arable fields and rough pasture, and constant back-breaking work was needed to maintain a reasonable standard of subsistence. In Minehead itself would have lived the remaining villeins; the smallholders who held land in the open fields and who worked the lord's manor as well as their own, and the serfs or slaves who worked primarily for the lord and for other freemen. The homes of all of these were grouped partly around the church near the North Field and partly around the mill above the South Field.

Monastic Landowners

By AD1100 a sizeable section of the manor of Minehead, one hide, about a fifth, had been granted by the first William de Mohun to the Benedictine Abbey at Bath as part of the endowment of a new priory to be built at Dunster. Presumably William had found a church established at Minehead for he was able to grant the abbey half of the tithes there as well. The benefaction was confirmed by the second William de Mohun and the boundaries of the hide of land specified. They ran from:

Horstonesdene by the Way called Wynneweye to Southdonnerugg and by the Kings Highway from Southdonnerugg to Stoneburge, thence to the water of Malferlegham, thence by that water to la Mulepoleshevd from Staunton, thence by a cross-way to the ditch on the other part of the way, and by that ditch to the way which extends beyond the cell next (?) of Staunton, thence by La Rygges to la Merchlane, thence to Wytestone, thence to Yaldych thence to le Wydepulle, thence to Horssawold and thence by the old ditch on the south part of the pool to Horscomscumbe.

Although it is not possible to identify every landmark the land clearly ran in a sweeping semi-circle from North Hill, between Bratton and the Parks, up Middlecombe Water, thence curving around to the edge of the manor of Staunton, and back to Whitestone (perhaps White Cross in the Parks). The map above gives some idea of the area of land held by Bath Abbey.

The third William de Mohun was a benefactor of the Augustinian foundation at Bruton and to these canons he granted the other half of the Minehead tithes and also the advowson of the church with certain lands to support it. This meant that the Augustinians were responsible for appointing a vicar of Minehead until the Dissolution of the Monasteries in the 1500s. The lands granted to the canons were developed as an independent unit, some being held by the vicar of the parish and the remainder by the canons themselves. A quantity of this arable land

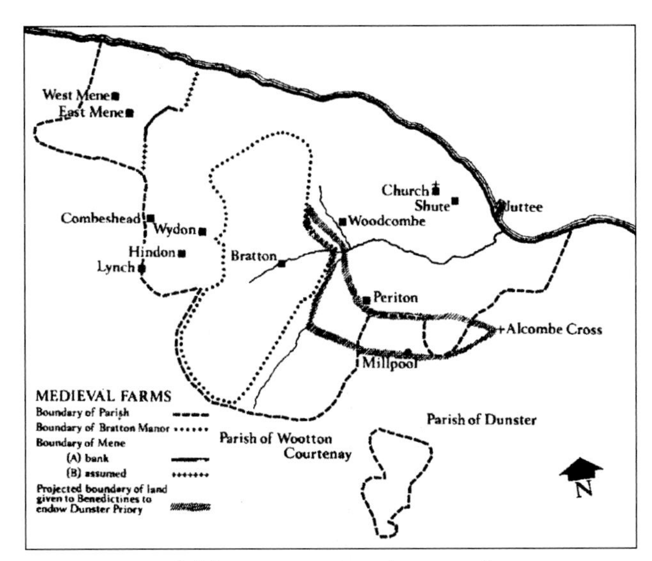

was at Derefolde, a name perhaps referring to an early park area. The canons also owned a water-mill. It is possible that this was the original demesne mill but copies of the charter granting it to the canons vary, one, in Chancery, omitting it altogether. De Mohun papers mention the lord's mill on several occasions and it was clearly a source of revenue to them, so it is most likely that the canons owned another mill. Possible sites are limited but could have been a little upstream from the lord's own mill or on the site of the later tucking mill below the town. This would bring it close to the late-medieval building often known as the old priory and raises the possibility of its occupation by monks in the period prior to the Reformation

The careful overseeing of these monastically owned estates can be assumed and the two groups of monks were jealous of their rights and dues. When in the 1340s the lord of Minehead bought two and a half acres of land to the south of Waterlane a dispute broke out as to which monastery should receive the tithes. It was only settled in Dunster's favour after a case in the ecclesiastical court. Both monastic landowners were, in the 1400s, receiving an income from the leasing of land for pasture.

It was during the 1400s that the present church of St Michael was built on its North Hill site overlooking the old medieval town. Parts of earlier buildings probably exist in the main walls and in the south porch which appears to be fourteenth century. The re-building of the church in the 1400s marks the increasing prosperity of the town and particularly the development of the mercantile element which brought new wealth to Minehead. The church is built of light grey sandstone which emphasises the dignified austerity of its style. The fine 87-foot tower is decorated with two popular medieval carvings which are representative of the teaching aids of the Church at that time. On the eastern face, St Michael weighs souls (*see right*). The monkeyish devil adds his weight to the cat-like sins placed in one scale but the Blessed Virgin Mary, sheltering human souls under her mantle, adds her beads to the good deeds in the other scale and thus outweighs the evil. On the south face is represented the Trinity showing God the Father supporting God the Son upon the cross. It was in these ways that the doctrines of the church were taught, though usually by more accessible pictures and carvings, to those who could not read or write.

Of this same period are the font with its charming figures, the priest's effigy and canopied tomb, and the chantry chapel with its wooden arch, once perhaps a sailor's guild chapel. The fine wooden screen of the Dunster school of carving was probably made at the end of the fifteenth century when the turret housing the stair to the rood loft was added to the church.

The church was served at this time by vicars appointed by the monks of Bruton, the last being Richard Fitzjames who eventually became Bishop of London. His illuminated missal, bequeathed to his successor in the See of London, Cuthbert Tunstall, is preserved in the church and is a fine example of early-fifteenth-century craftsmanship.

The ruins of the medieval Burgundy Chapel lie in a steep valley not far from East Myne. Tradition links the chapel with a founder shipwrecked while returning from France, but there is no written evidence to support this theory. It seems more likely that the chapel was built as a chapel of ease for the inhabitants of the isolated farms on the hill. Its name may be a corruption of Byrcombe.

St Michael with the Virgin Mary weighing souls at St Michael's Church. Note the devil on the left.

The variety of landownership within the manor of Minehead from the 1100s complicates any attempt to trace the growth of population and the development of cultivated land, particularly since documents relate in the main to that part of the parish held by the de Mohuns and incorporating Mene at an unknown date. At Domesday there were sixty-seven villeins, smallholders and serfs in the manors of Minehead and Mene. In a detailed extent of the de Mohun manor of the 1300s, ninety-three landholders are named. As we have seen the early figures may not include seamen. The later figure does not include certain freemen nor, probably, people living on ecclesiastical lands or sea-going folk. Nonetheless, the 1300s figure probably represents an increase of nearly 30 per cent of people working on the land since 1086 and this probably reflects the general pattern of population increase in Minehead by the early 1300s.

Fourteenth-Century Agriculture

An extent, or survey, of the manor of Minehead which provides details of the landholders owing homage and service to the lord of their holdings, exists amongst the Dunster Estate papers. It is not an easy document to date accurately since it is headed simply Edward. In William Prynne's catalogue it is ascribed to Edward III's reign (1355) but Hancock prefers the date 1300. In the same period lay subsidy lists exist for 1327 and 1331 and bailiffs' accounts are available for 1383-4; but comparison of names in these various documents is of little positive help in dating the extent since, although certain names and holdings do correspond, the documents are chronologically so far apart that such a comparison is of little value. However, the extent seems to provide a picture of a settled community rather than one affected by plague and famine, and this suggests that it should be given the earlier date of 1300 before the famines of 1315-17 and the outbreak of the Black Death in 1349 caused fundamental changes to take place.

The extent drawn up, then, in 1300, was witnessed by twelve substantial local jurors: Reginald Tonke, Gilbert de Pyryton, Nicholas de Comeshevede, Gilbert Chapelyn, John de Hyndon, Nicholas la Yurk, Richard le Preuere, Roger le Tracy, Roger le Heme, Roger de Wydon, and John le Childe. It depicts Minehead in the early-fourteenth century before any radical changes began to take place in the method of landholding. Ninety-three men and women are recorded as holding land from the lord. Five of these hold half a virgate, 24 acres, by suit and royal service. These include John le Selere, Robert Wyard, John de Pyryton, Robert de Bratton with a holding at Wydon and Ralph le Tort with a holding at Lynch. John le Selere, Gilbert Chapelyn, Robert de Bratton and Ralph le Tort hold land by charter and appear to own their own holdings with minimal payments to the lord. Robert Wyard pays 12d. and half a pound of wax worth 3d. Robert de Bratton pays six shillings a year. Robert Wyard and John de Pyryton's land is inherited through their mothers. Others who may have owned their own land in the manor include Reginald Tonke, Gilbert de Pyryton, senior, Nicholas de Comeshevede and Roger de Wydon who were witnesses to the extent but not mentioned within it, and merchants involved specifically in maritime activities and again not mentioned in the extent. The manor of Bratton and monastically-held lands also lie outside this survey.

Each of the ninety-three people named in the survey holds alone, or in part, a piece of land which is a fraction of a virgate in size. The holdings range from the 24-acre half-virgate through twelve acres, six acres, to one acre. There are also cottagers' holdings. The holdings are well established by this date and may even in some cases have been enclosed in blocks. Most of the ninety-three tenants performed services for the lord in return for their piece of land and also made customary payments in money and kind. These payments included larder rent, Peter's pence and Church scot; payments to the lord, to Rome and to the local church respectively. The services were specific works that had to be carried out on the lord's land or demesne, which would have been scattered alongside that of the tenants in the open fields.

These customary works are recorded in detail and give a clear picture of a manor where the demesne land was worked fully by the lord's tenants before they might turn to work on their own holdings. A man with a large holding and numerous services would not be expected to carry out all of them personally, but his family, both relatives and hangers-on, would have combined to fulfil these duties. Such a man was Roger Tracy who held a half-virgate and whose works are set out in detail and used as a yardstick for the assessment of other tenants.

Roger had to plough and harrow the land for wheat, oats and spring corn, although part of the work was limited by whether or not he was wealthy enough to own oxen. While the corn was growing he had to spend two working days each week in the back-breaking task of weeding the corn. Sensibly, the quantity of weeding to be done was not specified, for, as the clerk so rightly states, 'there is sometimes more weeding to be done than another.' At harvest time Roger had to help reap, bring his cart to assist in carrying the corn and remain at work until the harvest was home. Only then would he have been able to see to his own crops. Similarly he would have taken part in hay-making. Other tasks included digging in the vineyard, fetching a load of brushwood to the castle at Christmas, cleaning out the mill-pond and the water-leat and helping to make charcoal in North Wood, a fuel needed for providing fierce heat in the blacksmith's forge.

Roger was also responsible for travelling with the lord's retinue to Lyme in Dorset where the year's supply of salt (used especially for preserving meat and fish) would have been obtained and brought back to Dunster by pack animals. In 1428 a new salt store was built at Dunster Castle and perhaps a similar building existed at Minehead. Roger was also one of the group of men who went on behalf of the lord to Taunton, Bridgwater and Watchet to buy seed twice a year. This indicates that there was some interest in increasing the yield of crops with the regular introduction of new seed rather than reliance on seed locally produced. Each item of Roger's work is valued and for some works he was entitled to food for the day or small cash payments in lieu. At Christmas he was allowed a faggot of wood for his own fire from the load he carried to the castle and after his trip to Lyme was provided with his dinner. Roger's works represent a complete cross-section of the agricultural tasks carried out in Minehead in any one year and give us some idea of the farming economy based on the open fields in Minehead about 1300.

A less wealthy man, holding, for example, six acres of land, would harrow, if he had horses, once in winter and once in the spring. He would weed the corn for three days and reap and carry the corn and hay harvest. He would also dig in the vineyard. Three such men were Richard le Primare, John Childe and Roger de la Herne who had witnessed the extent. All these men also paid a small money-rent. Roger Tracy paid five shillings a year; William Hamond, who owed service for a six-acre holding, paid ls.6d. Cottagers such as Lucy Colroune and Lucy Londeberry paid 6d. a year and others 8d., 12d. or more. That such sums of money were available for annual payments by even the poorest peasants shows that there must have been much money circulating in the town in the 1300s. Doubtless food was being produced over and above the immediate needs of the farmers for sale locally to the merchants and maritime personnel, and also for export to the rapidly growing port of Bristol.

Besides the customary services of the tenants, certain of their rights are also specified in the extent. For example, all the men of Minehead had housebote and haybote in the North Wood; the rights of cutting wood to repair their houses and their fences. They also had the right of common pasture in the field against the gate of the court as soon as the sheaves had been carried to the barn, and on the Fenne and the North Marsh from Michaelmas, 29 September, until the feast of the Purification, 2 February. Other pasture was available while these fields were under cultivation and some tenants had extra specified common rights in certain places. Richard le Primare had common upon 'le Egge' [edge]. Other documents show rights of herbage, i.e. pasture and pannage, the pasture of pigs, in the Park, and of turbary, the right to cut turves, and of cutting wood for firewood and for repairing houses and fences as specified above. Each holding had its own particular rights and duties which were jealously guarded and which contributed to the whole manorial economy.

Fourteenth-Century Minehead: Changes in Landholding

By the last quarter of the fourteenth century the accounts of Richard Elys, the bailiff of Minehead, show that changes were taking place in the methods of landholding in the manor. In the accounts of 1383-4 we can see from holdings that are being re-let that, on average, land rents seem to have doubled since the beginning of the century. Roger Tracy in 1300 paid five shillings for his 24-acre holding. Now Roger Childe, Richard Elys and John Tuthorne each pay ten shillings a year for their 24-acre holdings while Henry Herputte pays 13s.4d. for his. A note about the new rent of John 'atte Herne' says that he pays it 'to release his works except that he shall give a ½d. for the work of the vine', and this seems to be the explanation of these higher rents. Some tenants were no longer performing their customary works but paying higher rents instead.

Besides these new increased rents for old holdings, there were also new rents for new holdings. Some of these were assarts, plots of land reclaimed from waste. Thomas Wysburgh pays 12d. new rent for a plot of waste between the park and the mill and Roger Smyth 4d. for a plot of waste ground near Sareborneshaye. Other people were adding extra acres to their holdings and certain wealthier men were taking over more than one complete holding. Roger Childe gave up his old holding but replaced it with two new ones.

Much of the land being annexed was demesne land which by 1383 was being let out on a large scale. Acres in the open fields were being let at an average annual rent of four shillings an acre: John Calynch paid twelve shillings for three acres in the north part de la lane while Margary Yeamste leased two acres in the field south of the lane for eight shillings. Altogether 142 acres of demesne land were leased in small blocks. It is possible that this was the period when the demesne land was enclosed, the fields of two, three and four acres corresponding with a series of small fields on the site of the open fields shown on the tithe maps of 1843. These fields reflected the pattern of strip-farming and in 1843 were generally let with smallholdings in the town, a practice dating from the time of the first leasing.

By 1384 winter grazing in the open fields and the fennes and meadow in Wetehull and at Tothhullbrigg was no longer available 'because all the land and meadow leased.' For some reason pannage was not available in North Wood and little wood had been sold. Common grazing remained available on the higher common lands, but other common rights were dying out because of the change to leasing of land for a monetary rent.

There were, then, three main changes that began in the mid-fourteenth century. Monetary rents began to take the place of the customary works as a common means of land-holding. Many substantial peasants increased the size of their holdings and demesne land was leased in small blocks to such tenants. These add up to a picture of increased agricultural activity throughout the manor, the deliberate expansion of farms presumably reflecting the influence of the profit motive. It is possible that the gradual commutation of works was accelerated by the outbreak of the Black Death which occurred in this part of Somerset in 1349. A loss in the number of tenants performing customary works might have encouraged the lord to let out that part of the demesne which could no longer be worked in the traditional way and to use the increased income from rents to employ labour or to buy food. It also gave the forward-looking tenants who were left the opportunity to consolidate and increase their holdings, to rid themselves of the tie of customary works and to produce food for sale in the town and for shipping to Bristol. The increase in acreage under cultivation shows that there were certainly no permanent ill-effects on the economy from the Black Death.

These changes begun in the fourteenth century continued throughout the fifteenth, and by 1435 most of the day works and boon works had been commuted although certain manual and autumnal works remained. By the time Edward IV held the manor most of these too had disappeared and one can imagine a fairly rapid finish to the process. One group of these manual works is referred to as 'churrys' or 'churrs' which may perhaps have some bearing on Minehead's unique street name, Cher.

Fifteenth-Century Minehead: Topography

It is possible to work out from documents quite an orderly and detailed picture of Minehead town in the later-medieval period. Minehead was by then already established on its three sites around the church on the hill, the mill by the stream, and at the foot of the hill near the jetty. Further afield were isolated farmhouses and hamlets including the separate manor of Bratton. The main road ran out of Minehead to the south west along the line of Bampton Street, branching off to the left to Alcombe and Dunster and to the right to Periton, Bratton and Porlock. To reach Wootton Courtenay and Timberscombe the track went up past Hopcott and over the hill, known today as Oway. More local roads led out from the market place to Alcombe and beside the park boundary to Woodcombe and Bratton. Pack-horses would have been a frequent sight on these rough roads carrying goods to and from the harbour in Minehead.

In the centre of the town, a stream ran from Bratton through the main street to the sea. A mill leat was trapped from the stream above the town and brought down through the meadow of Wetehull to the mill at the foot of Bampton Street. Bridges probably crossed the stream above and below the town; the latter was later known as Puddle Bridge but the higher may have been Tothhullbrigg. On either side of the stream and La Lane, or Waterlane, which ran beside it probably to the north below the lower bridge, lay arable fields known as the fields north and south of La Lane and basically the old open fields. The South Field was sometimes known as the Playland. These fields were, by 1435, probably divided into acre units; certainly the demesne area was (and probably partly enclosed as well). The tithe map of 1843 and another small manorial map extract of the early 1700s indicate an early strip system in the large fields surrounding the town, and by the 1400s many of these strips were fossilised into enclosed fields.

Although by 1843 all the fields were established and enclosed, in the 1700s certain larger fields were still subdivided into acre-strips or land-shares, the final enclosing taking place after that date. However, the main enclosure of two- or three-acre blocks probably had occurred by, or even at, the time that the demesne land in the open fields was first leased. Professor W.G. Hoskins writes of enclosure in the peripheral counties including Devon:

> *It seems likely that... the open fields were being enclosed into hedged fields during the course of the thirteenth and fourteenth centuries, at a time when records of the process are hard to come by.*

This comment seems to apply equally to the enclosure of open fields in Minehead.

Besides the big open fields, a number of smaller ones existed. Wetehull lay above the town alongside the stream and another small field lay against the gate of the court. This might have been the same field as that at Tothhullbrigg. Yet another field called Fullebrigg lay out towards the tiny manor of Staunton and this may be identified with the Bull Bridge of later days. A large area of summer grazing lay between the South Field and the sea and was appropriately known as La Fenne. Skirting the South

Field itself were other fields often under water in winter known as the North Marsh. A park for the husbanding and hunting of wild animals for the lord's table was also used for common grazing at times. Pigs could be put into the north wood to feed, so it was likely to have been an oak wood. The vineyard which featured so prominently in Minehead's medieval agriculture probably lay on the south-facing slopes of North Hill towards Woodcombe.

The water mill which belonged to the lord of the manor was situated on a site at the edge of the town where the mills at the bottom of Bampton Street now stand. The mill-leat was kept clean by customary labour under the direction of the keeper of the water-leat who was allowed the privilege of keeping one cow on the pasture beside the leat. The water in the leat would have been tapped from the stream at a higher point and diverted to drive a water wheel probably of the overshot type. The lord's tenants would have had to bring their corn to this mill to be ground. Only the men of West Myne were exempt from using the lord's mill and they paid the lord 12d. yearly so that they might grind their corn where they wished.

This raises the question of a second mill in the town belonging to the Augustinian canons which might have been used by the men of the West Myne, tenants of the canons and some freemen. Alternatively the men of West Myne might have used the mill of the manor of Bratton which would have been more convenient for them, or there might have been water wheels on one or two of the larger outlying farms such as Periton or Hindon.

The pound where straying animals were held was probably on a site at the top of Bampton Street where a field, Pound Close, later took its name from its proximity to the pound. Here the 'waifs and strays' were put until redeemed by their owners.

The park, first mentioned in 1279 and which was to be 'destroyed' and the land mortgaged in the early 1500s, stretched westwards beside the stream towards Woodcombe. In 1383 the acreage seems to have been 51 acres and in 1428 150 acres, which presumably marked a deliberate extension of parkland under Luttrell ownership. Field names such as West Park, Ball Park, Pit Park and Park Pales show that these fields were once part of the park. An ancient boundary bank and hedge running along the west of Ball Park near Fir Close seems to have belonged to the original park boundary.

The accounts of 1383 that were drawn up while Joan de Mohun was lady of the manor indicate that there was a group of buildings from which the manor and the demesne lands particularly were administered. They included a grange, a cow-house, a 'wynsellere' and other houses making up 'the Court.' There was also an old chapel which was eventually replaced by a new one. Although there is no mention of a house and no tradition of a manor house in Minehead, it seems likely that the group of buildings was under the control of a steward whose house would have adjoined this block. At one point the buildings are said to have been occupied by the lady, but since Joan de Mohun preferred court life to Dunster Castle, it seems unlikely that she was actually there for more than a brief visit.

Informed guesses can be made for possible sites for this group of buildings. The name of Tythings Court implies that it was the ancient site for the meeting of the Minehead tything, and this might well have been in a courtyard belonging to the lord of the manor. Alternatively the buildings might have been clustered around what is now known as Court Green, close to the demesne mill. This would be a logical site for them, less liable to flood than the Tythings Court site so close to the main stream. In either case a field could have stretched away to the west to form 'the field at the gate of the Court' or 'Courtygate.'

The market, which was established by 1461, included at least nine stalls and was held around the old market cross which stood on approximately its present site in Market House Lane. The annual fair, held at Michaelmas, was doubtless centred in the market place and fields below Middle Town. The market would have brought in regular sellers (and customers) from the nearby farms and hamlets who would have sold dairy produce and other perishable goods. Probably fish was also for sale. The fair, on the other hand, would have attracted a much wider range of pedlars and entertainers, who would have brought goods to sell, relative luxuries, and news and gossip from other places.

The maritime centre of Minehead in the early 1400s nestled at the foot of the hill where the North Field met the coast and the main stream ran into the sea. In 1421-2 Lady Margaret Luttrell contributed ten shillings towards providing a new 'juttee' for the town. This wooden structure jutted out into the sea making it easier for loading and unloading the small merchant ships. Fishing boats would have been pulled up on to the shingle. Presumably, without any man-made sea defences, a high shingle bank similar to that at Bossington protected the land at the highest tides, but it is reasonable to imagine a large area around the mouth of the stream subject to tidal movements. Further along towards Dunster, La Fenne and North Marsh, used as pasture in the summer, were for much of the winter under water.

The fishermen who lived in small huts at the foot of the hill could be divided into those who fished the sea and those who fished the foreshore by means of weirs and pools. The fishing rights belonged to the lord of the manor who leased them for an annual sum but reserved the right to claim any unusual

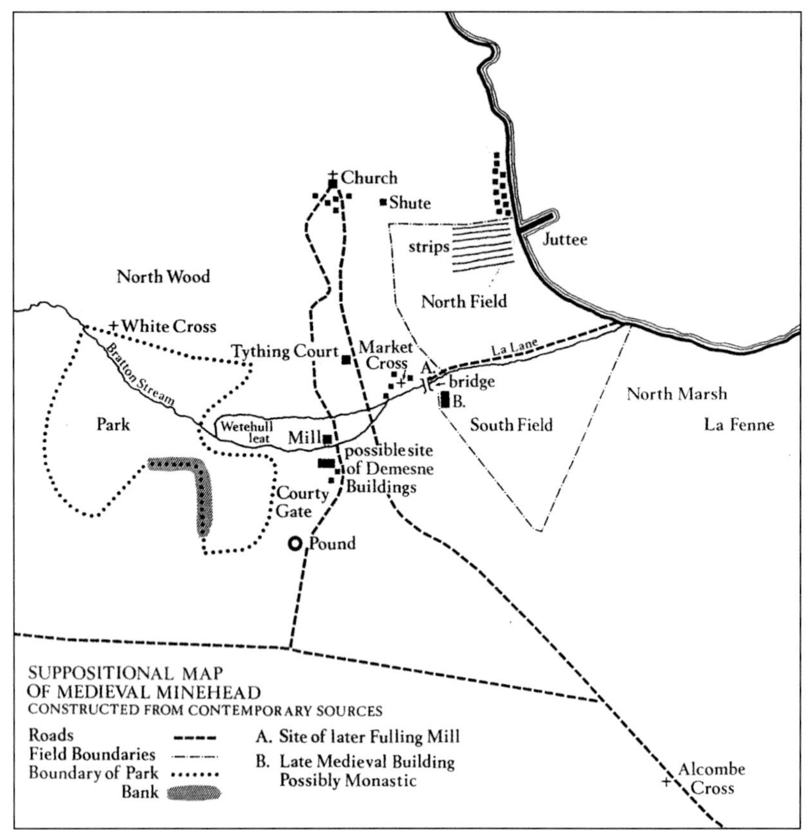

fish caught. Various references in the manorial documents can be found relating to the leasing of these weirs and pools which were situated along the shore between the high and low water marks. One pool remains today beyond Warren Point, Owl Pool, and also Big Weir, Little Weir and Martin's Weir. John Gilman describes a weir as:

> *... a low stone-built wall set with stakes and woven with wattles like a hedge. They were usually in the form of an angle with the apex inclined towards the sea and built in two rows, one for the spring tides and one for the neap tides. This form of fishing was very popular from the thirteenth century onwards. The reign of Richard II saw the introduction of constructed ponds and pools designed to stop the fish returning with the tide.*

These weirs and pools along the foreshore would have been a scene of constant activity for the fishing families living under the shadow of North Hill. Boats, too, went out from Minehead in search of fish in the Bristol Channel. By the 1400s some vessels were employed in trade between Minehead and Bristol, South Wales and France. The purchase of the Dunster estates by the Luttrells had given a special boost to trade with France since Hugh Luttrell's positions of responsibility in Normandy involved constant traffic between Minehead and various French ports. Supplies, particularly of Minehead fish, herrings, ling, milwell, congers and salmon, but also of other provisions, were shipped to France; while cargoes of wine sold in England contributed to the cost of each expedition. Roger Kyng, 'shipman' of Minehead, called at various ports to collect these supplies from the scattered Luttrell manors before finally leaving for Normandy. Another ship belonging to the port of Minehead was the *Leonard of Dounsterre* which, under her master, Philip Clopton, made the voyage to Bordeaux in 1418. Her sails had to be mended in port under the order of the reeve of Minehead. The bills for repairs show that there was no chance of this vessel leaving the port until quite seaworthy.

By the end of the fifteenth century, the king was regularly receiving Customs dues from Minehead showing that trade was well established. Tolls of the sea due to the Luttrells were left with the townsfolk who were responsible for maintaining the harbour. A problem then, as now, was keeping it clear of stones: in 1483 people were ordered to refrain from throwing small stones at the 'were'.

All this activity presupposes a group of buildings centred around the jetty where boat-building, storage, other maritime occupations and collection of dues could have taken place. By 1383 one 'Botehouse' at least is specified and later various small holdings, each called botehouse, imply small buildings where boats could be kept along with the other paraphernalia of fishing and shipping.

In the area surrounding the town of Minehead lay several small settlements. In a rental of 1407 there are seven distinct hamlets. These include Periton with five landholders, Woodcombe with six, Hyndon with seven, Lynch with three, East Mene with one, North Ridge with three and West Mene with six. All of these except North Ridge can be identified with their modern counterparts. North Ridge, from its juxtaposition in documents to the Menes, appears to have been on North Hill and was perhaps, with East and West Mene, originally part of the Domesday manor of Mene.

Substantial boundary banks, probably marking the Norman manor of Mene, can be identified at East Mene and although other medieval remains may exist it is probable that they were destroyed during the Army occupation of North Hill during the Second World War. All these hamlets are mentioned in the fourteenth-century extent of Minehead but, as we have already seen, could well have been of Saxon origin. Hedge-banks at Wydon indicate a pre-Norman origin too.

Chapter 2
The Manor of Minehead: 1485–1800

During the Wars of the Roses Sir James Luttrell supported the Lancastrians. He served his party faithfully, was knighted at the battle of Wakefield in 1460, but died early in the next year of wounds received at the second battle of St Albans. At the accession of the Yorkist king, Edward IV, most of Sir James' estates were confiscated, but his wife, Elizabeth, was a Courtenay and through the influence of her Yorkist family she was allowed to retain certain lands that were part of her jointure and which included the manor of Minehead.

The victory of the Lancastrian leader, Henry Tudor (*see Tudor Rose, above, found painted on the wall of the manor estate office*), at Bosworth in 1485, effectively ended the Wars of the Roses and restored the Luttrells to favour. Hugh, Sir James' son, once more enjoyed his father's possessions, though his mother disputed his right to Minehead. An agreement made 'at the chapel of Cleeve, the tuesday in the Whitsunday week in the first year of the reign of King Harry VII', gave Elizabeth for the duration of her life possession of all her jointure except the manor of Minehead and in order to hold this Hugh agreed to pay her a rent of eighty marks a year.

Thus from the very beginning of the Tudor period the Luttrell interest in Minehead was paramount and on the whole beneficial to the developing seaport of the sixteenth, seventeenth and eighteenth centuries, though this was not always appreciated by the merchants and shipowners of Minehead who often believed that they could control their own affairs better than the lord of the manor.

During this period, both at Minehead and generally throughout England, two manorial courts met regularly to conduct the business of the lord of the manor and to maintain the king's peace. During the reign of Henry VII the more important of these courts met twice-yearly in Minehead in the Town Hall and was called The Court of Law with View of Frankpledge, though by the end of the 1500s it was referred to by the more familiar name of Court Leet. The lesser three-weekly court probably met in the Tudor Rose room of the old manor estate office.

The Court Leet had two main functions. First it had to carry out the lord's business: to settle leases and questions of property, collect moneys owed to the manor, ensure that roads, streams, lands and houses were kept in good order, deal with straying animals and settle disputes among the tenants about debts, trespass or other matters. But also this court had to do 'the King's business'; that is to say it was concerned with matters of law and order, though later in the sixteenth century it gradually surrendered most of these powers to the justices of the peace. The dividing line between the business of the king and the affairs of the lord of the manor was rather vague as their interests often overlapped. For example, the Court Leet at Minehead elected through 'the homage', or twelve jurors, the officers of the court whose duty it was to ensure that the laws of England as well as the customs of the manor were observed by the tenants. At the Easter court each year two constables were chosen to keep the king's peace and a tithingman was elected for each of the manors of Minehead, Alcombe and Staunton to carry out the constable's orders. The duties of these unpaid policemen included presenting charges against offenders, compelling witnesses to attend the court and making arrests. They were also responsible for the enforcement of the assize of bread and the assize of ale which together regulated the weight and content of the penny, halfpenny, and farthing loaf of bread and its wholesomeness, and the measure and quality of ale sold by the licensed sellers of ale, most of whom in Minehead were women who thus supplemented their meagre incomes while their husbands were at work in the fields. To watch the activities of the bakers and brewers and to report offenders to the tithingmen there were officers elected each year called 'weighers of bread' and 'ale tasters'. There were also two 'keepers of the shambles' to supervise the butchers and purveyors of provisions in the market; two 'keepers of the ways'; two 'keepers of the waters'; and at a seaport like Minehead, two 'watchers of weirs'.

At the spring court of 1486 in the first year of the reign of Henry VII, some thirty people applied for a licence to sell ale and of these twenty were women.

Dunster Castle, home of the lords of the manor of Minehead, c.1930.

In 1492 twelve tenants were fined one penny each for selling ale before it had been sampled by the ale tasters. At the same court Robert Clemment was in trouble for taking unclean food to market, as well as for assaulting with his fists a certain Richard Butcher whose name suggests that he might have been a rival tradesman who had unkindly informed the keeper of the shambles of Robert's offence. Assaults were common and often more violent than this. Richard Bonaster attacked Alice Swerdes with a knife and drew blood, for which his knife was confiscated and he was fined. Donald Donkowe assaulted an unknown stranger with an old bucket which the court found of so little value as not to be worth confiscating. In 1504 there was an outbreak of stone-throwing involving Joan Power and Emma Smyth and Richard Carpenter and William Brannocke. In 1507 William Roche with a knife called a poniard drew blood from William Lynch, but Margaret Veale also drew blood when she assaulted Catherine Kerry with her 'washyn ketyll'.

At this court the weigher of bread presented John Baker of Watchet, John Baker of Cleeve, John Baker of Stogumber and Thomas Baker of Minehead for baking loaves that were under the statutory weight. It is interesting to observe that their surnames were all taken from their occupation. The transition from John the Baker to John Baker must have been very recent.

The Court showed an understanding of the need to isolate the victim of an infectious disease. A poor leper was ordered not to leave his house, draw water from the stream or infect it with excrement. Men and women who threw rubbish into the water or allowed their pigs to wallow in it were also amerced by the court, as were tenants who permitted their animals to stray into the marshes which were reserved for the lord of the manor, or even allowed them to wander about the lanes of the town.

All these multifarious problems were brought to the notice of the steward of Dunster Castle who presided over the court. However, decisions seem to have been made by the court as such rather than by any individual, and even the lord himself was subject to the customs enforced by his Court Leet.

The lesser court, called quite simply at the end of the reign of Henry VIII 'the manor court', met in theory every three weeks and in practice at Minehead about ten or a dozen times in the year. It was mainly concerned with the day-to-day business of the manor and in this the bailiff played an important part, presenting offending tenants to the court. When he neglected to do this he was himself amerced for inefficiency.

The more important Court Leet was attended by the principal tenants of the manor who, as 'the homage', formed a jury to hear cases for and against their fellow tenants. As we have said, they also elected the officers whose duty it was to serve both the manor and the parish, working closely with the churchwardens and overseers of the poor. These unpaid officials often gave their services reluctantly and halfheartedly, for they were loath to bring their acquaintances, friends and relatives to court. This is most evident in the behaviour of the constables who sometimes had to be bullied into doing their unpleasant duty. They carried a heavy responsibility for the maintenance of order but were usually uneducated though comparatively prosperous men, too much part of the community in which they lived and worked to be able to perform their duties without fear or favour.

Throughout the sixteenth century and during most of the seventeenth the manorial courts continued to function but with lessening authority, especially in the realm of law and order in which those useful servants of Tudor and Stuart administration, the justices of the peace, had taken over. The Latin records of the manor courts provide throughout the sixteenth century and the first half of the seventeenth a repetitive but detailed account from month to month of the common stuff of life in a small but growing and not unimportant seaport town.

During the Protectorate of Oliver Cromwell the manor court rolls were for the first time written in English. The leasing and surrendering of property and the little arguments about the non-observance of the customs of the manor continued to be the main concern of the court but there are no longer any records of criminal cases. At the death of a tenant the traditional heriot (or payment in kind) was still quite frequently required. When George Ford, the landlord of the Red Lyon, died in 1655, his widow, Joan, had to pay a heriot of a bushel of wheat. At Mary Slocombe's death the heriot was a goose, at Peter Teague's a hog, and the prosperous Lewis Baker's widow had to give to the lord of the manor a cow or £3 in lieu thereof. A tenant who did not occupy the house which he had leased was warned, then fined, and, if still absent, dismissed from his tenement. After a warning Diana Lynde was still failing 'to make her corporal and continual residence upon her copyhold' and for this she was amerced 13s.4d. Next year the penalty was doubled and she was threatened with a fine of £10, though at the ensuing court the fine was reduced to £4, which, however, she does not appear to have paid. Her late husband, Alexander Lynde, Esquire, was no doubt a man of some importance and she was herself a daughter of George Luttrell and must have felt strong enough to defy the Court Baron. Certainly Free Suitors like Hugh Trevelyan of Knowle and William Fry of Bratton Court, who lived at some distance from Minehead, seemed quite indifferent to the orders of the court to attend in person. Even orders to humble tenants to repair their cottages were not always obeyed and in 1657, to enforce such an order, Thomas Fugars, the bailiff, with John Bond, Henry Brooke, John Burnell and Peter Punter, were instructed to inspect the houses in the manor on St Michael's day to ascertain if they had been repaired. These records suggest that the manor court in the middle of the seventeenth century was already something of an anachronism, and that this was recognised by many of the tenants.

Sometimes a more unusual incident crops up. For instance, in the spring court of 1657, Mary Brooke, a widow, is presented for laying a trunk or hollow tree athwart the highway leading from Minehead town to Periton and so diverting the water, which flowed east-north-east along the highway, from John Roach's meadow which it had customarily irrigated, to one of her own called Broadmead. In such matters the court was still the only effective authority.

The powers and obligations of the lord of the manor and the rights and duties of his tenants were determined by custom and had been passed on for centuries from generation to generation. Not until 1647, after the turmoil of the first Civil War, was the manor court required to put down in writing details of the customs, this 'being a thing contrary to former use.' This written 'custumal' was presented by the whole tenantry to George Luttrell as the 'ancient and laudable customs' which must be strictly kept by tenants and lord alike. The first clause required attendance at the three-weekly court, excusing, however, seamen who were absent on a voyage. Following this came clauses concerning the cleaning of the lord's millpond and the obligation to use his mill; ploughing the commons and using them for grazing; giving evidence in court, though the witnesses were excused if the lord did not provide their dinner in return for payment of 1d. At the bailiff's summons the customary suitors, on the Eve of St John the Baptist, had to walk the commons 'from Hurstone to Dunster haven and from Oway and Periton Common (Hopcott excepted)', presumably as far as the seashore, in order to seek for stray animals. For this they earned a free dinner. Other duties included viewing the bounds of the manor with the steward and keeping the water-courses to the lord's warren clear.

A heriot was required at the death of a tenant and as much money as was needful to repair his cottage. A number of clauses regulated the granting of copyholds, the right to fell trees or cut turves and the obligation on a tenant to reside on his tenement and keep his wealth in the town where he had earned it. It cost nothing for one tenant to bring an action against another but he paid 1d. to withdraw and he was allowed to sue his neighbours in the manor court for sums not exceeding forty shillings. The lord's 'birds of warren' (i.e. game birds) and 'whale fishes, seal, porpoise, thornpolls, and great salmon' were protected. However, the most remarkable custom required:

... that the tithingman of Staunton every year upon Hock tuesday, being the third tuesday after Easter, in the morning before sun rising do bring into this manor a green bough and set the same in the place within the said manor where the Lord's Court have been kept most usually. And after he hath so done, he shall go to the next tenant's house within the said manor and call them and say Arise, sleepers of Minehead! three times, bear witness that the tithingman of Staunton hath done his duty. And if he do not the same he shall forfeit three shillings and fourpence.

Nor should we suppose that this strange custom was not enforced, for in 1603 the tithingman of Staunton was fined 6d. for 'not doing his duty in a hock-Tuesday.'

The strength of custom in the affairs of the old manorial system is, perhaps, the explanation for a dispute between Minehead and Bossington that was creating difficulties for the lord of the manor at the end of the sixteenth century.

The source of the trouble seems to have been an agreement between Sir Hugh Luttrell and Sir John Trevelyan made in June 1505, concerning the ownership of a part of North Hill. With Lord Fitzwarren, Sir Nicholas Wadham, William Wadham and John Sydenham as arbitrators, the two landowners allowed West Myne common to be divided into seven parts, six of which passed to Sir Hugh while the seventh on the Bossington side was given to Sir John Trevelyan who was compensated for the loss of part of West Myne common by a grant of Luttrell land adjacent to his seventh part. This presumably meant that the customary grazing rights of the village of Bossington had been changed. Minehead husbandmen could now graze their sheep as far west as Hurstone point on land which for centuries had been available to the graziers of Bossington. When few could read and communications were difficult it was not easy to make such an arrangement stick.

This must surely be the explanation for a strange document that claimed to be a note of the true bounds of the common separating the lands of Mr George Luttrell of Dunster Castle and Mr Arundel of Cornwall. Towards the end of Elizabeth's reign George Luttrell sought the opinion of an old man, William Stodden, of the parish of Selworthy, whose memory extended back sixty years to the time of Sir Andrew Luttrell. After tracing the bounds of the common on North Hill William described how in Sir Andrew's time 'the tenants of Minehead and the tenants of Bossington did meet' at East Hurstone commons head and there:

... the tenants of Minehead did claim from thence down right at Hurston and the tenants of Bossington did claim from thence down by a dike and so to go north right to a place called the Green Hole and so at great variance they did depart.

He added that there had been many meetings since at which Minehead 'did claim outright at Hurstone' but the tenants of Bossington held firm to their claim of common right 'as far east as the Green Hole and no farther.' Finally, 'for plainder proof' of ownership, William said that throughout sixty years he had tilled parts of West Myne common and paid Mr Luttrell 12d. for every acre so tilled. In spite of George Luttrell's attempt to bring a little order into this untidy situation, the dispute no doubt smouldered on with occasional eruptions when hard words were spoken and a few blows struck.

A more serious disagreement that troubled the Luttrells in Tudor times and indeed flared up again in the early 1700s concerned Minehead Park. Henry VIII's antiquary, John Leland, writing in his *Itinerary* shortly after Sir Andrew Luttrell's death in 1538, had this to say: 'There was a fair Park at Minehead but Sir Andrew Luttrell of late time destroyed it.'

To provide legacies of 400 marks for all his children except John, his elder son, Sir Andrew leased his manor of Minehead to Sir Humphrey Wingfield and Sir John Wyndham for 28 years. Two years after Sir Andrew's death Sir Humphrey Wingfield assigned his interest in this lease to Dame Margaret, Sir Andrew's widow, and she and Sir John Wyndham handed over the manor to her son, Sir John Luttrell, on condition that he would undertake to pay the promised legacies. Sir John was an ambitious soldier who had fought with distinction in France and Scotland and had been captured by the Scots at Broughty Craig. He had written to the Lord Protector Somerset to request leave of absence as his mother, Dame Margaret, wished to give back to him the manor of Minehead which she valued at £120 a year. He owed, he said, a great deal of money to his creditors and wished to accept his mother's offer whilst she was in the mood, 'for if she should take a fancy in her head to marry, I were utterly undone!'

His services in Scotland at that time were rated at too high a value for him to be spared from his post, but the deal with his mother went through, and he eventually returned to Dunster in 1550, though not for long, for soon he was planning with that intrepid sailor, Thomas Wyndharn of Marshwood, his half-uncle, a voyage to Morocco - but while he was at Greenwich waiting to sail he became an early victim of an epidemic of the sweating sickness and died in July 1551. However, just two months before his death, Sir John, anxious to ensure the payment of his father's legacies and others that he had himself undertaken, made a conditional sale of Minehead Park to his cousin, Hugh Stewkley, a lawyer described in these early papers as of London, though later the family moved to Hinton Ampner in Hampshire. For the sum of £230.13s.4d. Sir John mortgaged Minehead Park of 200 acres and valued at £20 per annum to Hugh Stewkley, unless it was redeemed by 1 May in the next year 'upon the fontstone in the Cathedral Church of St Paul in London between the hours of nine and eleven in the forenoon.' One is reminded of Antonio in *The Merchant of Venice*. Within three months, he believed, he would be able to pay his debt to Shylock over and over again, and so no doubt thought Sir John Luttrell. But within two months he was dead, and Dame Margaret, unaware of the closing date of the agreement, allowed 1 May to pass by without redeeming the Parks.

However, although she had apparently forfeited this valuable parkland, Dame Margaret 'being a wise lady' would not hand it over until the legacies had been paid, knowing that Stewkley was 'an adversary and one that hated her name.' She paid the legacies of 400 marks apiece and handed over her interest in the Parks to her second son, Thomas, who had succeeded Sir John as lord of the manor. More than a decade later, in 1564, the ownership of this land was still disputed, and very surprisingly the right of Samuel Hayrnan (a prosperous merchant of Minehead) to purchase part of the Parks from Sir Hugh Stewkley of Hinton Ampner was still being questioned as late as the early years of George I.

In 1619 a serious dispute in the manor court, which forced George Luttrell to seek legal advice, shows how the customs of the manor and the authority of its court were being called into question even in the early years of this century of change.

Henry Stephens had been granted by the lord of the manor a certain house and lands that belonged by copyhold of the manor court rolls to a widow, Joan Coffin. Her right to continue in possession of her property was disputed because of the conduct of her private life. To quote the lawyers brief: 'The sole question is whether the defendant, Joan Coffin... hath not forfeited her copyhold tenement by the custom of the manor for being unchaste.'

Ten years before, Joan's husband, John Coffin, had disappeared, and in somewhat mysterious circumstances if we are to believe the evidence of Walter Coffin, who heard 'a great stir and screeching noise ... in his house' on the night that he was last seen, and added that he now believed John to be 'dead long since.' In spite of the fact that Minehead was a harbour of good trade with 'divers persons' passing from 'thence into many foreign parts' nothing had ever been heard of him, and Joan also considered him to be dead. As his widow she could claim the copyhold according to the custom of the manor.

George Luttrell's lawyer could cite plenty of precedents for the expulsion of widows from their property for incontinence, taken mainly from the fifteenth century, but including some cases that George Luttrell himself had decided. Thomasine Gould and Alice Webber, because of their poverty, were, unfortunately for the plaintiff in this case, given compensation by the kindly Mr Luttrell when they were ejected, but whether this precedent turned the scales against Henry Stephens and in doing so changed an age-old custom of the manor is not known. Like the disappearance of John Coffin, the outcome of this strange case remains a mystery.

However, the Court Leet as late as the seventeenth century still occasionally concerned itself with criminal matters. In the first year of James I's reign the constables presented Robert Samuell for assaulting Thomas Shelley, bruising his head with a stick of wood and striking him so hard that he did 'sheed blod', for which offence he was fined 6d., but as has been said, the court was more commonly occupied with routine matters as tenants failed to observe the customs of the manor. By the end of this century manor courts had lost most of their importance, but they were still meeting in Minehead at the beginning of the next century as is shown by the first Parliamentary election of the reign of George I.

The Luttrells were Tories and, now that the Whigs were firmly in the saddle at Westminster, Government supporters in Minehead were able to challenge the result of this election because the constables, who were the returning officers, were still chosen at the Court Leet of the Tory lord of the manor and could therefore, with some justification, be suspected of prejudice. To establish the right of the constables to officiate as returning officers, many of the old manor court rolls were sent to Parliament to prove that these officers had been traditionally elected at the manor court, and that it had been customary from the beginning for the constables to officiate at Parliamentary elections. In 1728 the Court Leet was still functioning, for in connection with it there is a bill for seven dinners at 2s.6d. each, washed down by thirteen bottles of wine, ten quarts of spirits and unspecified quantities of toddy and ale. However, apart from electing the constables, there could, in the later years of the eighteenth century, have been little for this court to do that could not have been as well done in the estate office at the Castle.

But old ways died hard. In 1800 the Court Leet was still meeting. One, Crockford, was elected 'street keeper', a post described as 'an annual office of great antiquity in this parish.' As part of his duties he had 'to impound Hogs found at large in the street.' A little earlier, in 1793, William Graddon, a saddler, was sworn in at the Court Leet as 'searcher and sealer of leather.' The ale tasters and bread weighers may have gone, but the old baronial court had still sufficient authority to appoint one or two officers to supervise the tenants of the lord of the manor of Minehead.

Engraving of Minehead Harbour, early 1860s.

Wooden groynes were used to defend the harbour sea-front properties for centuries. Groynes on the beach, c.1900.

Chapter 3
The Port of Minehead: 1500–1800

By the end of the fifteenth century Minehead was a considerable seaport. The growth of trade during the reign of the first Tudor king had overstrained the modest resources of the estuary of the little creek, washed out by the Bratton Stream as it flowed into the sea at the foot of the present Blenheim Road, so Sir Hugh Luttrell, who showed a lively interest in the port and was always actively involved in its affairs, enlarged the capacity of the haven by protecting the mouth of the creek with a jetty.

Ships grew in numbers and tonnage. Trade expanded rapidly. At the accession of Elizabeth I only Minehead and Bridgwater 'on the Severn Sea' had port and Customs officials, apart from Bristol. As early as 1543 there were more ships of a suitable burden for service with King Henry VIII's developing navy registered at Minehead than at any other port in the Bristol Channel. Hugh Pawlett, who was commissioned by the King to make a survey of western ports to discover how many suitable vessels were available, reported that Minehead had four ships of sufficient burden. In harbour at the time of his visit were William Hill's ship of 70 tons and Robert Quirke's of 60 tons. Lady Luttrell's of 100 tons was in the port of London and Dennis Marranes of 60 tons was on a voyage to Ireland. There were thirty-seven seamen at Minehead and another forty at sea. The only other Somerset ship of sufficient tonnage, outside Bristol of course, was berthed at Combwich and belonged to Bridgwater and there were just thirteen sailors available to man it.

The Bridgwater harbour accounts for this period have survived and they show that the port of Bridgwater enjoyed a busy coastal trade with occasional voyages to Continental ports. By inference Minehead must have been trading at least as extensively as Bridgwater and the fact that larger vessels were based at her harbour implies that the Minehead merchants were more involved in traffic with foreign parts.

Back in 1480 there were three Minehead ships trading between La Rochelle and Bristol. In the Bridgwater papers of the time of Henry VIII Jasper Fernando's vessel, the *Salvador* of Aveiro in Portugal, is reported as arriving at Minehead, and similar reports name other foreign ships: the *Misericordia*, also of Aveiro, whose master was John Perez; and the *Anthony* belonging to John Raymond and Francis Fernando. Ships with Minehead owners are also frequently mentioned in these papers: ships such as the *Christopher* whose master was Richard Writte and whose first owners were probably William Hill, William Appewell, Harry Dale and Writte himself. Other reports concern the *Saviour* of Richard King and John Wyndham; the *Swan* of Thomas Wyndham and John Luttrell; the *Michael* of William Thomas; the *Martlet* (Martelot) of John Kerry, later to be part owner of the *Margaret* of 35 tons and master of Vice-Admiral Thomas Wyndham's flagship; the *Ann* of Thomas Vennicombe; and the *Tawdry* of Richard Laughill, perhaps an Irish skipper who had, like many of his countrymen, settled down at Minehead. Among the names of Minehead traders mentioned in these papers are those of William Dennell, who lived to be nearly one hundred years of age and whom we shall have occasion to mention again, and John Dowding whose family seems to have belonged to Combwich. In the Bridgwater harbour accounts Dowding's name occurs more frequently than any other merchant of our town and it is linked with the ship called the *Christopher*. In a later Minehead harbour paper he is said to be the owner of the *Great Christopher*, perhaps a larger vessel and a sign of his increasing prosperity. He was one of the first chief burgesses of the new borough established by the Elizabethan charter.

In the middle of the sixteenth century twelve ships and twenty barks belonged to the port of Minehead and twenty-nine shipowners were named, among them many of those already referred to in this chapter. As for the nature of our trade, with Bridgwater itself it was mainly in beans, coal, iron, salt, wood and wine, the last named no doubt imported from the Continent. Minehead records show that there was a more important trade in livestock and wool, mainly with Welsh and Irish ports, and that our sailors were landing good catches of fish, including the highly esteemed salmon.

It is remarkable that Minehead's little creek could handle so much shipping and that so many vessels found adequate shelter at a haven exposed to gales from the north-west. However, by the middle of the century the receding high water level and the consequent silting up of the estuaries, which had already reduced the trade of Dunster to insignificance, was closing the creek of Minehead to all but small ships. A parock or bank of shingle had formed at the mouth of the creek and a disastrous decline in trade was inevitable. Frantic efforts were made to restore the harbour to its earlier prosperity. It was probably at this time that a pool known as the Weir Pool was excavated in the place where Quay Street is at its widest and where today there is a lawn and shelter. This pool was filled at high water and was used, but obviously without effect, to flush out the anchorage as the tide fell. As the high water mark has receded over the centuries the depth of water in the old creek and later in the present harbour has gradually decreased and to this fact must very largely be attributed the loss of trade and prosperity in the port of Minehead and the town that depended on it. Our merchants and mariners had acquired self-confidence in a hard, competitive school; they did not doubt that, if the lord of the manor relinquished his authority to them, they would be able, by their own efforts, to save their port from extinction.

So it came about that at the beginning of her reign the leading citizens of Minehead petitioned Queen Elizabeth I to grant them a charter that would give borough status to the town and self-government to the port. They addressed their appeal 'To the quenes most excellent hyghnes our soverayn lady.' Their argument in summary is that 'whereas time out of mind' there had been a pier or quay at Minehead kept in repair at an annual cost of some £50 levied on the shipping using it, the decline in trade, which they attributed to recent wars, had so reduced the income of the port that they had been unable to afford the charges for proper maintenance. Unless, they continue, the necessary repairs were completed by the next winter the harbour would be virtually unusable and the consequences disastrous for the trade, not only of Minehead, but of the three most western counties, Somerset, Devon and Cornwall, whose markets depended on imports of 'cattle, sheep, wool, yarn, cloth, butter, stone, coal, oysters, salmons and other sundry kinds of fish and flesh.' The Welsh ports, from which many of these goods came, would suffer: a good point this, for the Tudors took pride in their Welsh descent. Her Majesty's Customs were already suffering losses by the decline in trade, another persuasive argument with the tight-fisted Elizabeth. Ships sheltering in stormy weather needed the port, an argument directed towards the great port of Bristol whose ships in foul weather so often needed a haven of refuge. As for unhappy Minehead, a hundred poor seafaring men had been driven from their homes 'to seek they know not where, to the utter undoing of your said town.'

They then proposed the remedy. They begged that they might be incorporated as a borough, with a portreeve and burgesses to manage its affairs; that all users of the port, apart from its burgesses and with some concessions to Bristol, should pay agreed wharfage duties for doing so, thereby ensuring an adequate income for the upkeep of the harbour.

Before the Queen and her council could reach a decision it was considered necessary to refer the matter to the lord of the manor, whose family for a century and a half had been responsible for the management and maintenance of the port. Part of Thomas Luttrell's reply in draft form has survived. As far as it goes this letter quotes from the petition paragraph by paragraph and comments on the arguments put forward. It is undated but is certainly of the same year as the petition, 1559. He doubted if as much as £50 a year had been spent in maintenance, but otherwise accepted the arguments of the petitioners without question and was even more emphatic about the need for immediate action; 'for if the same pier be not new made before the Feast of St Michael the Archangel next ... the same is not to be recovered and made (good) without the charges of a prince.' Thomas Luttrell's apparent willingness to acquiesce in this sacrifice of authority in Minehead may be explained by the extravagant and unbusinesslike conduct of his soldier brother and predecessor, Sir John, who left his family much impoverished in money and in lands when he died.

The decision to incorporate Minehead soon followed. The charter of 1559 begins by describing Minehead as an ancient town, situated on the seashore. It repeats the arguments in favour of a borough, and accepts Thomas Luttrell's emphasis on the need for urgency. Therefore, it continues, for the better government of the town, Minehead is to be constituted a 'free borough incorporate under the name of the Portreeve and the Burgesses of the same borough.' Its boundaries are defined as:

> *...the whole borough, through all the tithing of the same and through the within limits called the full sea marks and through all the water to the Fair Furlong [beyond Porlock] as far as the water called Donniford Water.*

This appears to give Minehead control of the five creeks of Porlock, Minehead, Dunster, Blue Anchor and Watchet, though a dispute with Thomas Luttrell about harbour dues for the Dunster haven at the mouth of the Avill took place just a year later and the Attorney General ruled in his favour.

The corporation was given various legal powers over property, law-making, apprentices, and so forth. The town was to be governed by twelve principal burgesses who were to be the common council of the borough to assist the portreeve and with him to appoint a steward. Among the twelve burgesses were John Dowding, portreeve, John Kerry, master of Vice-Admiral Thomas Wyndham's ship, James Fugars, who may also have acted as steward, William Dennell who lived to be nearly one hundred, and Robert Quirke, whose family was always in the forefront of Minehead affairs during this century and the next. The portreeve was to be clerk of the market and he and the steward were to be commissioned as justices of the peace.

The procedures for choosing the portreeve and for finding 'a fit and worthy man, learned in the laws of England, to be steward' were laid down. The burgesses had to nominate an honest and fit person to be sergeant-at-mace for making proclamations, arrests and so on. In a court of record the steward was empowered to hear and determine cases to the value of £40 and to impose fines. There was to be a prison, a weekly market on Thursdays and two marts or fairs a year, on 1 March and on Midsummmer Day. A court of piepowder would maintain order among the strangers at these fairs whose profits were to be 'for the proper behoof, use and utility of the portreeve and Burgesses.' In order to sell goods in the town the ships of strangers had to be licensed, but the merchants of Minehead were freed from all such tolls.

As it happened the most momentous clause was the last and briefest: the charter would be forfeited if the port was not properly maintained, a condition that the principal burgesses and their portreeve proved unable to fulfil.

That their new responsibilities weighed heavily upon them is shown by an agreement of 10 August 1562, between John Dowding and Joan, his wife, on the one hand and the portreeve and burgesses of Minehead on the other, by which the income from harbour dues was farmed out to the Dowdings for the seemingly insignificant sum of £8 per annum. It is difficult to see where the money was to come from for the repair and rehabilitation of the decayed harbour, and no doubt this is why the burgesses pocketed their pride and invited Thomas Luttrell to be 'principal burgess within this town of Menet.' The formal agreement of 4 February 1565 had been written by James Fugars and signed by eleven burgesses, nine of whom were among the first to be chosen. Their appeal for help to Thomas Luttrell was evidently successful.

Just a month before, a Writ of the Exchequer had directed Sir Thomas Dyer, Sir George Norton, Henry Portman and William Hatley to examine all the creeks and havens in the vicinity of the port of Bridgwater. Bridgwater itself, they said, was a thriving port, but Minehead was linked with insignificant Axewater as 'haunted with vessels bringing in victuals, salt, wine, coal and wood for which purpose they are fit to be continued but for little else.' They mentioned the growing heap of stones (the parock) at Minehead 'for the amendment whereof the inhabitants of Minehead are bound by their charter and do yearly travail thereupon.' They were also concerned about the collection of customs duties for the whole area as there was no provision for a customs house. However, the deputies to the Bridgwater customer, controller and searcher at Minehead, Robert Quirke, Thomas Pearce and William Beaumont respectively, had hired a house for 6s.8d. a year for which they received no allowance.

By 1570 a Luttrell paper makes mention of the claim that the pier was useless and in July of that year Thomas Luttrell, then Sheriff of Somerset, was writing to his wealthy friends and neighbours to appeal to them for help towards the cost of constructing a new quay which he had undertaken to build to his 'great charge with some assistance' and help of 'my good and well-willing tenants' (relations with the burgesses had obviously improved). He promised to erect such a pier as was never 'the like harbour in the West of England.' These letters were carried by bearers authorised by the borough and it was hoped that they would return with written promises from the subscribers whose names would be recorded at Minehead 'for a memory of your courtesy toward the said quay.' However, the new harbour works were probably never completed, though a pier called 'the newe key' was in use by 1605.

Thomas Luttrell died in January, 1571, and his heir, George, was a mere boy of eleven whose advisers may well have felt unable to meet on their own responsibility the heavy charges involved. A rough draft of a petition that probably dates from the end of the century and must have been written either by or for George Luttrell is entitled: 'Reasons why the Town of Minehead should not be incorporated by your majesty.' It is full of erasures and alterations and therefore difficult to decipher, but the main argument is clear and uncompromising: the town was better governed before its incorporation and was by this time overflowing 'with very dissolute and disordered persons.' The magistrates and burgesses were 'but simple and rude handicraft men, fitter to be governed than to govern others.' Because of their misgovernment and the many Welshmen coming to the town there had been frequent quarrels, affrays, bloodshed and 'some murders committed in Dunster, being the next market town adjoining.' Of the twenty-three tipplers licensed to sell ale by the portreeve only two were 'fit or able to give entertainment, whereby all vice and disorder [was] nourished and increased.' The once wealthy inhabitants were now living in poverty and the population sadly declined. The borough courts had become a laughing stock, and the fairs and market were almost defunct, but most serious was the loss of 'the very ancient and good harbour', that had, before Minehead was incorporated, as many as thirty or forty ships and barks belonging to it, whereas 'now there [were] but five and (those) very mean.'

George Luttrell now put forward some positive proposals. To the £600 that he had already spent on the old quay and the £200 subscribed by his friends and tenants, he was prepared to add another £1000. The most suitable site was already his, so that a harbour could be built in a 'fairer and fitter place.' All he asked in return that the town should no longer be incorporated. The advantages to the Crown were great; such a harbour as he intended to build would 'be able to receive Her Majesty's ships'; it would be the best port for transporting soldiers, ammunition and victuals into Ireland and for trade with Wales; and it would provide shelter, where there was none, for the shipping of Bristol and Bridgwater on the stormy voyage up and down the channel.

Above: *George Luttrell, builder of Minehead harbour in 1616.*
Below: *Minehead harbour. George Luttrell's work ended near the bows of the ketch in this modern photograph.*

Finally, whereas at this point and for fourteen years past the portreeve and burgesses had engrossed into their own hands 'such commodities and merchandises as are brought by sea', the new harbour would both benefit trade and increase the revenue of Her Majesty's Customs. Only the Luttrells had the wealth and the land to undertake so great and necessary a task. Just one condition had to be met: Minehead was no longer to be incorporated. The lawyer who worked on this draft seems to have been Thomas Stewkley and in general he (or another) toned down the language of the petition, erasing such phrases as 'that vile clique' (of burgesses). Clearly there was by this time a bitter feud between George Luttrell and the portreeve and principal burgesses of the borough of Minehead. No doubt as a result of this petition, a Writ of Exchequer of 26 November 1601

directed Sir Thomas Palmer, Thomas Mallett, John Pyne, John Trevelyan, James Clarke and Thomas Hughes to enquire whether the portreeve and burgesses had kept their harbour in good order. An inquisition taken at Nether Stowey on 11 January 1602 heard evidence on oath from seventeen witnesses, including George Carew of Crowcombe, steward of Dunster Castle, who affirmed that for the past twenty years the corporation of Minehead had failed to maintain its harbour which was choked with sand and stones, and 'altogether in decay', so that ships could not 'call at the port or stop there safely, without danger of being shipwrecked.'

An undated letter of this period signed by John Luttrell seems to show that George Luttrell's brother, John, was working on his behalf at Westminster. With Sir Nicholas Halswell and another person he had earnestly solicited the Lord Chief Justice Popham against incorporation:

> *My Lord's answer is that before he will signify his opinion of the cause he will have some of the chiefest of the town to be sent with some in your behalf before him; as by his letter shall be signified for that he taketh Lashbrooke (to be) an unfit man to be credited in so weighty a matter, being one whom I think my lord has just cause not to reckon of, but I assure you my lord is well conceited and inclined against the corporation and very desirous to find (in favour of) the harbour or anything else that shall be for the good of the country or public weal. He would have you to set onward with the work.*

Lewis Lashbrooke, whom Sir John Popham so obviously distrusted, was at this time one of Minehead's two Members of Parliament. Later he became notorious as an untrustworthy attorney and on this occasion had evidently been employed by the portreeve's irreconcilable faction to fight for the charter. However, nothing was decided until after the old Queen's death. A rough draft of a letter from George Luttrell to Roger Warre of Hestercombe, dated 20 August 1604, showed that some progress had been made. He asked his good friend, Warre, to speak on his behalf to Lord Chief Justice Popham, whose home was at Wellington, to explain that his efforts to pass on a letter from his lordship to the portreeve and burgesses of Minehead for communication to the principal inhabitants of the town had met with little success, because 'Master Portreeve', having arranged a meeting at the Town Hall at which the letter was to be read, failed to keep his appointment. Although those inhabitants who, in George Luttrell's words, 'preferred the good estate of the harbour there before the corporation' waited for him 'some two or three hours', they 'departed as wise as they came.' Since then it was observed 'the portreeve utterly refuseth to acquaint them or any of that sort, being all very honest men, with the contents hereof'.

George Quirke, the portreeve, and the traders who were supporting him, had petitioned King James for the continuance of their charter of incorporation. The decision had been referred to the Lord Chief Justice and he had appointed certain Somerset men (of whom Roger Warre may have been one) to advise him about the case, but before a decision was made, Lord Chief Justice Popham had decided to visit West Somerset himself. One senses that George Luttrell felt that he already had him on his side. His brother's letter had assured him that 'my lord is well conceited and inclined against the corporation', so he hoped that his lordship would continue to grant him 'still his honourable favour, as heretofore in his Majesty's time I always had, concerning the defaulting of that bad corporation.'

However, three years later, in November 1607, George Quirke was still signing an examination of a vagrant saddler named John Guppie as 'Portreeve of the said borough' of Minehead. The justices at the quarter sessions accepted his evidence and Guppie was found 'guilty and burned in the shoulder for a rogue.' By this time George Luttrell had lost his friend at Court, for Sir John Popham died in June of the same year. This examination must have been almost the last official act of George Quirke as portreeve, for at about this time the decision was taken to abrogate the charter that George Luttrell so much disliked. In 1609 he prepared a petition to Parliament asking that the right of Parliamentary representation should be withdrawn with all the other privileges that had already been forfeited. He claimed that Minehead, his inheritance, had no power to elect members of the House of Commons 'until the fifth year of the reign of the late Memorable Queen Elizabeth' when burgesses were chosen for Parliament 'by pretence of a new corporation.' No such power was granted by the Queen's Letters Patent, he maintained (though incorrectly), and certainly there was no longer any surviving authority for the right of election as 'the said corporation was dissolved in the sixth year of his Majesty's reign over us.' It would be a great indignity, he continued, 'for burgesses to be chosen for the High Court of Parliament without legal power.' It is strange to find a Luttrell at the beginning of the seventeenth century so anxious to give up a prerogative that his successors in the eighteenth century valued so highly for the influence and power that it gave them.

Another petition from George Luttrell for the restoration of the rights of the manor over the new harbour that he has started to build begins with a recital of the history of the destruction of the old pier 'by the violence of the sea and tempest whereunto it lay open,' of the no less troublesome 'blockage with gravel and stones and such like' and of the consequent decline in trade since the grant of the charter in 1559:

> ... *which being much respected and pitied by George Luttrell, Esquire, Lord of the Manor and Town of Minehead [he] hath of late erected a new harbour or quay which he intendeth to finish before Michaelmas next, and to keep and maintain the same as the charge of him, his heirs and assigns, Lords of the said Manor of Minehead.*

His new quay was to have 'a strong wall of rock 600 foot in length and 66 foot in breadth in the foundation.' It would project so far into the sea that 'at every dead tide' there would be 16½ feet of water and at 'high springs' 33 feet. 'So safe and spacious' was it to be that 240 ships, barks and boats 'of any burden' would be able to 'harbour there in all weathers in safety.' Already it had saved many ships from 'loss in tempest' and its equal could not be found 'within 30 or 40 miles.' 'Why now', he concluded, 'it was possible to cross to Wales in one tide and sometimes to come back again on the same!' Mr Luttrell left no argument unstated that could strengthen his case.

The Journal of the House of Commons for 28 March 1610 records that a new harbour had been built by Mr Luttrell at a 'great and extraordinary charge' of £5000 and in April the Lords gave a second reading to the same Bill 'for repairing and maintaining the quay or harbour of the Port of Minehead', though it does not seem to have passed into law at this time. The petition itself pointed out how great would be the cost of building and maintaining such a harbour and asked that proper charges should be approved for its use. There followed a detailed list of proposed duties to be levied on imported goods, based on an old tariff compiled before 1559 and renewed in 1594, but with considerable increases to allow for the severe inflation that afflicted those times. In this old list, 'all written out of a certain table which did hang in the Common Hall at Minehead to be seen of all', some 35 articles of merchandise appeared, ranging from a mease (500) of red herring for one halfpenny to a tun of French wine for 4d., a tun of Spanish wine from Andalusia for 6d., or a wey of corn (40 bushels) for 11d. The final agreed charges can be seen in a schedule of duties delivered on 22 September 1622, to George Ford, the wharfinger or water-bailiff of the manor, 'for the maintenance of the New Harbour.' The authorised charges were not quite as favourable as those requested in the petition, but they were usually double those in the old tariff and in the case of Spanish wine the duty had been trebled. There were also charges for keelage, rowlage, bearage, cellarage and measurage; cock-boats, however, were free and limestone could be imported for a mere halfpenny a ton. As we shall see, the dispute between the Castle and one-time burgesses still smouldered on, and this, no doubt, explains why those whom it was anticipated would refuse to pay were to be dealt with by way of 'distress as damage feasant for trespassing me upon my soil there.'

To underline the decline in the trade of Minehead, Dunster Castle drew up a list of thirty-two ships and barks that belonged to the port before the Elizabethan charter of 1559. The details were culled from the memories of three old sailors, William Dennell ('of the years near of one hundred'), Andrew Teague and William Morgan. A letter of 4 October 1609, from Robert Sydenham, evidently the steward at the castle, to a Master Morgan, was presumably intended for William. He was asked to invite forty citizens of the town, named in the letter, to meet George Luttrell's new ship when she entered harbour on the 23rd of the month, so that all could give their 'benevolence to the furthering and ending of the new quay here', which therefore by 1609 was already under construction. Robert Sydenham hoped that the vicar, Nicholas Browse, and his parishioners would also be present, but only twenty-three of the forty men on the list seem to have accepted the invitation, which, as they were invited to dine also, is surprising - and it is significant that no member of the Quirke family was among those invited.

Again a proportion of the inhabitants petitioned the king to restore their charter. In spite of the great expense incurred by George Luttrell in building the new harbour, the disgruntled minority of merchants and shipowners felt no gratitude to him. He counter-petitioned on 15 February 1620, stating that he had erected a new harbour, which was intended for the 'good and benefit of the town', near to the ancient port, but in a more convenient place and at great expense. Now, 'some few of the inhabitants' made more prosperous by the consequent increase in trade 'and puffed up with a desire for rule and authority (being men altogether unmete for the same)', were for their own ends seeking to recover the full borough status lost in 1607. 'Almost all the rest of the inhabitants of Minehead', as well as of places adjoining, had, he claimed, subscribed their names to his counter petition.

A reply of the same date from 'the Court of Whitehall', signed by Sidney Montague, found that the petitioner had been at great charges and that most of the inhabitants of Minehead had by signing the petition declared their unwillingness to have their town re-incorporated. Therefore His Majesty agreed that this should not be done, and issued an order to this effect which was 'entered with the Master of Requests and Clerk of the Signet.'

From this time until the Restoration in 1660 trade and prosperity in Minehead were very much on the increase. As a result, the population which had declined towards the end of Elizabeth's reign, began to expand rapidly. New houses were being built, particularly in Puddle Street, the business centre of the town, and also near the harbour. Records of twelve new houses in Quay Street alone have survived, including Roger Vyon's New Inn built by the Luttrells and leased to him in 1634.

Some harbour accounts for the period December 1647 to March 1649 give us an idea of the nature and extent of the trade of the town in this time of prosperity. Of the ports in the British Isles trading with Minehead, Aberthaw just across the Channel is most frequently mentioned and it is followed, but not closely, by Bristol and Watchet. There were sailings to and from Cardiff, Barry, Swansea, Tenby, Milford Haven and Haverfordwest in Wales. On the other side of the Severn Sea, Tewkesbury, Bridgwater, Porlock, Lynmouth, Combe Martin, Ilfracombe, Barnstaple, Appledore, Northam and Padstow were named. Among the ports on the English Channel were Topsham and Weymouth, and there is one reference to London. In the middle of the seventeenth century Minehead was in the forefront of ports trading with Irish towns: Carrickfergus, Strangford, Dublin, Youghal, Cork and Kinsale were prominent among them. Between 1660 and 1667 Minehead sent a fishing fleet to Newfoundland every year.

This period of boom in the history of Minehead brought to the town some new families who were to play an important part in its further development. The Alloways, an influential Quaker family, arrived at this time and so did the Haymans, one of whom, John, leased a house in Butts Green in 1618. Another member of the family, James, was resident in Youghal in 1672 which no doubt explains the frequent voyages between this Irish port and Minehead.

In 1667 yet another attempt by certain members of the trading community to regain control of the port because of 'some encouragement they then received' was frustrated by a writ of Quo Warranto in the Exchequer. A document of this year repeating the familiar story of decline between 1559 and 1608, presented the case against the portreeve and burgesses in some detail and attempted to show that they no longer had any legal rights to exercise authority in or over the port of Minehead. As a paper of 1716 puts it: 'a judgment was thereupon had against the inhabitants which also obstructed that design [i.e. for re-incorporation] and then they were quiet.'

Towards the end of the seventeenth century George Luttrell's splendid new harbour was unfortunately already beginning to silt up with pebbles and sand. This can only be explained by a steadily receding high water mark in this century as in its predecessor. In 1682 Colonel Francis Luttrell had strengthened the harbour wall on the seaward side 'by placing therein great rocks and stones' as a breakwater, and also no doubt in an effort to check the movement of pebbles around the harbour head.

However, in spite of these troublesome problems the trade of Minehead at this time was still considerable, as may be seen in a journal and ledger of the trading activities of William Alloway, junior, the prosperous Quaker merchant, for the years 1683 to 1686. His trade was mostly in wool, tallow, foodstuffs and wine and was mainly with coastal ports in the Bristol Channel and with Southern Ireland, but occasional, longer, voyages to Dunkirk, Bordeaux, Morlaix, the Canary Islands and even the West Indies are recorded. During one period of four months his income amounted to £157.15s.6d. Michael Bryant, Robert Deake, Christopher Devonshire (also a Quaker) and George Hayman were merchants with whom he had trading arrangements. Two of their ships were called *The Adventure* and *The Reformation*. The harbour accounts for 1666 to the end of the eighteenth century have been preserved. They give the names of ships, masters and merchants and details of the commodities carried to and fro, but they also record the expenditure by Dunster Castle on the clearance and maintenance of the harbour, and these charges seem always to have been increasing more rapidly than the income from port dues. So in 1701 an Act of Parliament was passed to help the Luttrells to meet these heavy charges and to provide funds for an extension of the harbour. This measure allowed the lord of the manor the benefit of certain duties for a term of twenty-one years.

When Colonel Francis Luttrell died in 1690 his son and heir, Tregonwell, was only seven years old, and his affairs were being managed by the boy's mother, Mary, 24, and by his uncle, Alexander. In 1696 Mary married Jacob Bancks, a Swede by birth and a captain in the English Navy, who sat in Parliament for Minehead from 1698 to 1713 and who was knighted in 1699. It was he who arranged for a survey of the harbour to be made in 1701. A London engineer called Dummer sent his man Thomas Surbey to Minehead on 9 July 1701 to examine the existing harbour and to recommend extensions or improvements that would help to keep it clear of 'sullage.' His 'Survey and Description of the Defects of the Pier at Minehead' is in the Somerset Record Office with his rather crudely drawn map showing the extension to the pier and the groyne which it was hoped would keep the harbour free from sand and stones. He found that at a spring tide the water at the pierhead rose 28 feet and on the same ebb the beach dried out three-quarters of a mile to the low-water mark, whereas on neap tides the rise was not above 22 feet at most and the ebb left the pier dry only 20

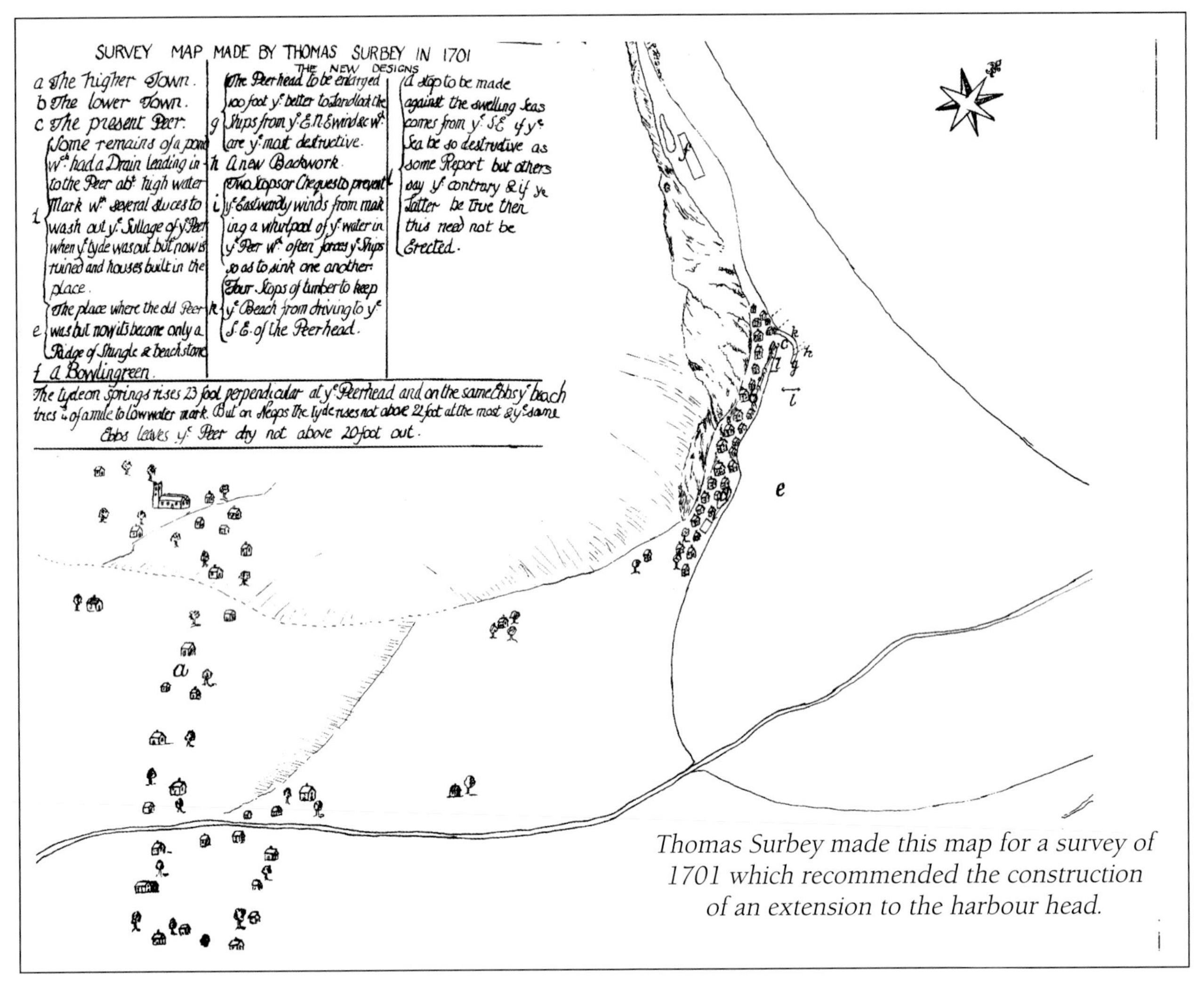

Thomas Surbey made this map for a survey of 1701 which recommended the construction of an extension to the harbour head.

feet out. He sought the advice of the masters of a number of ships, but in the account they gave him, 'the defects', he wrote, 'were as numerous and different as were the number of men I conversed with.' Although the main tide was a mile out, winds from certain quarters rolled the beach into the harbour and the resulting sullage had to be loaded into carts and taken about 200 yards into the 'wash of the sea'. His report waited for some days in Batson's Coffee House in London for Mr Dummer to collect it, but it eventually reached Sir Jacob Bancks with Thomas Surbey's bill for £30.14s.0d. (*see map, above*).

Tregonwell Luttrell, still a minor, died in 1703 and his uncle, Alexander, who succeeded him as lord of the manor, signed a contract with Daniel Dennell of Cannington on 22 July 1704, to build a new head by 25 December 1705, 120 feet long 'with timber trees firmly locked together and piles to the north side towards the sea.' This framework was to be filled with stones, and a groyne 100 feet in length was to hold back the drifting pebbles at the back of the old pier. The work was to cost £1509, a figure soon raised to nearly £2000, with free timber from Langridge Wood, near Roadwater, valued at £900. The contractor also had the right to collect the harbour dues until the project was completed.

Minehead and the Luttrells owed much to the perseverance and steadiness of Madam Dorothy, whose husband, Alexander, had died in 1711. Her son and heir, also named Alexander, was six years of age and the full responsibility for the management of the estate had to be borne by his mother, described by a contemporary as 'the great good lady at the Castle.' She was determined to pay the heavy debts incurred by the extravagance of her late brother-in-law, Colonel Francis Luttrell, and at the same time to meet the costs of the new work at the harbour which were increasing year by year.

In 1706 her husband had borrowed on a mortgage of the manor of Minehead from Sir George Rooke, the famous admiral who had married Tregonwell's sister, Mary, first a sum of £3000 and then a further sum of £1000. After six or seven years Daniel Dennell at last completed a wooden extension to the old pier which, as agreed, he had filled with stones, but already 'the sea worms had gotten into it whereby the timber on the back side of the quay was very much perished and decayed.' It was clear that much more would have to be spent, so the Luttrell family and some of the Minehead merchants petitioned Parliament for an extension of the term of years during which duties could be levied on certain goods to meet these mounting expenses. An account was submitted which showed that Dunster Castle had spent £3885.8s.7d., whereas harbour dues over a ten-year period had yielded just £1775.8s.7d., leaving the Luttrells over £2000 out of pocket.

On 8 January 1713, a new contract was concluded with Daniel Dennell whereby he agreed, for a sum of £700, to build a strong stone wall to encase the timber frame, 12 feet wide at the base and tapering to 6 feet at the top of the outside of the pier, and 8 feet wide at the base to 4 feet at the top on the inside, 'allowing to every rope of wall 20 feet long two hogsheads of good lime.'

However, Dennell became increasingly difficult to work with. He kept pressing Dorothy Luttrell for more and more money in excess of the sums agreed in the contract. When this was not forthcoming he 'left and ran away from the work, cheating the poor workmen of their wages and without making any restitution or satisfaction to Madam Luttrell.'

Dorothy Luttrell, 'the great good lady at the Castle', completed the extension to the harbour in 1714.

Thomas Chidgey of Watchet, the chief mason, and his men were still available, and at this critical moment Joseph Alloway was appointed supervisor. His father, William Alloway, had been a devout Quaker, but Joseph, because of his marriage by a priest to Mary Brooke in 1687, had been forced by the Somerset Quarterly Meeting to leave the Society of Friends. Like others in his family he became a prosperous merchant and he was obviously also a decisive and capable man. Before Christmas the outer wall of the 'New Quay was finished to content and done very firm' for the expenditure of a further sum of £441.15s.6d. with an additional £54.16s.6d. for 'Mr Alloway's trouble and charges.' By an agreement signed on 1 May 1714, Joseph Alloway undertook for £300 to encase in stone (according to the original plan), the inner wall of the harbour, and by Christmas this also was finished. He added some groynes in an attempt to control the movement of the stones, placed some cranes on the quay and fixed massive timbers to the quayside to protect the wall of the harbour and the hulls of the ships that were moored to it, some of this work apparently at his own cost.

But Dorothy Luttrell's troubles were not over. At Christmas, 1715, a great storm shattered the sea-facing wall at the top of the pier, broke the wharfside in Quay Street and demolished a number of houses there. Once again, in May 1716, Thomas Chidgey, the master mason, came over from Watchet to repair the damage. Every year some £20 had to be spent in clearing the stones and sullage from the harbour. Jonathan Dibble and Hugh Bevin alone were paid £54 for this work. At the end of this year a group of inhabitants, egged on by political opponents of the Luttrell interest, encouraged, no doubt, by the Whig government that came into power at the accession of George I, submitted a petition to HRH the Prince of Wales, Guardian of the Kingdom:

> *The humble petition of the Gentlemen Merchant Traders and Principal Inhabitants of your Majesty's Ancient and Loyal borough and Port of Minehead, requesting the restoration in full of the Elizabethan charter, with authority to make by-laws for the more regular and peaceable government and entertainment of the inhabitants of the said borough and strangers resorting thereto.*

In answer to this Madam Dorothy, and the trustees appointed to help her to manage the affairs of her son Alexander during his minority, made an effective reply by quoting figures which showed that no adequate return had been received by the family for the very large sums of money already expended or likely to be required in the future for the improvement and maintenance of the harbour.

The merchants of Tiverton, backed by a few importers from Taunton and Minehead itself, also petitioned Parliament. They had already shown their hostility to Dunster Castle by refusing on a number of occasions to take their wool to the Town Hall so that it could be weighed on the beam provided by the lord of the manor, a service for which they were required to pay a duty. They now demanded that Watchet should be made a staple port for the import of wool, hoping thus to escape the payment of this duty altogether. However, it was pointed out to Whitehall by the trustees that Watchet had no Customs facilities whereas at Minehead there was a Customs House with ten officers: to move the wool trade to Watchet could not be 'of advantage to the Government (whatever it may be to some private persons).' Furthermore, the recent improvements to the port of Minehead enabled ships of 300 or 400 tons to berth there, but Watchet had only 'a very incommodious dry harbour or creek, not having water in it (unless at Spring Tides) for a ship of above 15 or 20 tons'; and

if Minehead harbour were not maintained ships trading between Bristol and the West Indies, and even those of Watchet itself, would have no shelter to run to in tempestuous weather. Indeed the case against transferring the wool trade to Watchet was so strong that even Sir William Wyndham of Orchard, who at first backed the Tiverton merchants, withdrew his support.

A great many drafts and copies of petitions to Parliament or the sovereign for the last years of Queen Anne's reign and the opening years of George I have survived in the Dunster Castle muniments, but they are very repetitive and add little to what has already been said.

A petition to King George I, designed to obtain the signatures of as many Minehead men as could be persuaded to sign it, begins by stressing the absolute dependence of the town on the trade of the port 'having no resort of travellers, being in the remotest part of your Majesty's County of Somerset.' One cannot escape the impression that the Luttrell advocates, in the draft petition at least, were apt to overstate the case against incorporation: a claim, for instance, that the Crown collected annually £6000 in Customs duties in one draft was expunged from a later one. However, the basic argument against incorporation was unanswerable: the upkeep of the harbour was always more expensive and less profitable than some of the Minehead traders were prepared to recognise, and only the Dunster Castle estate had the resources to maintain it properly. The authority of the Luttrells over the port was rightly confirmed.

The battle for the port of Minehead had been won for the lord of the manor and during the next few years the town enjoyed a prosperity even greater than that which followed the completion of George Luttrell's harbour just one hundred years before. It was at this time that Daniel Defoe, the novelist and old Monmouth soldier, made his *Tour Through the Whole Island of Great Britain*. Minehead he considered to be the safest harbour on this side of the Channel and a fine port:

No Ship is so big, but it may come in; and no Weather so bad, but the Ships are safe when they are in: And they told me that in the great Storm, Anno 1703, when the Ships were blown on Shore, wreckd and lost, in every Harbour of the County, they suffered little or no damage in this.

The Trade of this Town lies chiefly with Ireland, and this was for many years the chief Port in these Parts, where wool from Ireland was allowed to be imported; but that Liberty is since enlarged to several other Ports, by Act of Parliament.

The Town returns two Members to Parliament. It is well built, full of rich Merchants, and has some Trade also to Virginia and the West Indies. They correspond much with the Merchants of Barnstaple and Bristol, in their foreign Trade. What has greatly contributed to the Improvement of Minehead was an Act passed in the 12th and 13th year of King William III, which was continued by an Act of the 10th of the late Queen Anne, for recovering, securing and keeping in Repair, the Harbour of Minehead - In pursuance of which, a new Head has been built, the Beach cleared, and a great Progress made in the Piers and designed Works.

At this time Minehead enjoyed its years of greatest prosperity and expansion. Among the prominent merchants there are repeated references to Thomas Holwill, Joseph Alloway, Nicholas Hayman, Silvester Deake, George Devonshire, Edmund Baker, Hugh Paine, William Barrow and John Williams. Between 1718 and 1740 the import of wool from Ireland alone amounted, according to Collinson, to an annual average of nearly 30 000 stones, while a decade later an average weight of Irish wool of about 10 000 stones per annum provided the town with a yearly profit of some £500. Other valuable imports included linen cloth (estimated by Collinson to be worth £126.5s.5d. in 1726), bay yam and various hides and skins, while during the same period Collinson considered oak bark and grain to be the most valuable exports.

Throughout the eighteenth century there was a steady trade from South Wales, mainly with Swansea, in coal, in culm for burning lime, and in live animals. For example, William Gemlett, whose ship was named the *Sochable Friends*, landed twenty-eight chaldrons of culm, and a brig from Wales in 1738 brought over twenty-five cows and five horses. Sometimes more unusual cargoes were unloaded. John Forrest, the water bailiff, reported to the steward at Dunster Castle in June 1770 that there had been 'pretty many ships in this week among them a vessel from Genney which... discharged some camwood, beeswax and Elifands teeth.' It is not mentioned what old key duty it paid.

The Act of Parliament mentioned by Defoe was passed at the end of the reign of William III. Renewed in 1712, and at various other times later in the century, it authorised the lord of the manor to make charges for the use of the harbour and to make provision for the appointment of trustees to assist in running the affairs of the port. These trustees met regularly at one of the better hostelries in the town. In July 1757, George Squier, landlord of the Plume of Feathers, entertained them; in June 1769 John Martin's George Inn was chosen for their meeting. However, the cost of maintaining the pier in good repair and of clearing the harbour of silt was always too great to allow them to pay off entirely the heavy debt incurred during Queen Anne's reign, which one Luttrell draft petition put at £15 000, though this figure is certainly exaggerated.

In 1770 the trustees obtained from Henry Fownes Luttrell a loan on a mortgage of £9718.5s.5d., though Robert Davis, who led the political opposition to the Luttrell interest in Minehead, claimed that this sum was an over-estimate, and that just a decade before the debt had been as little as £2000. Nevertheless, by the end of the century it had grown to £20 000 and of one thing we can be certain: the cost of maintaining Minehead harbour was always outpacing the calculations of the trustees, of the Castle estate and of the merchants who traded from the port. These losses can only be explained by the reduction in the depth of water in the harbour at a time when ocean-going ships were increasing in tonnage.

The removal of silt and stones from the harbour was a persistent, growing and expensive problem for the trustees throughout the century. There are repeated references in the harbour accounts to payments for clearing away the stones. In 1755, for instance, eighteen men and four tossers were employed. The labourers were paid 10d. a day, the tossers 1s.1d. and two carters with their horse butts cost 6s.2d. As another example, in 1758 the contractors for the removal of stones were paid 1s.6d. a load and between 1753 and 1756 the cost of this work exceeded the income of the port by £95.19s.1¾d. Very soon after the completion of the New Head, the work of clearing the beach had to start all over again. Some accounts of 1720 refer to the use of baskets for gathering the stones and tipping them into the carts, and in 1773 Sarah Bumold supplied John Jenkins and his son with nine shillings' worth of ale during the nine days that they were working on the quay, which provides an interesting comparison with the rate of pay, one shilling a day for a labourer and 1s.6d. for the foreman.

Damage from heavy seas to the structure of the pier and the wharfside along the quay was more spasmodic but even more expensive when it occurred. A reference in the Blathwayt correspondence from their Porlock estate reported storm damage at Porlock in 1770 and added that Minehead harbour was said to have suffered £200 worth of damage.

The depth of water in the harbour steadily diminished: soundings taken by John Short in December, 1753, gave the maximum depth as 27 feet 6ins, though this could not have been made during a high spring tide. There was certainly much more water than there is today, and John St Albyn, the steward of the manor, reported near the end of the same month that fifteen or sixteen ships were in, and that all were afloat one and a half hours before high water, including two foreign merchantmen, both large, and one of Minehead's largest vessels, Captain Gregory's *Molly*.

An undated schedule of duties, probably prepared to meet some of the charges incurred for extending and maintaining the enlarged harbour, is not dissimilar in many of its details to that of 1622, but masters of ships were required to pay more and to observe certain rules for the general safety of the shipping that now crowded the port. The heaviest penalty was imposed for melting tar on board ship, no doubt as a fire precaution. For this offence

A painting of 1735 showing the enlarged harbour.

masters could be fined £2.10s. In 1740 Minehead ships were charged one shilling for keelage, ships from other English ports 1s.4d. and foreign or outlandish ships two shillings. It is not clear how long vessels could remain in port for these charges but a letter to the Blathwayts of Gloucestershire from John Perkins, their unsalaried water bailiff at Porlock, suggested that the keelage charge was made for every tide. He had been asked to prepare a schedule of charges for Porlock and he required time to consider it properly, it being near the port of Minehead:

> *... where they pay three or four shillings a boat or small vessel if they lie there but a tide. Which heavy charge is laid on that harbour for paying about three or four thousand pounds and interest that have been laid out on that quay.*

He was confident that no skipper would pay these exorbitant charges who might find a safe harbourage six miles down the coast for a shilling or 1s.6d. Perhaps he was right and the decline of the port was accelerated in the 1700s by the heavy charges that the harbour trustees felt impelled to make.

The schedule of duties referred to above, among much that is familiar, lists a few strange new charges:

> *For the use of the Pecks a bushel of coal or in money 6d.; For every ton of greenery or saltory weares 3s.4d.; and after the list of keelage charges ships are required to pay 4d. for each of their Round Topps.*

The tale of woe continued, but in 1771 the water bailiff, John Franks, could cheer up his master at Dunster Castle by reporting that Richard Watkins in 'the *Febe*' from Bristol had entered port, 'bown for Darkmouth.' In 1791 John Fownes Luttrell's sloop *Industry* was repaired by the shipwright, Thomas Manston. Captain Richards was sailing this little ship of 20 tons across to Swansea for coal and culm during the last quarter of the eighteenth century, as was Captain Matthew Craig in another little bark. Grahame Farr in *Ships and Harbours of Exmoor* writes of the *Dolfyn* of Holstein in 1760 coming in with lemons from Oporto, but there could have been little foreign trade late in this century and in the next paragraph Farr writes that in 1792 Minehead as a port had been outstripped by Ilfracombe.

To curry favour with the electors, John Langston, the political opponent of the Luttrells in the 1796 election, built a ship and named it after himself in an attempt to revive the port's fortunes, but he was fighting the processes of nature and his efforts, like those of the harbour trustees, were doomed to failure.

Let us conclude with some words about the port of Minehead from Collinson's *History of the County of Somerset*, written in the last decade of the eighteenth century:

> *About the beginning of the present century upwards of forty vessels were employed to Ireland. Many others were engaged in the West India, Virginia and Straits trade; and four thousand barrels of herrings were at that time shipped here annually for the Mediterranean. But all this is now nearly at an end: the trade is lost; the herrings have left the coast; and there are at present only five or six vessels belonging to the port.*

Chapter 4
The Parliamentary Borough: 1559–1832

As we have shown, Minehead was a place of considerable importance in the first half of the sixteenth century. The little creek which flowed into the sea at the foot of the present Blenheim Road somehow managed to accommodate ships of up to 100 tons in burden, but by the middle of the century the once thriving trade was already threatened by the silting up of the creek with stones; and this was happening at a time when the Luttrells, who had financed all our previous harbour works, were disorganised by the untimely death of the distinguished soldier, Sir John Luttrell, which left his family deeply in debt. When, therefore, some of the principal inhabitants of Minehead petitioned Queen Elizabeth for a Charter of Incorporation, believing that they could manage their own affairs better than the lord of the manor had done for them, their request was not opposed by Dunster Castle and in 1559 Minehead became a borough with a portreeve and Common Council of burgesses to govern it and with the right to return two members to her Majesty's High Court of Parliament at Westminster. Every householder within the parish of Minehead and the manors of Alcombe and Staunton in the parish of Dunster who was not in receipt of alms was entitled to vote, a wide franchise for the sixteenth century.

By the early-eighteenth century, Thomas Gage, a candidate, in a petition defined the voters of Minehead as 'inhabitants and pot boilers', that is to say every householder with a hearth on which he could boil a pot; but more properly Minehead was an inhabitant householder borough. The votes, of course, were cast in public, so that the candidates knew exactly who had voted for them. As most of the houses were leased by the manor, a candidate in the Luttrell interest started with a considerable advantage, increasingly so as the seventeenth merged into the eighteenth century, the age of the pocket-borough and the all-powerful patronage of its wealthy owner. However, at the beginning of the seventeenth century the patrons of the borough were still asking for favours rather than giving orders. Thomas Luttrell sat in the Parliament of 1562, his son George, who built the new harbour in 1616, was elected in 1584 and George's brother John represented the borough in 1586 and again in Armada year. By this time George Luttrell was engaged in a bitter struggle with the portreeve and burgesses of Minehead with the object of persuading the Privy Council to annul the charter. In a draft petition entitled 'Reasons why the Town of Minehead should not be incorporated by your Majesty', George Luttrell described the magistrates and burgesses of the town as 'but simple and rude handicraftmen who are fitter to be governed than to govern others.' They returned one of their number, James Quirke, to the Parliament of 1592, and their choice of Lewis Lashbrooke, a Minehead lawyer who lived at Butts Green, to represent their interests in 1601 and to fight for the retention of the charter, showed them to be poor judges of character. The Lord Chief Justice considered 'Lashbrooke to be an unfit man to be credited in so weighty a matter,' an opinion which Lashbrooke's arrest in 1628 for interference with the work of the Customs officers fully confirmed. Evidence was given against him by those he had 'grieved and unjustly molested, troubled or sued', and at the end of his long life he was still named at the head of a list of Somerset attorneys who had 'given many testimonies of their ill affection to the public peace.' The abrogation of the charter in 1607 ended the incompetent rule of the portreeve, George Quirke, and his burgesses, but George Luttrell was unable to persuade the Privy Council to take away also the Parliamentary franchise, a privilege greatly valued by most of his successors, though for some reason distasteful to him. Thus, for more than 200 years two members continued to be returned for Minehead, with just one exception - 1614 - the notorious Addled Parliament, when Minehead was the last borough in English history to fail to hold an election when required to do so by the Sheriff.

During the troubled years of Charles I, Edmund Wyndham of the loyal Kentsford branch of the family, sat for the town, sharing the seat with Thomas Luttrell and later with Thomas Horner, descendant of Little Jack Homer of Mells and a Roundhead. The election return for the Short Parliament of April 1640 has survived. It is signed by one of the constables, Rice Jenkins, who was also the harbour master. The

High Sheriff was notified that two 'men of good understanding, with Knowledge and discretion for causes concerning the work public of this realm' have been chosen to represent the borough. One was Francis Wyndham (who hid Prince Charles at Trent during his famous escape after Worcester), but the other successful candidate, Alexander Popham, preferred to sit for Bath, which had also elected him. The signatories to this return included Robert Quirke, the elder, and Robert Hayman, members of two famous Minehead families, and, of course, Lewis Lashbrooke, who in spite of his evil reputation continued to play a prominent role in local affairs, though he was never again returned to Westminster.

In the famous Long Parliament Sir Francis Popham and his nephew, Alexander Luttrell, represented Minehead. At the death of the latter in 1642 Thomas Hanham of Caundle in Dorset was chosen to succeed him, but during the Civil War members suspected of Royalist sympathies became unacceptable to Cromwell and the radical Independents. Hanham committed the indiscretion of visiting Charles I at Oxford in 1644 in search of peace. He even attended the Royalist Parliament there and not surprisingly he was disabled as member for Minehead. Next year, at the age of seventy, he was begging to compound for his error; pleading that his journey to Oxford was 'induced on pretence of making a happy peace' and that he remained there 'but ten days'. However, he paid heavily for his moderation and was eventually fined £968.

In the confused period between the first Civil War and the Restoration it is difficult to trace the precise history of our Parliamentary borough. Two men who supported the triumphant Independent party were elected in 1645: Edward Popham, the brother of Jane Luttrell, inherited his father's old seat, and Walter Strickland, Parliament's ambassador to the Dutch Republic, was elected to the other. A reference to 'our Burgiss' James Nelthorpe in Thomas Skelton's letter to William Leptratt may imply that Nelthorpe had been sitting for Minehead in the Rump Parliament, which had been dissolved just two days before Skelton wrote his letter, though he would not have been aware of this at Minehead. After the introduction of the written constitution known as the Instrument of Government in 1654 Minehead ceased to be represented as a separate borough until after the death of the Lord Protector. His son, Richard, summoned a Parliament under a different franchise and this assembled in January 1659. Richard Hutchinson was elected to represent Minehead but he preferred to sit for Rochester which had also returned him. A new election was ordered on 17 March 1659 for the vacancy created at Minehead, but no bye-election is known to have been held and this short-lived Parliament was dissolved on 22 April 1659.

During the reign of Charles II two Francis Luttrells, father and son, sat for Minehead. The elder was joined in the Convention of 1660 by his brother-in-law, Charles Pym of Brymore, a son of the great Parliamentarian, and in 1661 by another Wyndham from Kentsford, Hugh, son of Edmund, whose tombstone in front of the altar of St Decuman's Church at Watchet accuses Charles II of ingratitude:

Here lies beneath this rugged stone
One more his Prince's than his own;
And in his martyr'd father's wars
Lost fortune, blood - gain'd nought but scars;
And for his sufferings as reward
Had neither countenance nor regard.

The younger Francis became our MP at the age of twenty and continued to sit from 1679 until his premature death in 1690. He was opposed to James II's measures to free Catholic and Protestant Dissenters from all disabilities. Whitehall was informed that 'Francis Luttrell (who will not comply) hath so much interest there (i.e. at Minehead), that it will be difficult to oppose him.' He and his fellow member, Major Nathaniel Palmer of Fairfield, those 'violent churchmen', met the Prince of Orange at Exeter and raised a regiment in his support. Francis Luttrell's brother, Alexander, succeeded him as our member and he was joined in 1698 by Captain Jacob Bancks, RN, a Swede who had married Colonel Francis Luttrell's wealthy widow, Mary. She was the daughter and heiress of John Tregonwell of Milton Abbas in Dorset, a lady whom Captain Bancks had gallantly rescued from a disastrous fire at her London home. A defeated candidate, John Sandford, disputed his election because he was a foreigner and had used bribes, treating and other undue means to get himself elected. Whatever methods were employed by Captain Bancks they were very successful, earning him a knighthood in the following year and ensuring his return for Minehead in seven successive Parliaments. No wonder that in gratitude he gave us the statue of Queen Anne that now stands in Wellington Square.

The first election of the reign of George I in 1715 led to a troublesome dispute between the four candidates. The vaguely defined franchise which allowed householders in the electoral area of Minehead, Alcombe and Staunton to vote, had to be interpreted at each election by the two constables of Minehead, who were the returning officers. These men were usually of yeoman stock and of small education. They were appointed annually at the Court Leet of the lord of the manor, and inevitably they were suspected by political opponents of the Luttrells of being too easily influenced by the Castle. The Tory party was tainted with Jacobitism; the fifty-year supremacy of the Whigs was just beginning; now, they thought, was the time to attack the Luttrell and Tory predominance in the borough.

This long supremacy of the Whig party changed the political balance of power in Minehead, a fact that the great lady, Dorothy Luttrell, who was managing her son's affairs during his minority, did not at first understand. In 1715 Sir William Wyndham and Sir John Trevelyan, Tories and fervent Jacobites, were returned in the Castle interest, but their opponents petitioned against the partiality of the constables. Dunster Castle was forced to contest a costly legal action, involving the despatch of the old manor court rolls and other historical evidence to Westminster, to prove that the constables were, and always had been, the legal returning officers for the borough. The election was declared void and a new writ was issued, though time was allowed for some of the discontented inhabitants, led by the Quaker merchants, to petition Parliament for the restoration of the Elizabethan charter. To avoid conceding this Madam Dorothy Luttrell agreed to give her support to a Whig running-mate for Sir John Trevelyan. It seemed certain that they would both be returned, but so determined were the supporters of the charter to further their cause that they forwarded to the Sheriff, before the actual polling was completed, a return unsigned by the constables, and with just forty-eight signatures on it. To poll publicly some two or three hundred voters in'tallies of ten', as was the custom at Minehead, was a slow business and it was far from complete on the afternoon of the allotted day, Thursday, 11 April 1717. Edwin and Gage, who were opposing Trevelyan and his Whig companion, James Milner, requested a postponement until nine o'clock next morning. In the meantime a Quaker called Boys was sent posthaste to the Sheriff, who was obviously himself a Whig, with the aforementioned unsigned and illegal return, giving a majority to Edwin and Gage. This return the Sheriff accepted and he at once dispatched it to London. The polling at Minehead did not finish until three o'clock on the Friday afternoon and when the constables' messenger with the legal return finally found the Sheriff at Shepton Mallet next day he refused to have anything to do with it. The Whigs at Westminster would no doubt have been pleased to add another member to their enormous majority, but they dared not condone such a palpable fraud. They referred the decision to the Committee of Privileges who by a majority of sixty-nine awarded the seats to Trevelyan and Milner.

In 1722 Madam Dorothy was informed that if her family gave its support to a second Tory candidate this would be 'a certain way to vacate both seats' and even to bring about the restoration of the charter that she wished at all costs to avoid; so she agreed to share the two seats, keeping one for her family and giving the other to the Whigs. Alexander Luttrell was chosen for Minehead in 1727 and 1734. At his early death in 1738 the Castle gave its backing to the eccentric Thomas Carew of Crowcombe Court whom Horace Walpole described as:

> *... a crazy zealot who believed himself possessed by the devil till he was cured by his apothecary's assuring him he had met the devil on the stairs coming from him.*

Throughout this period the Luttrells shared the two seats between their own man and a Government nominee. This way the citizens of Minehead had someone close to the seat of power in Westminster who could take care of such important matters as patronage - appointments to posts in the Customs and Excise for example - about which the good people of Minehead were much concerned, and this is why an examination of the poll books, many of which are extant, shows the same man giving one vote to 'the natural interest', his lord of the manor, and the other to a Government candidate. With our present preoccupation with party this seems to be a strange procedure, but an electoral borough in the eighteenth century was a financial asset and it was accepted that all who could were entitled to make the most of it.

This pattern was broken briefly when Henry Fownes married the Luttrell heiress, Margaret, in 1747, and adopted her surname. He was convinced that his late father-in-law's great debts were almost entirely due to his enormous election expenses. 'I too plainly see', he wrote, 'the rock my father Luttrell foundered upon to run myself headlong into the same danger.' At this time he was not interested in politics and had decided to sell his manor of Minehead and with it his political influence.

From 1727 until his death in 1742 Francis Whitworth of Blackford had been the Whig representative returned to Parliament by Minehead. His son Charles at that time was too young to succeed him and John Periam, a Devonshire man, took his place. In 1747 Charles Whitworth resolved to stand himself and, as the other candidate, Percy O'Brien, was also both wealthy and influential, Periam decided to withdraw. He considered that his income was insufficient to win votes against such strong opposition, but William Hayman assured him that with the support of Dunster Castle he could still win enough votes to defeat the Egremont candidate, O'Brien. He hesitated and at first resigned his interest to Thomas Carew. However, when Carew received less support than had been expected John Periam returned to the fray. He was given no encouragement from Henry Fownes Luttrell however, and the fickle voters swung over to Whitworth. As Hayman said: 'They are a wavering people and when money is in the case nothing but that will fix 'em'. Periam's vacillation was a great embarrassment to William Hayman who believed that for the time being his influence in Minehead had been destroyed. In a long letter to H.F. Luttrell of 1 June 1747, he summarised the political situation in Minehead. Money was the key to success, he wrote, in any borough 'be it ever so small where the right of election is in the populace.' He went on to describe an incident in our electioneering which brings vividly to life the political excitement of those Hogarthian times. Whitworth had sent an old servant of his father named Husk to sound out the town in order to discover if his interest was superior to O'Brien's. While Husk and Whitworth's supporters 'were at the Quay firing guns and displaying colours', Percy O'Brien's agent appeared 'at the Feathers, where he elegantly treated' his supporters until he was interrupted by the arrival of Husk and his company who had 'returned from the Quay and were crying up their friend Whitworth.' O'Brien's supporters poured out of the Plume of Feathers shouting for their man 'and by the throwing up of their hats happened to hit one of the other party in the face, which caused a fray which might have set the Town by the ears.' However, 'while the better sort of people were fighting, the mob, happening to be pretty sober, remained quiet and it was soon quelled.'

Hayman concluded that the election was likely to be lively, 'both parties being now warmed with resentment', and for his part, unless Mr Luttrell needed his help, he had decided to remain 'a mere spectator of the confusion and, at present I may almost say distraction, of a heated people.' In the same year, Charles Whitworth sent an extraordinary letter to H.F. Luttrell, proposing that their families should share the representation of the borough as Whitworth's father and Alexander Luttrell had done. 'The situation of Minehead,' he wrote:

... induces the inhabitants thereof to make choice of their members, the one upon the natural interest, the other upon that which may be serviceable to them. It was upon this footing that they approved of Mr Luttrell and my father... These I believe you are sensible are the only two material interests in that town, though every place there is a floating squadron. As I am determined to stand the General Election at all hazards, I think it will be for both our interests to unite together which I dare say will be to the entire satisfaction of the constituents.

Mr Luttrell declined the proposed pact and allowed two Whigs to be returned unopposed, but this letter illustrates very well how the great men manipulated the borough to their own advantage.

Henry Fownes Luttrell's indifference to politics devalued his Minehead estates at a time, as we have said, when he was thinking of selling them - or so his business adviser, Conand Prowse, believed - but when his political opponents were prepared to spend money so lavishly in order to win the 1754 election, he came reluctantly into politics by giving his support to Henry Shiffner of Ross in Herefordshire, a wealthy merchant in the Russian trade, with a house in St Petersburg, and by so doing he inaugurated the most active period of electioneering in the 270 years' history of the borough. Lord Egremont was rumoured to be prepared to back his candidate, Daniel Boone, with £10 000, while Charles Whitworth was said to be ready to sell his estates at Blackford to win a seat. Egremont spoke to Pitt's ally, the great manipulator, the Duke of Newcastle, who pressed Whitworth to drop Shiffner and support Boone, offering him £1000 of Secret Service money to add to the £1500 of his own that he was ready to spend on the election. In the event Whitworth received 283 votes, Boone 178 and Shiffner just 145. Shiffner protested 'with fussy zeal' that Lord Egremont and his candidate, Daniel Boone, had bribed their voters and that Boone's income was below the £300 per annum that would qualify him to stand as a candidate. However, the Tory Club, the Cocoa Tree, which had agreed to support Shiffner's petition to the House of Commons, let him down. 'Attendance is promised,' he wrote, and continued:

... notice is given of the day, and all goes swimmingly till the critical minute; then one is out of town, another at home and a great many at the bottle and hardly any at the place of action.

In fact it was one of Shiffner's own supporters who was found guilty of bribery, a judgment that elicited from Mr Luttrell this comment: 'No justice is to be expected, at least in this part of the world.'

H.F. Luttrell's support this time had been too little and too late, but now he and his adopted candidate sedulously nursed the borough in preparation for the next general election. It is surprising how openly bribery and corruption were practised in our elections, and this in spite of the formidable oath which each voter had to swear before he declared his vote. This oath is given in full in a pamphlet entitled, 'A Caution against Bribery and Perjury or False-swearing necessary to be perused by all Christian electors whom it may concern at the next General Election of Members to serve in Parliament.' There followed a series of questions and answers with thinly disguised names attached to them. For example, 'Has any person given me any money... and asked me downright for my vote? Yes: Lord Eg-nt.'

It is remarkable how easily these men, from the highest in the land to the lowest, not excepting the clergy, reconciled their consciences to giving and receiving bribes and to various forms of unlawful persuasion. James Hensley, at this same election of 1754, evaded the issue by casting his vote before he could be given the oath, much to the indignation of the mob. As early as 1723 the Luttrell's election expenses amounted to £459.4s.7d. One hundred voters were paid two guineas; fifteen sailors £1 each for loss of voyages; Captain Bastone was given £4; the expenses of Joseph Alloway (who earlier had finished the new harbour head) were £8.18s.4d. and the vicar's were ten guineas. By 1761 the usual gift to a voter had risen to three guineas, and by 1768 some fifty men, mainly sailors, 'given to' in the presence of four witnesses, were each presented with four or five guineas. On this election alone Henry Fownes Luttrell spent, in a couple of years £1868.5s.9d. A note is added at the foot of these accounts: 'The bearer Floyde says he has had nothing. Therefore give him five guineas and also his brother when he calls upon you for it.' Another device was to bring voters in from the country to occupy empty houses a few weeks before an election. George Bryant's house had no windows and was full of birds a fortnight before one such election, and Henry Williams confessed that his was not even furnished a week before the poll.

The potboilers of Minehead expected also to profit from their right to vote in many indirect ways and they were not usually disappointed. For example, in 1760 the more prominent citizens were entertained to dinner - and what dinners they were! - at the George Inn in Puddle Street and the Plume of Feathers in Frog Street - while 169 of the less important voters were given supper washed down with vast quantities of ale at fifteen taverns in Minehead and Alcombe. A few years later the leading gentlemen were being invited to Dunster Castle to dinner, some to dine in the Great Room, and others, less important no doubt, in the Little Room; but the high spot of social persuasion was reached in 1775 when seventy voters and their ladies were invited to a splendid supper and a ball.

Just before this glittering occasion Mr Luttrell took legal opinion about the legality of 'treating electors.' He was assured that he was fully entitled to entertain his 'friends' before the writ for a general election had been published. If 'friends' happened also to be voters, so what! The humble voters, 'the poor fellows', were not forgotten either. They were kept happy with enormous quantities of liquor and with sports and pastimes like the races run in the field behind Thomas Collins' house near the quay. At four o'clock sailors in sacks were invited to compete for a pair of handsome trousers, won, and no doubt proudly worn, by John Summers. Landsmen raced for a hat and there were two women's events, both won by a fast young lady, John Brewer's daughter, who lived near the Vicarage gate. Her prizes were a pair of stays and a handsome shift and there were also pairs of pumps to be run for by young girls tied back to back. There were less pleasant ways too of keeping 'the poor fellows' up to scratch. In 1770 the Dunster steward had added a pencil note to his voters' list: 'To make an example of John Hill, Gregory Horn, Thomas Edbrooke, Richard Moore, John Reed and John Tudball,' but John Wickland must have had a change of heart; his name is crossed out. Not all of them could be frightened. Isaac James and his wife heard William Beckford declare 'he had no intention to vote for Mr Luttrell in future and that if he would not give him the money he might keep it and be damned.'

Back in 1715, during the disputed election, 'the Quakers and Dissenters' were accused of being 'the occasion of all this strife and discord' in the borough. The small, prosperous and influential Quaker community in particular continued to spearpoint the opposition to the Luttrells until the first years of the nineteenth century. To discourage him, their leader in 1764, Robert Davis, had his rents increased and had to send back the keys of his malthouse because he could no longer afford to lease it. The Revd Leonard Herring, the vicar at that time, took a keen interest in politics, hunting and cockfighting, writing long and lively letters to his patron, Mr Luttrell, about all three. Robert Davis he described as 'the long-headed quaker who keeps close quarters' because 'his party is ruin'd to a standstill', and when in 1767 Luttrell at last decided to stand for Parliament himself Herring considered that 'Mr D's' scheme would 'be knocked to ten thousand times ten thousand pieces' and that their opponents would 'have their chins down to the fifth buttonhole.'

These elections were often the occasion of verse if not of poetry. In 1768 this doggerel appeared, inspired by Robert Davis and the Whig opposition to the Luttrells:

Come fill up your glasses, replenish your bowls,
And drink a health round to all jolly free souls:
We'll laugh at oppression, be merry and gay,
To the call of fair freedom, brave boys, come away.

In Freedom we're born and all Slaves we disdain;
We always are ready,
Steady Boys, steady!
We'll Scheme and we'll Conquer again and again.

Ye sons of oppression who wish to enthrall,
And stupidly think to make Slaves of us all,
To very small purpose, you take all those Pains,
Tho' you've got a few Dastards who hug their
own chains.

Above: *The high walls in Brook Street, Alcombe, behind which William Davis chuckled with satisfaction* (see page 47).

Left: *The procession at the uncontested election of 1774 arriving in the market place on polling day.* (R.G.L)

The fourth verse seems to have been aimed at William Hayman, a notable supporter of the Luttrells:

Proud Ha'man a tree for poor Mordecai rear'd
And fell in the Snare he himself had prepar'd,
Young Ha'man take Warning, before 'tis too late,
That you may deserve not the very same fate.

Before 1832 Parliamentary elections were the occasion for processions, festivities, horse-play, noise, bustle and even violence. In October 1774, following hard upon a successful canvass of the town, Henry Fownes Luttrell and his son, John, met their supporters at Alcombe Cross at 10 o'clock and joyfully proceeded to the poll at Minehead.

First came the colourmen with their flags, two ringers with hand bells, three drummers and four fiddlers. Also there were gunmen, whose gunpowder was an expensive item. The two constables, Richard Cox and John Bryant, each with his staff of office, were followed by the two candidates, hats off and very gracious. After a pause for refreshment at Cox's house, the cheering mob descended Friday Street into the market place. The crier called for silence three times. Mr Warren read the Sheriff's precept, William Hayman swore in the two constables and Lawyer Bastone read the Bribery Act. Finally the candidates offered themselves, and the officials and burgesses adjourned to the nearby Market House for the poll, as the customary outside platform or hustings was not used at Minehead until after the disastrous fire of 1791 which destroyed the Market House.

As there was now a Tory ministry under Lord North there had been no necessity for any concessions to the other party and the Luttrells were returned unopposed. They thanked the electors, were given three cheers and were borne aloft by the chairmen to Richard Cox's house. On 11 October the return was sent to the Sheriff, to be followed a little later by a loyal protestation to King George III from the constables, merchants and inhabitants of Minehead, supporting his determination to tax his rebellious American colonies.

To the Luttrells Minehead must now have seemed to be as safe as a pocket borough. The strength of the political power of the lord of the manor at Minehead is demonstrated by a letter of October 1774, written by the Prime Minister, Lord North, in his own hand. He assured Henry Fownes Luttrell that he had no intention of challenging his right to choose the two candidates and to dispose of the patronage of the borough, which, he said, was 'entirely in [their] hands' and had never been considered 'a Government borough'. However, complacency led John Fownes Luttrell to the very brink of disaster. The leader of the Whigs in Minehead, Captain William Davis, was a member of the the Quaker family whose activities throughout the eighteenth century had kept politics in the borough alive. He was a nephew of Samuel Johnson's physician, Dr Brocklesby, also a fervent Whig, who had been born in Minehead and sometimes intervened in its politics. He died in 1797 a few years after he had contributed £50 to a fund organised by William Davis for the homeless people whose houses had been destroyed in the fire of 1791.

In 1796 William Davis was able to stir up a furious agitation which ended in another contested election. Many houses were in disrepair - no doubt following the great fire; the Luttrell's agent was autocratic and unpopular, even with his own supporters; a loud-mouthed bully was in charge of the Poor House; and there were irregularities about the assessment of the poor rate. This was enough for Davis. He found two Whig candidates, John Langston and Admiral Pole. Although J.F. Luttrell was given plenty of good advice by his well-wishers, which can be summarised as 'Confide in the people', the atmosphere in Minehead was electric. 'Wild rumours were afloat that a multitude of electors opposed to Mr Luttrell were to be arrested.' The slanging and counter-slanging was vicious. The poll was so close that in the end the agents of Luttrell and Langston arrived at a compromise which allowed one from each party to be returned, but left out Admiral Pole, whose backers were only persuaded to agree to this when they were threatened with charges of bribery. William Davis, behind his high walls in Brook Street, Alcombe, must have chuckled with satisfaction at all this, but Nemesis awaited him.

In the very next election in 1802 both the Luttrells were returned to Parliament, so John Langston, hurt by the fickleness of his supporters, decided to cut his losses by selling his Minehead property to J.F. Luttrell and getting out before he had incurred any more expense. He did his best for his supporters by making a bargain with his opponents that, if he withdrew his petition challenging the legality of the 1802 election returns, they would withdraw their prosecutions of his backers. He also tried to defend the (many) poor men who had supported him by exacting a promise from Mr Luttrell that there would be no victimisation, but in this he does not seem to have been entirely successful.

FIDELITY REWARDED! TYTHES RAISED! RENT ADVANCED! AND POOR'S RATES TO BE CHARGED ON TENANTS!

To the Electors and Inhabitants

OF MINEHEAD.

Gentlemen

THE late unparalleled *Exactions* of the CASTLE in charging the POOR'S RATES on the Tenants, contrary to all former Usage or Example in this Borough, as well as the present *daring Attempt* of Mr. GALE to lay us under an *intolerable Contribution* with respect to the SMALL TYTHES, which have already been *doubled* within the last Twenty Years, appears to have aroused the dormant Spirit of the Electors and Inhabitants of this Town and Borough.—We now see, that notwithstanding all our *Exertions* to serve Mr. LUTTRELL, we are to expect nothing in return but *Ingratitude and Insolence* at the Hands of him or those under him.—But before we submit to the *Chains of Despotism,* thus attempted to be rivetted on us and our Posterity, let us make a noble and vigorous Struggle!—Let us convince Mr. LUTTRELL, that although we stood forward *in his Interest,* we do not intend to be treated like SLAVES.—Call to mind the Year 1796, when though many of us took no Part in *the Glory of that Day,* yet if such an Opportunity should again offer, which it is very probable may be the case, we are determined no longer to be made Fools of, but convince the OPPRESSOR—

THAT WE ARE MEN!

FELLOW PARISHIONERS, stand forward for your RIGHTS; begin with insisting on a liquidation of the COW MONEY Accounts, secured to the Parish by *Act of Parliament*: for though Mr. LANGSTON suffered an Infringement on our DEAREST RIGHTS, let not that discourage us from doing our Duty.

Be firm and We shall prevail,

TYTHE-MEETING, Minehead, May 26th, 1804.

PINK & GREEN.

DRAKES, Printers, Fore-Street, TAUNTON.

The libellous broadsheet which finally destroyed the Whig opposition to the Luttrells.

Undeterred by this setback the indefatigable William Davis returned to the fight, but this time he over-reached himself. In 1804 his rash vituperation and scurrilous broadsheets led to a charge of libel. A pamphlet entitled 'Fidelity Rewarded!' was taken to a printer at Taunton by Robert Young, a nephew of William Davis, and the printer was told that its author was Francis Pearce of Bratton, though in fact it was written by an Irish Quaker friend of Davis named Beale, 'a violent opposer of Mr Luttrell's interest in the borough.' Francis Pearce had changed sides because his tithes had been increased. On the Sunday following the meeting concerning the tithes he met Davis and Beale on his way to church. They told him that they would see him in the afternoon and, as Mrs Pearce was indisposed, they gathered at a Mr Ward's house and there agreed jointly to subscribe to the cost of printing Beale's abusive broadside. This challenging leaflet attacked in detail 'The late unparalleled exactions of the Castle', accused Mr Luttrell of 'ingratitude and insolence' and called on the electors not to submit to 'the Chains of Despotism.' It encouraged them by reminding them of their success in returning John Langston, a Whig, in 1796, but rashly described Luttrell as 'the oppressor', and hinted that he was less than honest in his handling of the funds of the Cow Charity. Dated 26 May 1804, at the Tithe Meeting in Minehead, this was such a highly provocative pamphlet that Mr Luttrell's supporters were bound to react with vigour.

John Fownes Luttrell who in 1802 gained absolute control of the borough.

Pearce was so angry about the tithes that he was easily persuaded to subscribe more than the others to the pamphlet's cost, and boasted that he would tell Mr Luttrell to his face that he had written it himself, adding that if such a man as Luttrell were living in Ireland 'he would soon be blown up.' Davis did his best to incriminate Pearce by printing the letter in which he had offered to increase his subscription. 'Do you think', he asked the protesting Pearce, 'I meant to make a Rod for my own back?' But his associates turned against him, and Albert Pell of Exeter, a lawyer whose advice had been sought by Mr Luttrell, had no doubt 'that the paper in question [was] a most gross scandalous libel' and that Davis and Beale, with their accomplice Robert Young, were guilty. A rough draft addressed to the Somerset court, of an indictment of William Davis, late of Dunster (i.e. Alcombe), merchant, John Beale (his Irish Quaker friend who wrote the pamphlet) and Robert Young (his nephew), 'being persons of wicked, envious and malicious minds' who intended to 'injure, scandalize and vilify the good name and reputation of one John Fownes Luttrell', shows that Davis had already been driven from the town by his rashness, and by the date which it gives for the libellous broadsheet, 26 May 1804, it positively identifies 'Fidelity Rewarded!' as the document in the case. Davis made a final attack on Pearce, describing him as that 'poor maniac of Bratton', but this case seems to have brought to a close the century-long struggle of the Davis family and their supporters to win Minehead for the Whigs.

Langston had spared no expense in nursing the borough. He had built a ship and forty houses, including the Woodcombe cottages, but all in vain. The lord of the manor was now the absolute master of his borough. Those powerful merchant families who had supported the Whigs during a great part of the eighteenth century had seen their trade and the influence that it gave them depart, or, like the Hobhouses, had left the town for a more commodious port. As Gladys Bradford has written in her preparatory notes for the first volumes of the *Victoria County History of Somerset*:

> *The history of the borough in the eighteenth century is the record of the gradual decline in prosperity and importance of the town, and increased bitterness in electoral conflicts as the dwindling population made corruption profitable.*

There was no further contest in Minehead until the election of 1830 set the country alight in the passionate struggle for Parliamentary reform, though once again and for the last time the Luttrell interest prevailed.

In the historic debates leading up to the Reform Act of 1832 Mr Luttrell and his agent, William Leigh, put up a vigorous and ingenious defence, arguing that the combined population of Minehead and Dunster would easily justify the retention of at least one seat, but Lord John Russell, a Whig, was unimpressed and coldly remarked that the matter in dispute concerned the borough of Minehead, not Minehead and 'Dunsford.'

So, in spite of its many contested elections Minehead was placed in Schedule A among the despised rotten and pocket boroughs to be disfranchised of both its seats. Between 1802 and 1830 the Luttrells had been too successful. A few contested and close-fought elections then might have saved at least one seat, but for nearly thirty years a single family had completely dominated elections in Minehead and this was fatal to the Parliamentary borough. After 270 years of often exciting, but sometimes inglorious, political history, our little town with its shrinking population and declining prosperity sank, for a few years, into an obscure torpor until it was awakened by the coming of the railway and the developing phenomenon of the seaside holiday.

Chapter 5
War, Privateering and Smuggling

Sir Hugh Luttrell, a supporter of the House of Lancaster in the Wars of the Roses, who had been deprived of his estates by the Yorkist King, Edward IV, was restored to prosperity after the Battle of Bosworth when the Lancastrian King, Henry Tudor, succeeded to the throne. Sir Hugh appreciated the importance of Minehead as a seaport and accordingly enlarged the capacity of the haven in the little creek by building a jetty. He was appointed Vice-Admiral of Minehead. In this capacity he presided over an enquiry into a curious dispute between William Keste of Swansea and Robert Basher of Minehead.

During the summer of 1497 Basher had hired a vessel from Keste that he proposed to use for fishing off the Irish coast. In return Keste was to receive one-seventh of the catch or one-quarter of any freight that was carried by his pykard. However, Perkin Warbeck's arrival in Scotland in November 1495 had provoked a state of war with England and the pykard was seized by the Scots. Basher had to pay them £400 in order to redeem her, a large sum that seemed to convince him that he now owned her, though not unnaturally Keste thought differently. A prolonged and acrimonious dispute followed that was referred to the Vice-Admiral and a jury of twelve Minehead men. They decided that the pykard should be returned to Keste on condition that he paid one-seventh of the ransom, but this Basher felt to be so unjust that even after he had been threatened with Star Chamber proceedings he obstinately refused to return the borrowed boat. William Keste was a tenant of Sir Charles Somerset to whom Sir Hugh Luttrell wrote in despair, seeking his forbearance and deploring the fact that unless Basher could be persuaded to yield, he and the jury of Minehead seamen would have to make the arduous journey to London to explain why the royal writ had not been executed. However, it is unlikely that in the end Robert Basher was able to escape the stern justice administered by the first Tudor king and his council.

The isolation of Minehead and its remoteness from the seat of power at Westminster no doubt encouraged such lawless practices as smuggling and piracy, but its seclusion did not insulate the ships and seamen of Minehead from the calamities of war.

For example, in 1530 the Privy Council 'were moved with pity for certain poor women, wives of certain poor mariners', some of them Minehead men, who had been seized off the coast of Spain. In 1533 and 1534 Thomas Cromwell was repeatedly reminding himself to send for the men of 'Myned' to answer the charge of plundering a Breton ship, and to discharge their debt to the King for the compensation that the Government had paid to the Bretons. Richard Sare, once a resident of Minehead, was, at Exeter, tried though acquitted on a charge of piracy. His later adventures in the north of England and in battle with the Spaniards and Bretons would make good material for a romantic novel.

Thomas Wyndham of Marshwood near Blue Anchor, a renowned captain in Henry VIII's growing navy, the master of whose ship was John Kerry of Minehead, was not above a little privateering or even piracy on his own account. In 1540 he was accused with Thomas Dale of seizing part of the valuable and easily disposable cargo of pepper and cloth from the *Jesus*, a ship of Portugal - with whom we were not at war. Some of the cargo had been passed on by Wyndham to his friend, John Luttrell, and both men were deep in trouble as late as 1546 for failing to restore their ill-gotten gains. At about the same time the Privy Council was authorising the Mayor of Bristol and officers of Minehead to recover a cargo of rice, almonds and molasses taken from another Portuguese ship by 'a ship of Mynnet' owned by John Hill and John Dallin. The prominence of Minehead at this time as a port on the Severn Sea is remarkable when we remember how seemingly insignificant was its creek and the little jetty that sheltered it. In 1543, in alliance with the Emperor Charles V, Henry VIII unnecessarily and unwisely declared war on France. As part of his preparations the King ordered a survey of the ports to discover how many merchant ships there were of sufficient tonnage to be incorporated in the Royal Navy. One of his commissioners, Hugh Pawlett, certified on 15 May 1544 that Minehead had four suitable ships of 60 to 100 tons, adding, 'There is no other ship or balinger belonging to Somersetshire but for one at Combwich pertaining to Bridgwater.' Further evidence of the importance of Minehead is contained in a map of the coast of Somerset reproduced by Emanuel Green in *The Preparations of Somerset Against the Spanish Armada*. It probably dates from 1544 and shows either planned or completed defences along the Somerset coast. Porlock Bay is guarded by two round towers, each supporting an enormous cannon. At Minehead is a battery of guns sited where the present harbour stands. War with France almost automatically led to war with Scotland. While John Hill of Minehead was raiding the Breton shipping and had taken two or three prizes, two other Minehead ships, the *Saviour* and the *Tawderey*, were attached as unarmed transports to an expedition that had been dispatched from Ireland in 1545 to raid the west coast of Scotland. In the next reign Thomas Wyndham and Sir John Luttrell were fiercely engaged on the east coast of Scotland, supported no doubt on board and on shore by men of Minehead.

An interesting document in the Trevelyan papers dated 14 June 1555 shows how the system of beacons was used to give warning of an invasion. When Queen Mary married Philip of Spain England was dragged unwillingly into war with France. The instructions for the watch at the beacons on Cleeve Hill, which would have given warning to Minehead, are very precise. If any number of unidentified ships were sighted, one of the three beacons was to be fired. Should seven or eight ships approach within four miles of the land two beacons were to be lit. And in the event of a landing which was too strong for the local militia to repel all three were to be lit 'or else not'. (The temptation to light all three must have been great.) The neighbouring beacons at Hangborough above West Quantoxhead and at Selworthy overlooking Porlock Bay would then be lit, and the message would pass to the pairs of inland beacons which, when both were lit, acted as a summons to the militiamen of Quantock, Brendon and Exmoor to assemble at their places of rendezvous. On this occasion they were not required, but there must have been many false alarms when perhaps friendly ships in convoy took shelter under the lee of the shore.

By the middle of the century the silting up of the harbour referred to previously had destroyed its usefulness for the larger ships. The Elizabethan 'Commissioners in Somerset upon the sea coasts', who were ordered in 1577 to enquire into accusations of piracy, no doubt visited Minehead, but there is no evidence to suggest that they found any pirate ships based in a creek that was now of little use to anything larger than a fishing boat. Our largest ships in 1588, when the Spanish Armada was almost ready to sail, were of 35 and 46 tons, and there were but few seamen to man them. A number of Minehead men were among the pikemen and shot of George Sydenham's company of militiamen, and once again, as in 1555, the beacons at Cleeve and Selworthy would have been manned and ready, but Minehead had no part to play on this occasion.

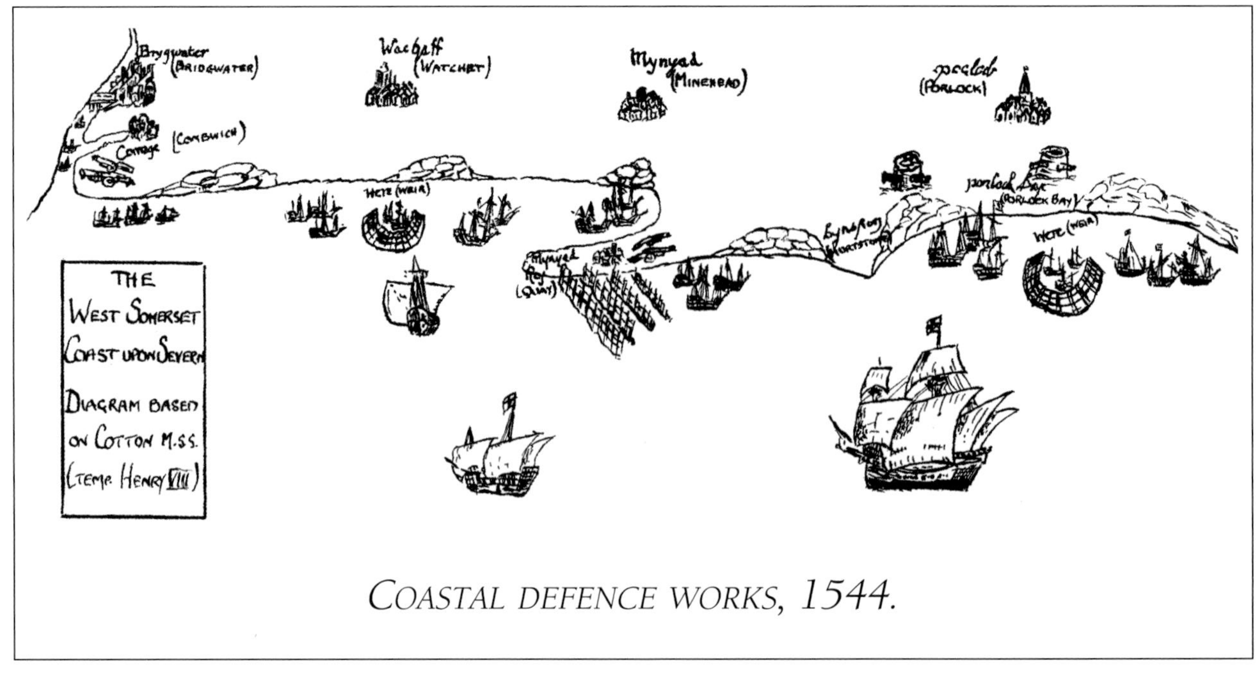

COASTAL DEFENCE WORKS, 1544.

Early in the seventeenth century Minehead attracted the attention of the King's Council through the activities of Lewis Lashbrooke, a dubious attorney who in 1601 had served the borough as one of its members of Parliament. He was a man of substance who lived at Butts Green. As early as 1611 he had been accused of malpractices, but in November 1628, a warrant for the arrest of Lashbrooke and his brother-in-law, John Baker, was issued by the Board of Admiralty. They had been accused by the Customer, Comptroller and other officers in the Port of Bridgwater and the Creek of Minehead of interfering with their work. They were brought to London on 18 December and discharged four days later, having given their bond 'to attend the Board the second Star Chamber day of the next term.' In March 1629, the case was referred to the Lord High Treasurer of England who on 24 April 'desired his Majesty's Attorney and Solicitor General to examine the business and make report thereof.' Meanwhile Lashbrooke and Baker, having given good security and promises of good behaviour, returned home where the former at least, still unrepentant, continued to pursue his evil courses; for in 1632 three justices of the peace were ordered to examine those whom he had 'grieved and unjustly molested, troubled or sued' and to award him 'an exemplary punishment', but once again he seems to have been too clever for his accusers.

Is this the first detailed account of smuggling in the history of Minehead? It may well be that this was the nature of the accusation that brought about his arrest. However, the petition from the Customs officers and inhabitants of Bridgwater and Minehead has not survived and we may never know the exact nature of his offence. He continued to figure prominently in Minehead affairs and he seems very shrewdly to have married his daughter to the Harbour Master, Rice Jenkins, but such a man inevitably made more enemies than friends. He was imprisoned by the Royalists in 1643 and by the Parliament in 1645. Some time before his death, which at last overtook him in 1655, he was named at the head of a list of Somerset attorneys 'who have given many testimonies of their ill-affection to the public peace [and] do yet constantly practice.'

But we must return to the early years of Charles I before misfortune and tragedy had overtaken this well-meaning king for whom the times were 'out of joint.' The completion of George Luttrell's new pier in 1616 had given once more to our seamen the opportunity to do work of national importance. In July 1626, Minehead was considered important enough to be included among the twenty-four seaports in England and Wales that were ordered to fortify their harbours against the threat of a Spanish invasion. In the next year letters of marque were issued to Thomas Lee and Hugh Davies of Minehead to take pirates, possibly French or Spanish privateers; but there were also Algerian corsairs operating in the Bristol Channel and this commission may have been aimed at them. At the same time Bridgwater and Minehead together were ordered to impress fifty sailors for Buckingham's ill-fated expedition to La Rochelle. The privateers were not unsuccessful. Henry West had seized a small Biscay prize laden with pitch and resin; John Chekley of Capton had captured the *Croissant* of Normandy with a varied cargo; and in November 1630, Sir John Drake had prepared a list of prizes brought into Minehead, a tenth of whose cargoes were due to the Government.

However, because the Spanish privateers were even more successful, the merchants of Minehead and Bridgwater petitioned Charles I to be allowed to provide and arm a ship to protect their trade with Ireland. Henry Hastings, captain of the *Dove*, with the support of Robert Pawlett, a Customs officer, and other merchants, was able to arm his 80-ton ship and man her with a crew of fifty seamen. They were quickly successful in driving away the Biscay privateers from the trade route to Ireland, so with their letter of marque they sailed towards the Azores, hoping to claim a prize or two for themselves. They soon captured a richly-laden Portuguese ship, but they were deprived of this and their own ship by a Dutch captain, Cornelius Te Kint, who after a hot fight overwhelmed the *Dove*, took her men into captivity, ill-treated and humiliated them, and finally carried them in his ship, the *Peter*, to Rotterdam where they were at first imprisoned and later forced to work to buy back their own property. Ever since the massacre of Amboyna relations between the two Protestant and commercial nations on opposite shores of the North Sea had been far from friendly. The States General showed little inclination to compel the arrogant Captain Te Kint to recompense the owners and the crew of the *Dove*. Robert Pawlett petitioned the King over and over again for justice, and just before the outbreak of the Civil War his widow, Anne, was granted letters of reprisal against the Dutch, though in such troubled times she could hardly have made much use of them.

A Bristol petition of 1634 shows with what impudent bravado the Barbary corsairs sailed their pirate ships into English waters. The *Abraham* reported that as she was entering the Bristol Channel she saw two little barques, bound out of Minehead with passengers for Ireland, fall into the hands of a Turkish man-of-war. Goods and people alike were seized by the raiders. The King was asked to send a warship into these waters to defend our ships from these desperadoes. At about the same time a night raid on the Somerset coast had led to the capture and enslavement of men, women and children from isolated farmhouses near Weston, and a few years before, in 1627, an extraordinary scene was enacted in St Michael's Church when a ship's boy, who had been captured by the Turks and taken to Algiers, was arraigned before a number of learned and self-important clergymen and ordered to abjure the Mohammedan faith that he had accepted in order to save his life, and to do penance for not wishing to become a martyr in his early 'teens. The poor puzzled lad stood in the centre of the church and listened to as much as he could understand of two interminable and pedantic sermons preached by Dr Edward Kellet of Bagborough and Henry Byam, rector of Luccombe, which occupy seventy-four pages of *A Return to Argier* (1628). The sermons are introduced by a brief account of the young man's adventures which unfortunately does not mention his name:

> *A countryman of ours, going from the port of Minehead to the Straits, was taken by Turkish pirates and made a slave at Argier, and living there in slavery, by frailty and weakness, forsook the Christian religion and turned Turk and lived for some years; and in that time, serving in a Turkish ship, which was taken by an English man-of-war, was brought back again to Minehead, where being made to understand the grievousness of his apostacy, was very penitent for the same.*

He was reconciled to the Church by the Bishop of Bath and Wells, and the two learned sermons were preached on the third Sunday in Lent, 1628, the day assigned for his public penance in St Michael's Church. Edward Kellet made much of the fact that he had allowed his captors to dress him in Turkish clothing and had even worn the lock of hair by which the followers of Mahomet hoped 'to be lifted up to Paradise', but he does not say that the young sailor wore these clothes during his public penance, as has previously been implied in published accounts of this incident.

By 1634 Charles I had been ruling without a Parliament for five years. Desperate for money, he turned to an old custom which allowed him, when our shores were threatened by invaders, to demand a ship for the navy from the maritime counties. The first writs were issued in 1634, but in 1635 when Minehead was ordered to contribute £60, a sum only exceeded in Somerset by Taunton (£100), Bath (£70) and Bridgwater (£70), there were loud protests which Professor Barnes believes must have been supported by Thomas Luttrell, a justice of the peace; but they achieved a reduction of only one guinea.

The outbreak of the appalling Civil War in Ireland in October 1641 greatly increased the importance of Minehead. The commodious new harbour was soon in use for the transport of soldiers and supplies to Waterford and Cork. Some 300 men, ostensibly as a reinforcement in Ireland, were detained in Minehead during the spring of 1642, much to the annoyance of its Parliamentarian citizens who had to billet them. After a complaint to the House of Commons on 18 May it was ordered that the 'mere Irish and papists' at Minehead should be at once shipped to Ireland.

Roger Mainwaring, Bishop of St David's, whose sermons in support of the King's absolute power preached in the early years of his reign had given great offence to the leaders of the Commons, was well rewarded by his royal master. Now, with the clouds of war gathering, his arrest was ordered. In flight from Wales the old Bishop was seized as he landed at Minehead with his wife of twenty-two.

At the end of July 1642, the Marquis of Hertford led a party of the King's supporters from Charles' headquarters in the north into Somerset, hoping to raise an army in the county. He received only a few recruits and after some skirmishing around Wells and Sherborne the mounted men of this little force, about 160 in all, rode to Minehead where they expected to find a number of vessels to ferry them over the Channel into Wales. However, Thomas Luttrell had married Jane Popham, an ardent Roundhead, and in this crisis she seemed to have taken command at the Castle, ordering her musketeers to fire on the sixty men that the Marquis had sent to demand its surrender. Sir Ralph Hopton was the most experienced soldier among the Royalists. His advice to march to Clevedon instead of Minehead had been rejected. He knew that the Luttrell influence alone would ensure a hostile reception, and also that the merchant classes, the seamen and the textile workers, who were predominant in Minehead and Dunster, were generally opposed to the King. The Cavaliers had arrived in Minehead on Wednesday 22 September. The leaders were so closely beset in a strong inn that according to a Roundhead correspondent they dared not 'look out of doors.'

On the Friday morning news was received that Parliament's Lord Lieutenant of Somerset, the Earl of Bedford, was close in pursuit and that afternoon his soldiers, both horse and foot, were observed about four miles away on the hill between Watchet and Blue Anchor. Hertford was now at his wits' end and was willing to listen to Hopton whose advice he had scorned so disastrously just four days before. It was arranged that Hertford and the gentlemen volunteers should embark that night in two little coal boats for Wales, while Sir Ralph and the more experienced officers would ride with the horse and dragoons into Cornwall. It seems certain that Minehead was in such an uproar that the Cavaliers were forced to embark with more haste than dignity.

Hopton and his troopers no doubt covered the embarkation by sealing off the narrow entrance to Quay Street. They then made tracks for the open country, riding first to Dulverton and then doubling back to Exford, crossing the lonely Exmoor uplands and down through Torrington to Sir Bevil Grenville's house at Stowe in Cornwall. In a letter to Sir Ralph Hopton the Marquis of Hertford wrote of their 'disastrous fortune at Minehead and Dunster, occasioned by the multitude of your countrymen's evil dispositions and cowardly behaviour', but Hopton came quickly to the defence of the men of West Somerset, assuring the marquis that they would fight bravely enough against a foreign invader but that it was 'not warrantable by God's laws' to fight against one's friends and neighbours. He, poor man, did this ceaselessly for the next four years, until having commanded the last of the King's field armies, he was driven into exile.

In January 1643, a Royalist fleet manned by Welshmen blockaded Minehead harbour, cutting off the supply of food and coal, while a landing party under a Captain Pawlett terrorised the countryside and made a futile attempt to capture Dunster Castle; but after the loss of one man the raiders transferred their attentions to Barnstaple.

In 1643 Hopton's advance into Somerset and through the county to Lansdown had liberated Taunton from Parliament and persuaded Thomas Luttrell that, despite his Roundhead wife, it was time for an accommodation with the royal army. Accordingly he handed over his castle to Francis Wyndham who became its governor and defended it bravely until the spring of 1646. The effect of this change on Minehead is difficult to assess. At about the time that Wyndham took command of the Castle, Minehead's parishioners dismissed their Royalist vicar, Robert Knolles, and all the evidence suggests that their sympathies stayed with Parliament throughout the war. Most seem to have agreed with the Clubmen in other parts of the county and country, whose main concern was to protect their lands and homes from the depredations of both armies. Hancock quotes some doggerel verses two of which read:

Ise had zixe oxen t'other day,
And then the Roundheads stole away,
A mischief be their speed;
I had six horses left me whole,
And them the Cavileers have stole,
God's sores they are both agreed.

How I doe labor toile and zweat,
And 'dure the cold, hot dry and wett,
But what dost think I gett,
Hase just my labor for my paines,
These Garrizons have all my gaines,
And thither all is vitt.

In August 1644, General Middleton, the Parliamentarian leader in east Somerset, reported that he had driven the infamous and brutal Sir Francis Dodington and eight other colonels to Minehead, 'whence they seem to have retreated to Ilfracombe.' The long and stirring defence of Taunton during this winter must have roused sympathetic feelings in Minehead and perhaps gained a few recruits as well. Its relief in 1645 by the New Model Army under Fairfax and Cromwell and the rapid collapse of Bridgwater, which followed the defeat of the King's last field army at Langport, was welcome news to the people of Minehead.

The siege of Dunster Castle by Robert Blake, soon to be famous as an admiral, began in the following autumn. It had unpleasant repercussions for some of the small group of active Royalists in Minehead. Lewis Lashbrooke, who earlier in the war had been imprisoned by the King's party and fined £40, was in October 1645 arrested by Colonel Blake and forced to pay the Roundheads £100 to which the Committee for Compounding added another fine of £54.14s.0d. Rice Jenkins had paid a trooper to serve under Francis Wyndham, the Royalist governor of Dunster Castle, and he informed the committee that this had cost him £161; even so they exacted a fine of a further £38.

Dunster Castle in November 1645 was a formidable fortress. The old medieval keep stood on the top of the steep and treeless Tor. For a long siege the water supply was uncertain, but to take such a castle by storm was well-nigh impossible without a battery of the heaviest cannon. As the Royalist resistance in the West collapsed Blake received more and more reinforcements. Mining the walls proved unproductive; arms, ammunition and supplies were brought to the Cavaliers from Barnstaple by Colonel Finch; Minehead was raided and partially destroyed by fire by General Goring's ill-disciplined Cavalry. However, the King's last army under Hopton was defeated at Great Torrington and the fall of Exeter finally convinced the resolute defenders of Dunster that further resistance was futile. On 21 April Sir Francis Wyndham marched out with all the honours of war granted to him by a generous and humane opponent. So the ringers of Minehead rang long and lustily for a handsome reward of 4s.8d. to mark the final defeat of the hated Cavaliers or perhaps, more accurately, to celebrate the end of nearly four years of unpopular Civil War in Somerset.

If we are to judge by the number of references to Minehead in the State Papers, the years between the first Civil War and the restoration to the throne of Charles II must surely have been the busiest in the history of the port. During this period the harbour was at the most active stage of its development, and was most used by ships directly or indirectly in

Government service. The cruel Civil War in Ireland continued unabated, and now that the fighting in England had subsided, men and supplies were available to be sent there. Minehead became their principal point of departure. There were great opportunities for enterprising men in trade with southern Ireland and it was at this time that the prosperous merchant families of Crockford, Hayman, Devonshire and, a little later, Alloway, established themselves in the town.

As early as 1644 Francis Bishop, master of the the *John* of Minehead carried to Ireland 3000 pairs of shoes and stockings with caps and coats for the troops, which earned him £14.13s.0d. In 1647 shipping was ordered to be in readiness to transport Colonel Long's regiment to Ireland and £1000 was to be sent to Minehead to pay for quarters at 6d. a day for each soldier. At about the same time Captain Nathaniel Bullocke arrived from Youghal with a cargo of wool. He was the Government agent at Minehead for the requisitioning of ships and the impressment of sailors required for service to and from Ireland. In a petition to Quarter Sessions at Ilchester he described himself as the owner of the good ship *Patience* of Minehead, and claimed to have had experience of trade with Youghal, Cork, Kinsale and other Irish ports over a period of thirty years. However, his great experience did not save him from rather tactlessly commandeering some ship's carpenters who were working on one of Robert Quirke's vessels. This upset the influential Quirke, 'very potent and owner of shipping' with 'many sailors and servants under his command', who 'did very violently assault and cruelly beat... with a cudgel' poor Captain Bullocke, warning him to keep away from the quay, and preventing him from fulfilling his obligations to the Government.

Cromwell sailed in the *John* from Milford Haven to Ireland in August 1649 in two convoys totalling more than a hundred ships, some of which must have belonged to Minehead. In the previous June the Government agent in Bristol, James Powell, had been ordered to hold all ships in Bristol, Minehead and other Bristol Channel ports in readiness for this expedition, to provision them with beer and biscuit and to send them on to Milford Haven. In the autumn Minehead and the other ports were required to find transport for 5000 recruits and 700 horse, and to pay for these Powell received over £6000. Colonel Farr's regiment of foot marched from Sussex to Minehead for transportation to Ireland.

These were indeed busy and exciting times for the sea-faring people of the town but they did not bring immediate prosperity.

A petition of the next year addressed to Quarter Sessions at Bridgwater tells a sad story of disaster at sea and misery at home. Six vessels pressed into service for the transportation of soldiers and horses to Ireland sailed from the harbour on 5 January. Two days later they were caught 'in a great tempest' and five of them 'were cast away on the coast of Ireland.' About a hundred 'poor widows and fatherless children' were being kept alive by parish relief, but the numbers requiring help were still increasing and the problems of the churchwardens and overseers of the poor had been magnified by an outbreak of plague. All this had come on top of the disruption caused by the English Civil War; to a town troubled with many refugees from that in Ireland; and to a port whose ships had been plundered by Royalist privateers and whose citizens had paid £1300 in fines.

In the spring of 1650 Cromwell returned from Ireland but the war continued, and so did the busy participation of Minehead in the ceaseless traffic that was its consequence. Our port was one of twenty-six in which an agent of the Lord Deputy of Ireland was settled expressly to transact this business. Our man was John Bond. In April 1651 he was ordered to arrange for the quartering and despatch of 800 soldiers. In October he was warned to prepare to receive the military stores from Taunton Castle which was being dismantled, as Dunster Castle had been. He received forty barrels of powder, twelve packs of match and twenty-four barrels of musket balls, with instructions to pass them on to William Cooper, the quartermaster of Captain Bagnall's Horse, whose ship, having sailed from Milford Haven, had been driven back into the Channel by contrary winds and had found shelter at Minehead. Bond was sent £200 for this work, £150 for the transport of recruits and £600 for the 800 impressed soldiers. There are many such entries, and Minehead now was clearly on the road back to prosperity.

The sequestration of the estates of Royalists, the arrest of their persons and the seizure of their property was sometimes a profitable business for Commonwealth men who could bring themselves to benefit from a fellow countryman's misfortune. Prebendary Hancock describes how one, Robert Nagle, petitioned the Parliamentary Committee for the Navy for permission to proceed against Richard Pettingall, who had seized prizes in excess of the value that his letters of marque granted him. Nagle overreached himself and died in a debtor's prison. Thomas Skelton, a Minehead Customs officer, had no more success in an unworthy attempt to prosecute a Royalist sea captain, William Balthazar, who was trying to make his peace with the Government. On 22 April 1653, Skelton wrote a long letter to William Leptratt 'at the Harp and Ball by Charing Cross' asking him to assist with the prosecution of his captain and to recruit the help of James Nelthorp, 'our burgess and my friend', and others, all of whom he promised to reward out of a sum of £168.18s. which was owed to Balthazar by Jasper Gill, a Bristol merchant. Balthazar's wife and his lawyer, Hugh Muttlebury, whom Skelton described as a 'grand cavalier and forsworn enemy of mine', were on their way to London to petition the Council of State. They were to be forestalled at all costs. However, Leptratt knew his man and commented that Skelton was 'still thirsting after the money.'

William Balthazar had been a captain in the King's Army from the beginning of the Civil War. When the Royalist armies collapsed in 1646 he had been given the command of the Fort of St Mary's on the Isles of Scilly. When this fort fell to Parliament he was commissioned by the exiled Prince Charles as a sea captain and he engaged in privateering off the coasts of Ireland and Wales. He was apprehended by Skelton and committed to prison by the judge at Taunton Assizes. After long drawn-out legal proceedings, during which time he was successively a prisoner in Ilchester gaol, the Tower of London and Newgate, Balthazar was released on bail in December 1653. It is pleasing to record that as he had endeavoured to avail himself of the pardon that had been offered to mariners in foreign service, it was considered that Skelton had prosecuted him more from motives of malice and greed than of patriotism. At this point the envious man's nerve failed him: he did not proceed with the prosecution of this seemingly loyal and straightforward officer whom he had described as 'a grand tory and pirate of Brest.' Captain Balthazar was then released from Newgate on 20 January 1654.

Active service in Ireland was as unpopular in the seventeenth century as it is today. Even Captain Bullocke, who had himself commandeered so many ships for the government, stood off-shore when the *Patience* was herself in danger of being pressed into service. The press gangs were busy and Captains Hewitt and Pene, who were responsible for recruiting in the West Country, reported that they were being violently resisted in Barnstaple and Bideford but, they continued, 'we think the sword men could procure in thirty days 400 men in Bristol Bay, 50 in Minehead, Watchet and Porlock and 20 in Bridgwater', and it was to his home town, Minehead, that Captain Henry Hatsell sent for seamen for the *Lily* that he was fitting out at Plymouth.

During the Interregnum distinguished travellers were often seen in Minehead, such as Colonel Robert Sanders, the Governor of Youghal, and his family, the Countess of Cork, Justice Cook, the Earl of Barrimore and the powerful if unpopular Lord Broghill and his lady. Minehead ships continued to carry the nobility to and from Ireland after the Restoration, among them the Earl of Roscommon and the Earl of Orrery, a new title created by Charles II for the wealthy and influential Lord Broghill. In 1671 the King's yacht, the *Merlin*, was in harbour for at least eight days waiting for Sir Robert Southwell. The Cromwellian wars with the Netherlands and Spain subjected our mariners to attack by Dutch and Spanish privateers and naval vessels in the open waters west of Lundy. A petition from the inhabitants of Barnstaple, Bideford, Ilfracombe and Minehead appealed for 'two small, nimble frigates' to be stationed at Ilfracombe and Kinsale to give protection to the convoys. Two frigates are named in later papers, the *Fox* and the *Grantham*, and they may have been sent in answer to this appeal. The *Grantham*, was storm-driven to Lundy, and while her captain was on shore her cables parted and she drove all night and next morning to Minehead where she procured a pilot 'by whose industry with God's providence they now ride safe.' The *Fox* had twelve vessels in one of her convoys, laden with corn for Bristol and Minehead.

The Restoration of King Charles II made little difference to the maritime history of Minehead. Trade with Ireland flourished and frigates during the Dutch wars were still required to protect the convoys. The Government agent was now a certain John Maurice whose correspondence with James Hickes in London kept the Admiralty well-informed of occurrences at this remote but not insignificant port. He reported anything that might have concerned the King's Council from the suspicious behaviour of dissenting preachers to the discontented foot post who carried letters every week from Taunton to Sherborne, where he met the horse post, and then back to Taunton, a distance of one hundred miles, for which he used to be paid six shillings but at that time received only 4s.6d. Maurice was not surprised that he was discontented and begged for an additional half-a-crown a week for him. Most of Maurice's letters, of course, concerned the movement of shipping. In June 1666, during the first Dutch War, the *Harp* had some forty ships in convoy, fourteen or fifteen of which belonged to Minehead. Standing in close for shelter off Worms Head, this large convoy was mistaken for a French fleet and caused considerable perturbation among the Welsh people along the shore. He reported the rejoicing of Minehead folk at the naval victory in the Downs and their sorrow at the 'disaster to the glorious city', the Great Fire of London. The sea was clear of capers and pickeroons (Dutch privateers) and ships were arriving safely with beef, butter, tallow and hides, their masters much encouraged by their success in losing neither bark nor goods since the beginning of the war. He wrote that during summer as many as twenty barks had arrived in one day laden with cattle and sheep, adding that beef was sold for ½d or ¾d a pound in Ireland at that time.

However, in the seventeenth century, a seaport and disaster were inseparable companions. In the

Minehead Harbour showing the Customs House (thatched) and a warehouse (right), c.1890.

very next year, 1667, Maurice was afraid that twenty or thirty barks laden with cattle had been lost at sea in a storm. Some had taken shelter at St Ives but others reached Minehead only to have their bullocks and sheep seized by the constables in obedience to a recently-passed Act of Parliament that forbade this trade. Such an incident was the origin of the 'Cow Charity.' The *Mary* had been reported lost with all hands and there was great distress reported among the relatives of her crew. The 400-ton *Jacob* of Bristol, a Dutch prize, had been driven ashore. There was no news of the *Friendship* of Minehead that sailed to Lisbon ten weeks since. The *Unity* was lost off Milford Haven, though all hands were saved, and the *Agreement*, a French ship from the Bermudas, driven ashore east of Minehead quay, lost all her cargo of oranges and potatoes in spite of an all-night vigil by the 'best of the town'. To these natural disasters war added its tally of victims and an unnamed ship voyaging from Ireland to Minehead was reported from Swansea as having been taken by two Dutch capers. All these misfortunes occurred between 1667 and 1672, but on the whole Maurice's reports are of successful voyages and it is clear that at this time Minehead enjoyed a diverse, vigorous and prosperous mercantile life.

At the end of the reign of Charles II the question of the succession to the throne was dividing the nation so sharply that civil war seemed to be not far away. Colonel Owen, a Whig and a Dissenter, as he was about to embark for Ireland was arrested by Richard Sandys, the senior Customs officer of Minehead, who reported to Mr Secretary Jenkins that this man was suspected of being involved in 'a horrid plot', presumably to assassinate Charles and his Catholic brother, James. He was examined by Sir William Wyndham and other justices, and enquiries were made in London about his background. In Dublin he was reported as having said that some 80000-100000 fighting men were lost (presumably to the King) in London alone by the recent legislation against dissenters. No real evidence was uncovered to convict him but he appeared before a justice of the peace, William Lacy, and was held on suspicion and finally released so that he could continue on his journey to Ireland where he was to be re-arrested. However, in some way he evaded arrest, for the Dublin authorities could not find him and suggested he might still be in hiding in Minehead - possibly true, for Sandys complained bitterly of the inadequacies of the constables, often 'poor mechanics', too frightened to act. Previously they had refused to arrest Owen until Sandys had agreed to accompany them personally. A suspected accomplice, a Taunton man, Thomas Slape, alias Seeley, alias Rumbold, was discovered in Exeter and another notorious enemy of the regime, Richard Bowers, an officer under Oliver and an ensign at the siege of Dunster Castle, described in an earlier paper as an Anabaptist of Dunster, was also arrested by Sandys on the road to Bridgwater. However, he was released by the justices only to be re-arrested as he hid in a garret. That all this was something more than the excited imaginings of a self-important Customs officer is made evident by the desire of King Charles to examine Owen himself, which prompted a message from Secretary Jenkins to the Mayor of Bristol to 'spare no charges' in effecting his arrest.

West Somerset was so isolated by distance and bad roads and its coastline was so sparsely populated that it inevitably became a haunt of smugglers. The Customs officers at Minehead, if they were men of integrity, were kept busy controlling the undercover activities of merchants and their seamen. In 1670 the Customs House itself had been robbed of its casks of brandy and rum and in 1682 Richard Sandys had other matters to engage him than a hunt for conspirators, for in that year William Culliford, Surveyor-General of Customs, visited Minehead to investigate certain complaints that he had received.

He had been informed that some of the Customs officers were themselves concerned in running contraband goods. James Hellier, a tidesman, was suspended and recommended for dismissal, while Henry Clement, another tidesman, a servant of Dunster Castle, at first confessed that he was a smuggler and later denied what he had said after some encouragement from his master, Colonel Luttrell, who obviously was more deeply involved in the affair than he should have been. A Minehead shoemaker who lived on the quay, Peter Bond, had attempted to uncover the illegal behaviour of Hellier and his accomplices, but with the connivance of Colonel Luttrell his enemies turned the tables on him. Bond was kept in prison from Saturday until Wednesday, which was market day, and then 'being hard bolted with iron shackles' he was drawn through the town at the cart's tail and publicly whipped, receiving over one hundred stripes from one of Luttrell's Dunster servants, no Minehead man, according to Bond's evidence, being willing to treat him so cruelly.

Bond had described how he had seen forty packets of cloth and other merchandise landed at night from a Bristol ship for which Hellier was the tidesman, and carried by men whom he was able to identify, to the house of a merchant who lived on the quay, Thomas Wilson, and then hauled by ropes into the courtyard of his house. He also stated that wine and brandy from the ship of Samuel Crockford had been secretly landed and conveyed to this merchant's cellars, and that even the pious Isaac Davis was not above bringing ashore a little contraband from his ship, the *Diligence*. In the indenture of his apprentice, John Harding, the puritanical Captain Davis was most explicit about the morals and behaviour of this young man; perhaps he missed the beam in his own eye!

Further evidence of smuggling of a like nature was given by John Fry, a Minehead mason. This time the ship was the *Merchant's Adventurer*, but once again Thomas Wilson's house was the repository for four hogsheads of wine and some casks of brandy and other liquor from the aptly named *Swallow*. Hooker's wagon from Taunton seems to have taken away most of it, but no doubt some found its way to Dunster Castle and perhaps to the Vicarage. A Bridgwater Customs officer in 1679 had seen sixty hogsheads of illicit tobacco landed at Minehead from the *Encrease* on her way back from Virginia before he could begin to check her cargo.

Although these matters were reported to various officials in Minehead, these gentlemen showed a strong disinclination to follow up the evidence; and it seems certain that many influential men in the district were themselves benefiting from a trade that did not seem to them particularly reprehensible. Even Joseph and Benjamin Alloway, the sons of the justly respected and prosperous William Alloway, the leader of the Society of Friends in Minehead, were involved in an attempt to defraud the government by importing about '1200 pounds of stems, butts and offal of tobacco mixed with liquor, intending to draw back about twenty-two pounds sterling from the Government.' For this and other breaches of discipline they were eventually expelled from the Society of Friends.

Indeed, as we have seen, the Customs officers themselves were not very trustworthy. Richard Sandys, the collector, who was in charge at Minehead at the time of William Culliford's investigation, was himself misappropriating Government money. He died insolvent in the autumn of 1684, owing the Treasury £466.0s.2d., a sum never recovered. His predecessor, Josias Walker, was dismissed in 1679 owing £140 which he finally paid back in 1680. The worst offender at this time seems to have been Thomas Wolstenholme, whose brother, Sir John, had influence with the Lord Treasurer, Godolphin. He was already collector at the end of William III's reign in 1699. On 7 May 1705, he surrendered his patent to Francis Webber for £700 and was in debt to the Crown for the Minehead collection for the very large sum of £1600. His brother had the impudence to petition Godolphin for the post of Commissioner of Customs for Scotland for Thomas, who by 1707 had absconded from Minehead and disappeared. Needless to say this request was refused.

During the time that Thomas Wolstenholme was in office as collector, the last and greatest of Louis XIV's wars, the War of the Spanish Succession, had broken out. Wolstenholme reported that several 'dangerous persons' who had been French privateers in the previous war had been seen at Minehead in the summer of 1701. His letter to our members of Parliament, Sir Jacob Bancks and Alexander Luttrell, was supported by the signatures of seventy-five inhabitants of the town and requested that the MPs should petition the sovereign for the provision of 'a convenient number of great guns' for its defence. This was necessary because Minehead, 'a staple port', was so exposed that a single privateer could destroy it. Seamen known to be Irish, French or Dunkirk privateers in the war of William III had been seen in the town and had in their cups made threats about what they were going to do to Minehead when the new war broke out. It was pointed out that the quay had 'a noble platform' and 'ports for seven guns', and that there would be room for three more when the new harbour head was built. Minehead would provide the gunpowder and gunners if the Government would send along the ordnance and accessories. Thomas Wolstenholme added that the Customs House itself would be in danger, with all the important papers and records lodged in it.

The estimated cost of what was required for the defence and security of the borough is given in some detail in a later Luttrell paper. Four iron culverins (not seven as requested) and six six-pound bullets for £137.16s.0d., carriages for these, £25. Round shot about £25. Ladles, sponges, ladle staves, cases of wood for cartridges, funnels of plate, crows of iron, linchpins, spikes, forelocks, a small melting ladle, about 1000 nails, beds and touches (ordinary and extraordinary). Such a detailed list suggests that Minehead was considered important enough to be given at least a good part of what its anxious inhabitants had asked for.

An appointment to a post in the Customs House was much coveted in seaport towns and the power of influence of these appointments was of value to a Member of Parliament who stood for the party of the Government. There were eleven officers at Minehead: a collector, a comptroller, a searcher, two land waiters, two tidesmen, two boatmen and two coal-meeters or supernumerary tidesmen. Together they earned annually £492, of which the collector's share was a handsome £250. The comptroller earned £40, the searcher £30 and the others proportionally less. At the end of Anne's reign the revenue to the Queen was said to be very considerable.

During the wars against Louis XIV Minehead equipped a number of privateers to operate against the merchant ships of France. Captain William Hayman's *Wincanton* of 100 tons was articled in December 1709, and the *Queen Ann*, owned by Andrew and John Hare and William Alloway, in September 1710. She was of 200 tons, carried sixteen guns and a crew of forty. The armament of Captain William Rogers' ship of 100 tons, the *Three Brothers*, is given in some detail. She carried eight guns, with six barrels of powder and thirty rounds of great shot for them. Her crew of thirty was armed with twenty muskets, four blunderbusses, three pairs of pistols and twelve cutlasses. Privateering was, of course, a risky operation, as the misfortunes of Robert Paulet and the *Dove* in the reign of Charles I have shown, but it could also be profitable. In 1710 Sir William Wyndham, Vice-Admiral of Somerset, petitioned for permission to award a French ship in harbour at Minehead to her captor. She was valued at £1466 but the Admiralty ordered Sir William to sell her 'at her Majesty's best advantage' and then to reward Captain Clarke's mate, Bering, and eight seamen principally responsible for her capture in a suitable manner.

These wars were profitable in other ways. Once again troops and their supplies had to be shipped to Ireland for the campaigns for William of Orange. In June 1689, the regiments of the Duke of Schomberg's army of 25 000 men were ordered to march to Milford Haven, Liverpool, Bristol and Minehead. Some 400 vessels were required for their transport and even if Minehead provided the smallest part of the fleet the quay must have presented an animated and colourful scene during that summer. Magazines of supplies were accumulated at Bristol, Minehead, Liverpool and Chester, and, in spite of the silting up of the harbour and the effect that this was having in reducing the burden of the vessels able to use it, the port continued to be employed in carrying soldiers and supplies across the Irish sea at least until 1694. It seems likely that, with the completion of the extension to the pier during Queen Anne's reign, Minehead continued to enjoy a considerable share in Government shipping, although the end of the campaigning in Ireland reduced the usefulness of the harbour to the State.

Although war with France was almost incessant during the eighteenth century we have found no further reference to Minehead privateers. By mid-century the harbour was again silting up to such an extent that keeping it clear of stones and sand cost the Trustees and the Castle more than the diminishing trade yielded in harbour dues. It comes as no surprise to hear that late in the century, Captain Aaron Floyde's privateer, the *Tartar*, had to operate from Bristol. Great times they must have been when little Minehead mattered in the councils of the nation, but at last they had ebbed away with the tide.

There are indications, however, that throughout the century some of the merchants and sea-captains of the town continued to find smuggling a profitable side-line. As the legitimate trade of the port declined, the temptation to run contraband into Minehead must have been great. As early as 1726 Alexander Luttrell, still in his early twenties, was obviously involved in some way in rum-running. A letter that he received from Henry Gale, a lawyer of the Inner Temple, shows that a trial was pending on a charge laid by the Commissioners of Excise. The case was to be heard in London, and his legal adviser clearly anticipated that it might go against the young lord of the manor, in spite of the efforts that he promised to make in his defence. How this ended is not known, but the fact that once again, as in 1682, a Luttrell was involved, however indirectly, with the smugglers, prepares us for the most bizarre of the smuggling stories of eighteenth century Minehead - when the smugglers of the town and their backers were able to effect the dismissal from his post of a seemingly honest and highly efficient Supervisor of Excise.

In February 1759, Thomas Withers of Stogumber, a butcher, was prosecuted at Crowcombe for being in possession of some Irish soap which had been smuggled into Minehead. He was fined £3 by the justices, Thomas Carew and Dr Camplin, but after the hearing he approached William May, the Supervisor of Excise at Bridgwater, at the Three Lions Inn in the village. He volunteered to act as an informer and, as he had been for years involved with smugglers, May jumped at the chance of using him, but in doing so he himself walked into a trap.

He gave the rascally butcher from Stogumber a written undertaking to pay him five guineas for any information that would lead to the seizure of contraband goods to the value of 'ten dozen of soap'; but the plan went wrong from the beginning. Withers sold some contraband tea to an innocent woman. May at once reported this to the Board of Customs and Excise and was told not to prosecute the woman 'as she was ensnared into the offence.'

In employing Withers, William May had been guilty of an error of judgment which he had admitted quite frankly to his superiors. He had no reason to expect anything more than a reprimand and he continued to seek out wrong-doers in Minehead with his usual diligence, among them William Blake of Friday Street, a prosperous merchant and shipowner, who had been accused of 'harbouring uncustomed soap' and 'selling brandy without a licence.'

However, Blake had influential friends who had succeeded in delaying the hearing of the charges. Philip Harrison, 'one of those most trusted by the smugglers' was the landlord of the inn at Alcombe Cross. There May heard that his enemies had conspired together to deny the evidence that they had previously given. In an affidavit prepared by the Minehead attorney, Francis Bastone, they accused him of being a dishonest troublemaker who had planted contraband tea on a frightened and innocent woman. The information was sent to the Commissioners of Excise and an enquiry into May's conduct was set on foot.

The aggrieved Supervisor wrote to his superior, the Collector at Castle Cary, a letter which seemed to exonerate him completely. He indicated how Withers had been so generously bribed by Blake and his friends to deny the evidence he had given, that 'from a smuggler of the lowest class, obliged to trudge about on foot with his goods to his back' he had been transformed into a prosperous trader, mounted on a good horse, supplied with a brace of pistols, and directed by his new friends to use them on any officer who stopped him on the road or tried to 'enter his house without a constable.' Minehead was described as 'the fountain that supplies the whole country with Irish soap and most other run'd goods', yet few seizures of contraband occurred there and this, May wrote, the dishonest traders attributed to their influence as Parliamentary electors. By using this influence they had appointed local men to their Customs House and in so doing had made Minehead into 'a kind of free port'. 'The little interruption it hath met with of late makes my behaviour no longer to be borne with,' May concluded, and he was right. Within five days of the despatch of this letter the Commissioners of Excise had discharged their conscientious Supervisor and appointed a successor from Cockermouth where the Wyndhams had wide estates.

William May immediately appealed against his dismissal. His letter was supported by sworn statements from his fellow officers, by letters from the Mayor of Bridgwater and the soap boilers there, but most important, by a statement from three justices of the peace. Sir George Trevelyan, Thomas Carew and Dr Thomas Camplin. Significantly there was no word from Minehead or from the Wyndhams or the Luttrells. The three justices described the practice of smuggling at Minehead as 'notorious' and believed that its 'most vigilant officer' had been removed because he knew too much. For Withers, 'now a smuggler, then an informer' they showed the utmost contempt, and they had no doubt that - unless May was restored to his station - no one, perhaps not even a magistrate, would dare to oppose the practice of running goods 'as is most notoriously carried on at Minehead.'

These arguments made no impression on the Commissioners, so the magistrates wrote to the great William Pitt himself during his year of victories, when it is unlikely that he could spare much time for the affairs of Minehead. Their letter revealed that William May was not the first Customs officer at Minehead to suffer from being over-zealous, but nothing more is known of this strange affair, so interesting for the light that it throws upon the methods and attitudes of smugglers, Customs officers, electors in a potwalloper borough and the gentry, who in spite of their wealth and power, depended upon these electors for a seat in Parliament. There seems little doubt that on this occasion a confederacy of illicit traders, unopposed by the local gentry and perhaps even supported by the most influential of them, was able to frame a conscientious and honest officer.

St Michael's Church, Minehead, from above Postboy, c.1890. Note the sheets drying in the centre field and the numerous thatched farms. Cleveland, built in 1887 for Thomas Lomas, can be seen top left.

Robert Quirke's almshouses, c.1900.
The stump of the Market Cross can be seen beside the lamp post.

Chapter 6
Church and Chapel: 1485–1800

When the King's antiquary, John Leland, visited Minehead during the later years of the reign of Henry VIII, he wrote that part of the town 'runneth steep up a long hill, in the top whereof is a fair parish church.' During almost fifty years of the Tudor period the parishioners of this church worshipped God in the manner of their medieval forefathers, but when Leland came to Minehead the Reformation had already begun to make profound changes, some of which, as we shall see, were to enlarge the place of the church in the secular life of the community. As the manor courts declined in importance, so the churchwardens took an increasing share of responsibility for local government.

At the accession of Henry VII in 1485, the fine tower of St Michael's, 87-feet from base to pinnacle, had not been built. Francis Eeles places it at the end of the fifteenth century. In style it resembles the solid structures of Devon and Cornwall rather than the more ornate Somerset towers, but it stands as an impressive monument to the prosperity of Minehead in early-Tudor times, a prosperity that was due to both the developing trade of the seaport and to the textile industry which was being practised widely and successfully throughout West Somerset. The rood-stair turret and the finely carved screen must have been added shortly after the tower was built. The date 1529 which appears on a stone shield outside the east window of the north aisle suggests that considerable alterations were made to the medieval building during these years and the Tudor rose with the initials R.H. beside it on the battlements of the south porch, removed since Hancock's time, indicate that further changes were made to the fabric during the reign of Henry VIII.

The late-fifteenth-century tower of St Michael's Church on North Hill.

The first vicar of the parish in Tudor times was Richard Fitzjames. He was a distinguished churchman, warden of Merton College, vicar of Minehead from 1485 to 1497, almoner to King Henry VII in the next year and successively Bishop of Rochester, Chichester and London. He was among those who met Catherine of Aragon on her arrival in England in 1501 and he held the bishopric of London until his death in 1522. Dr William Gilbert, founder of Bruton School, became vicar of Minehead in 1507 and he was also a man of distinction. His affairs at Bruton must have taken precedence over Minehead, but he did not relinquish his benefice here until 1522. Walter Cretyng was the incumbent from 1526 to 1533 during the decisive years when Henry VIII, the Reformation Parliament and member for Taunton, Thomas Cromwell, the King's Vicar-General, were effecting the separation from Rome. Cretyng surrendered his benefice at Minehead to become a canon residentiary and Vicar-General of Wells Cathedral. By 1536 he had been appointed Archdeacon of Bath, an office which he held until his death in 1557. At that time he was wealthy enough to be able to leave £60 for distribution to the poor. He was also a pluralist, holding the benefices of South Brent and Evercreech concurrently with Minehead.

Indeed, it is unlikely that our parish saw much of Fitzjames, Gilbert or Cretyng, for they must surely have looked upon remote Minehead simply as a source of additional income, leaving a poorly-paid curate to take care of the church in their absence. This practice was not uncommon even as late as the eighteenth century when the Revd William Moggridge of Minehead also became Porlock's rector.

Walter Cretyng's successor, John Richards, however, seems to have been resident in Minehead, for his burial in 1548 is one of the first to be recorded in the parish registers. There is a considerable gap before the institution of the next known vicar, John Tilly, in 1561. He seems to have been speedily followed by John Rise, whose death in April 1562 made way for yet another pluralist, one Thomas Williams,

The early-sixteenth-century rood-stair turret.

who was also rector of Old Cleeve from 1565 until his resignation in 1572.

Coincident with the Reformation great changes were taking place in the position of the parish in the community. At first only an ecclesiastical institution, the parish gradually acquired secular functions which it was now possible for the King as Supreme Head of the Church of England to develop through the orders of his Privy Council or the decisions of Parliament. Churchwardens retained their ecclesiastical duties but they were also given new responsibilities as the principal agents of local government in the parish, working with and under those notable officers of Tudor government, the justices of the peace. Orders for the keeping of parish registers were first made in 1538, and sixty years later, at the end of the reign of Elizabeth I, instructions were issued that copies of these registers were to be sent to the diocesan registries, back-dated to the beginning of the reign, although at Minehead burials were already being recorded as early as 1548, during the reign of Edward VI.

Nicholas Browse was instituted as vicar in 1585 and he held this office for half a century. At his death in 1635 he was described as 'both grave in years, and sober in manners, painful in his cure and patient to his parish.' His ministry began when England was threatened by invasion from Spain and when Minehead had been depopulated and impoverished by a disastrous decline in trade, but when he died at the age of eighty-three the new harbour had been erected and the town had made a remarkable recovery. New houses had been built, especially along the quay, and many merchant families, soon to be prominent in our history, had migrated to Minehead, while older ones, like the Quirkes, became more prosperous. The most famous member of this family, Robert Quirke the younger, was a witness at the bishop's court in a strange case that occurred in 1628, towards the end of the long incumbency of Nicholas Browse.

Gradually, since the last years of the reign of Elizabeth I, pews had been constructed on each side of the chancel. Mr Browse, in his evidence to the court, stated that when he was installed as vicar only two seats, his and the parish clerk's, had been erected in the chancel, though there were seats (probably benches) along each wall 'where the youth heretofore sat to sing psalms in at prayer time.' However, the rectory and parsonage properties had been leased to Conand Prowse, and about thirty years before the date of this inquiry he had introduced two pews alongside the parish clerk's which were used by him and his family. His rights in the parsonage were bought by James Quirke and Robert Bond as joint owners and passed on by them to their descendants.

The proprietors of the rectory properties were responsible for the repair and maintenance of the fabric of the chancel, and as some compensation for this they assumed the right to introduce more seats into the chancel and even to let them to other parishioners. By 1628 this privilege had not been challenged by anyone and for just under a year John Quirke's widow, Mary, the late Robert Bond's daughter, had been letting the two pews next to the clerk's seat to the merchant, Thomas Bishop, and the Customs officer, Robert Pawlett.

However, that troublesome lawyer, Lewis Lashbrooke, had drawn up Robert Bond's will and he knew that no mention had been made of seats in the chancel when the various bequests were made to Bond's daughter and her future husband, James Quirke's son, John. On Easter Day, 1628, before morning service, Lashbrooke's manservant, Thomas, pulled out the nails which temporarily closed the pews normally used by Bishop and Pawlett, so that Lewis Lashbrooke and his brother-in-law, John Baker, could occupy these seats. When Bishop arrived Baker rudely expelled him by thrusting his elbow into him and Lashbrooke, in an audible voice, ordered both aggrieved gentlemen to depart as they had no right to be there. For that morning they retired to the vicar's seat and from Easter onwards never again occupied their places in the chancel.

Such an unseemly disturbance in the parish church and on the most important day of the

Christian year was a matter for the bishop. His court heard lengthy depositions from ten leading parishioners, including Thomas Attwill who had been parish clerk for thirty-three years. All the witnesses affirmed that it was a long-established custom for the owners of the parsonage to use or let seats in the chancel, but the legal rights of the proprietors may not have been so clear and no doubt a clever lawyer like Lewis Lashbrooke was able to make a lot of trouble for the Bishop of Bath and Wells, the ageing vicar of Minehead and some of his principal parishioners.

These church courts were not always treated with proper respect. There is a case in 1623 of a Minehead man accused of fornication failing to appear before a jury of his neighbours when ordered to do so by the archdeacon's court. In the same year Thomas Hill of Minehead arrived at this court, when it was sitting in Wiveliscombe, quite drunk. When he was ordered to do penance for his offence of adultery he said he 'would attempt another wench first' and further insulted the judge by offering him a paper which he audibly proclaimed was 'something that came from the bawdry court.'

The surgeon, John Paul, was reported by the vicar, Nicholas Browse, for not taking communion at Easter and for frequently absenting himself from church. He was probably a Puritan but might have been a Roman Catholic. Recusants were so harshly treated that they naturally avoided publicity and this, no doubt, explains why so little is known about Roman Catholics in Minehead, though there were some in the town. For example, Richard Sturd, a Minehead man who was a servant of John Trevelyan of Knowle, was presented to the archdeacon's court as a recusant in June 1623.

Nicholas Browse and his church benefited from the growing prosperity of the town. Already in 1607 one wealthy parishioner, Francis Pearce, had added a new bell to the belfry. The Jacobean table and chairs and the carved pulpit are also of this period. Shortly after putting up his almshouses (*see page 62*), Robert Quirke, in 1634, gave the church the painted boards which were then placed behind the altar and are now to be seen on the north wall of the nave. In 1638 a new organ was bought from a Bath organ builder named Serridge for £90, a large sum of money in a year when four collections of the poor rate brought in only £87.19s.2d. The yearly salary of the organist, Rice Jenkins, the harbour master, was £10.

The churchwardens' accounts show recurring and heavy charges for the maintenance of the bells. The date 1639, that could once be seen on the porch, refers to extensive repairs to the loft over it. In the same year the stonework of the tower was renewed and for this George Chapman fetched stone from the quay on his sledge. That the churchwardens could afford to spend so much on the fabric of the church must surely be an indication of the growing prosperity of the parishioners.

Nicholas Browse had been able in 1610 to purchase the advowson of his vicarage. In 1622 he sold it to his son, Philip, 'for the fatherly love and affection that he beareth to the said Philip,' who paid him £30 immediately and promised to pay a further £40 at his father's death. For the use of the house and lands the old vicar paid a rent of £13.6s.8d. to his son and daughter-in-law, Mary. Eventually the advowson passed to their son, Nicholas, who experienced hard times during and after the Civil War, when he was pleased to earn a little by keeping the church registers. In 1652, during the Interregnum, he became vicar of Minehead, but he died in 1666 while his five children were still young. In his will he empowered his 'good friends and neighbours', Samuel Crockford and John Burnett, to sell the advowson and invest the capital for the benefit of his children. This was not finally done until 1695, by which time all his children were dead except his daughter Willmoth, though there were two grandchildren, both named Nicholas and both infants. The advowson was sold to the vicar, Robert Stone, for £140 and as the annual profits were assessed at between £60 and £80 he should have been pleased with his purchase. At his death in 1701 it passed to his widow who married the Reverend William Moggridge, vicar from 1709. He in turn sold the advowson to the Luttrell family in 1718 and it is still in their hands.

But we must return to the reign of Charles I and to Nicholas Browse, the elder, who ended his long incumbency of St Michael's in 1635, hardly aware of the war clouds that were beginning to gather on the horizon. However, his successor, Robert Knolles, could not escape them. He was a Royalist who was expelled from his living at some time after 4 May 1643, by the supporters of the Parliamentarians who were in the ascendant at Minehead. He seems to have held other livings in Gloucestershire and he may not have spent much time at Minehead.

The old Vicarage house in Higher Town.

Certainly he maintained a curate, a Mr Heathfield, later described as a lecturer, whose name appears in the examination of the reported apparition at Minehead. This, of course, was the notorious affair of Widow Leakey's ghost. Some judicial matters were still the concern of the ecclesiastical courts and this inquiry was conducted by William Pierce, Bishop of Bath and Wells, assisted by two eminent justices of the peace, Dr Paul Godwyn and Sir Robert Phelipps.

During the reign of James I old Susanna Leakey had lived at Huish Champflower where her younger daughter, Joan, had married the rector of the parish, Dr John Atherton. In the spring of 1623 her elder daughter, Susan, gave birth to an illegitimate child a few miles away in a lonely house at Runnington near Langford Budville, where, no doubt, she had been sent in the vain hope that her misconduct would not be discovered. By the middle of June Susan was being accused of an incestuous relationship with her sister's husband, the young rector himself, but the records of the court of the archdeacon of Taunton give no indication that charges were preferred against Dr Atherton. He must have found a way to scotch the embarrassing rumours that were rife in his parish, though Susan, as an unmarried mother, was declared excommunicate and remained so for some time.

Perhaps in order to escape from these embarrassments, Widow Leakey moved to Minehead to live with her elder son, Alexander, a prosperous merchant with a large house on the quay. Here she died in 1634 and her burial on 5 November is duly recorded in the parish register.

Her son-in-law, Dr Atherton, apparently quite unabashed by what had been said about him at Huish Champflower, made rapid progress in the Church. He was a good scholar and in some way he won the confidence of the great Earl of Strafford, Lord Deputy of Ireland. In 1630 he became prebendary of St John's, Dublin, though he continued to hold his benefice at Huish until 1636 when he was installed as Bishop of Waterford and Lismore. However, his later career suggests that there may have been some justification for the accusation of incest made by some of his parishioners at Huish Champflower in 1623, for in 1640 he was hanged in Dublin for the crime of sodomy.

The story of the apparition which caused such a sensation in Minehead that Bishop Pierce felt it necessary to investigate it personally, was first circulated by Alexander Leakey's second wife, Elizabeth. At the inquiry she informed the Bishop and the two magistrates that her mother-in-law on her death-bed had told her that she would return after her death 'in the devil's likeness.' About six weeks later, while she was in her bedroom, Elizabeth claimed that she had heard knocking and other noises 'which went away like a drove of cattle.' She said that her nephew, John, who died in the next year at the age of fourteen, had complained during his sickness that 'he could not be quiet for his grandmother.' Gradually her stories became more circumstantial and melodramatic. Three weeks before Easter, on her way to bed with a book in her hand, she saw the old lady sitting in a chair 'in her full proportion and in her usual apparel.' Frozen with fear she stared at the spectre for a quarter of an hour, until with a mighty groan it vanished.

Mr Heathfield, the curate, in whom she confided, assured her that it was all her fancy but about Allhallowstide, at her husband's storehouse near the harbour, at seven o'clock in the morning, she saw her mother-in-law again, and six weeks before Christmas, while her husband was on business at Weymouth, the ghost appeared for the third time to Elizabeth, 'she being in a chamber making herself ready and handsome to go abroad.' This time she found the courage to speak to it: 'In the name of God do me no hurt', she pleaded; and she received the comforting, indeed flattering reply, 'I cannot; God is with thee.' In brief, old mother Leakey asked her to do two things: first she was to deliver a bond to her deceased son William's wife, Lordesneare, at Barnstaple and to collect a gold chain from her to give to Alexander; secondly, she said, she had been ordered to go to Ireland in order to give a mysterious message to her sister-in-law, Joan Atherton, a message which she declined to repeat to the investigating magistrates, but would reveal to King Charles himself if he ordered her to do so.

In concluding her evidence Elizabeth said that she and her husband both believed that they were the victims of witchcraft. Alexander had suffered severe losses at sea and she suspected that a particular woman was the witch, but would not name her.

The next witness to be called was the curate. He testified that after a christening party at Mr Rono's he had called on Elizabeth Leakey. At about nine o'clock at night he retired to the yard 'to make water' and as he turned to come in again he saw just a few feet from him the apparition of old mistress Leakey. She was wearing her usual dress - a black gown, a kerchief and a white stomacher - and by the light of the candle shining through the kitchen doorway he was able to see her face very clearly, but he 'being affrighted, made all the haste he could to go away.' Later Elizabeth had told him that she had seen the apparition follow him as he took to his heels.

Widow Leakey's old servant, Elizabeth Langston, produced a colourful account of a visitation by the ghost 'in the shape of a little child, shining very bright and glorious.' She saw this strange vision as she sat with her children in front of the fire on Christmas Eve, or so she said. It is in her evidence that there is a reference to 'a shrieking voice' which became so much a part of those ghost stories

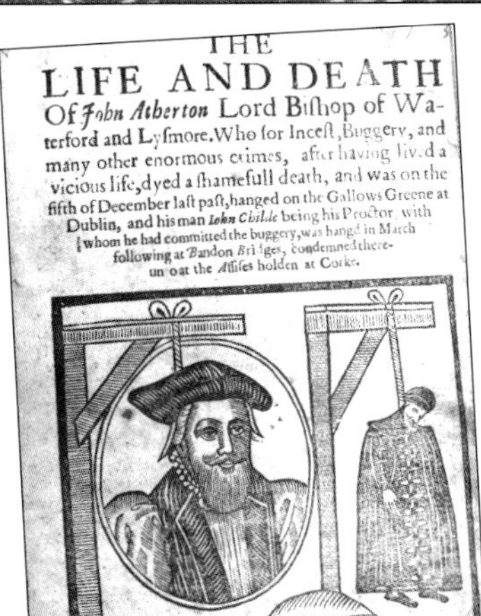

THE
LIFE AND DEATH
Of *John Atherton* Lord Biſhop of Waterford and Lyſmore. Who for Inceſt, Buggery, and many other enormous crimes, after having lived a vicious life, dyed a ſhamefull death, and was on the fifth of December laſt paſt, hanged on the Gallows Greene at Dublin, and his man *Iohn Childe* being his Proctor, with whom he had committed the buggery, was hang'd in March following at *Bandon Bridges*, condemned thereunto at the *Aſſiſes* holden at Corke.

London Printed, 1641.

Above: *The ghost of Mrs Leakey from a cartoon by George Cruikshank.* Left: *Title page of verses written after the execution of Dr Atherton and his proctor.*

recounted by sailors who thought they heard it in the whistling wind during a storm at sea.

Elizabeth Leakey's own servant, Eleanor Fluellin, confirmed some of her mistress' evidence, but had little to add to it. Two other witnesses, Lencatelli, an Italian mountebank, and a sailor called Garland, could not be found, and Elizabeth's husband, Alexander, was so unwilling to appear at the inquiry that he 'was down of the gout' on one occasion and absent from Minehead on another.

The bishop and the two distinguished justices of the peace must have spent many hours hearing this evidence and the irritation that they felt at wasting so much valuable time can be sensed in their summing-up. They found Elizabeth Leakey's evidence quite unreliable. She contradicted herself by giving one version of the affair to the rector of Luccombe, Dr Henry Byam, and another to the bishop's inquiry at Wells. She also contradicted the curate's evidence insofar as he was quoting her, and she became entangled in a web of falsehood about the gold chain which, in any case, was worth only thirty shillings and had been brought from Bermuda by William Leakey, Susanna's second son, as a present for his wife, Lordesneare. Heathfield, the curate, they found to be 'a very fantastical man' and the reference to the great christening feast, which the report interposed in brackets towards the end of his evidence, seemed to hint that he might not have been entirely sober when he saw the ghost. Elizabeth Langston was dismissed as 'a silly poor woman often distempered with drink' and Eleanor Fluellin was described as 'a wanderer' who would do anything she was told to do by her mistress. Garland the sailor was 'an idle fellow... employed by Mr Leakey', the Italian mountebank's evidence was worthless. They concluded, reasonably enough, that 'there never was any such apparition', but that Elizabeth Leakey, 'an understanding woman, but bold and subtle enough', had invented the story for some purpose of her own which the investigation had not discovered. Some scurrilous verses written about Dr Atherton's crime and shameful death on the gallows can hardly be used as evidence, but the suggestion that the secret message which Elizabeth had to take to Ireland was a warning to her brother-in-law to mend his ways may have been true. It is not necessary to believe that she had received the message from the departed widow Leakey: these were superstitious times and she may have hoped to frighten the erring bishop with a voice from the grave that she had herself invented for the purpose.

Mother Leakey's ghost is such an enduring part of the mythology of old Minehead that it seemed worthwhile to treat the story rather fully, especially as the little details incidental to the inquiry help us to understand better the manners and beliefs of the early-Stuart period.

DISSENT

The Civil War and the Puritan Interregnum gave birth to Protestant Nonconformity. The dissenters left the Church of England and formed their own societies unhampered, except in extreme cases, by legislation or state interference. However, some dissenters were so uncompromising in their attitudes to Church and State that they almost invited persecution. The Society of Friends, or 'quakers in the sight of the Lord', came into being under the inspiration of their remarkable leader, George Fox, who visited Minehead in 1668. Their absolute faith in the guidance of 'the inner light' and their determination to live according to its guidance in defiance of all human authority made them appear to be a dangerous minority that might, if given too much rope, overthrow all ordered government.

The Quakers were soon active in Somerset and, with the arrival of William Alloway, senior, at Minehead before the Restoration, a branch of the Society of Friends was soon established here, proving much more influential than might have been expected of such a small group of people. By 1663 William Alloway had married Susannah Lynd and become a prosperous merchant. He leased two houses, a cellar at the quay and some land for which he paid £207, a large sum of money for such a transaction in Minehead at that time. His absolute commitment to the Society of Friends soon earned him a reputation as 'one who freely received them [the Friends] and readily gave up his house to the Lord's service.' Among the Minehead families who attended the meetings in his house in Butts Lane were the Devonshires, the Clothiers, the Bonds, and the Davises. The last named family succeeded the Alloways as the leaders of the little Quaker community, and in the eighteenth century they became the focus of the political opposition to the Luttrell family in the Minehead elections. John Davis, a mariner, who married Joan Pare in 1686, was presumably the ancestor of Robert and William who successively kept politics alive in our Parliamentary borough until and beyond the last properly contested election of 1796.

The Minehead Quakers, like those in many other places, showed those seemingly contradictory traits of selfless humanitarianism far in advance of their times and of provocative hostility to the Establishment. Their care of the poor and the sick was remarkable. The minutes of monthly meetings are thickly interspersed with references to charitable gifts, such as the one authorised at Ashill in 1680 which gave William Bond fifteen shillings for the relief of Alice Evans and instructed William Alloway to assist him in caring for her. A little later William Alloway, junior, was given five shillings for Sybil Easton, 'a poor impotent woman', and his mother, Susannah, twenty shillings for the ailing wife of William Thorne. Although they were not chosen as churchwardens it was common for Quakers to be among the overseers of the poor. In 1681, when William Alloway, senior, held this office with a certain Towhill, a sum of £5 was given to William Paul, the surgeon, for the care of a sick woman, Mary Buck, and a like sum was promised to him if he cured her. It seems likely that this was a personal act of charity and that William Alloway donated the money. In 1722 three of the four overseers were members of the Society of Friends, George Devonshire, Robert Davis and Richard Brocklesby. The latter had married Mary Alloway and was on a visit from Ireland where he normally lived. Their son, Richard, born during this visit, became a famous physician and attended the great Dr Johnson during his last illness. In 1738 Robert Davis was responsible for a pension scheme and a hospital for sailors and their dependents, which the politicians at Dunster Castle believed was depriving their candidates of the poor man's vote. Thirty years later they countered it with their own society for Mutual Benefit and Assistance. The charitable activities of the Quakers, however, continued in Minehead at least until the end of the century. After the disastrous fire of 1791, William Davis, who liked to be known as 'the poor man's friend', started a subscription list to help the homeless. The first subscriber was Dr Richard Brocklesby with a gift of £50 and altogether the fund raised £4000.

However, the respect which their acts of charity earned them was often counterbalanced by the anger which their antagonism to authority provoked. In 1683 William Bond, Henry Mattock, Christopher Devonshire and Susannah Alloway were committed to Ilchester gaol for refusing to take the oath of allegiance and for not attending their parish church which Friends disparagingly named 'the steeple house'. They refused to pay their fines and two of them, Bond and Mattock, were in prison a year later. They also objected to paying tithes to 'the so-called priest'. After a disturbance in David Webber's cornfield at Porlock in 1667, five Quakers, among them Bond and Alloway from Minehead and Mary Webber, the farmer's wife, were charged with causing a riot by resisting that 'so-called doctor of divinity', Hamnet Ward, the rector of Porlock, when he tried to collect his tithes by seizing some of the corn as it was being harvested. However, it transpired that William Bond was not even present in the field and counsel for the defence of the others successfully pleaded that, as the rector was not entitled to his tithes until the harvest had been gathered, the Webbers were defending only what at the time belonged to them. They were found not guilty, but the angry justices who heard the case ordered them to take the oath of allegiance, which they knew Quakers could not do as they believed that all oaths were barred by Scripture; so they were sent back to prison.

Mary Webber's case was heard separately. She was also acquitted and re-arrested, charged with non-attendance at church. She was evidently less securely imprisoned than the men and she 'took an opportunity to take her liberty and to go about her occasions.' In other words she escaped from custody and returned to Porlock, whence she was fetched by the son of the infuriated gaoler and his man with two horses. She remained in prison for six years, but her unconquerable spirit seems to have been as great a trial to the Society of Friends as to the magistrates. Her husband, David, fell from grace and she was said to have 'manifested herself to be of a perverse spirit' which no doubt the gaoler at Ilchester would have been able to confirm. As she had 'departed from the way of truth' she was expelled from the Society of Friends.

Such independence was exceptional in women of the seventeenth century, but the confidence which their religion gave them seems to have lifted some Quaker women above the passive role that was accepted by most of their female contemporaries.

Katherine Evans and Sarah Chivers landed at Minehead in 1664 after a voyage from Ireland. They remained for a few days and then set out 'toward their outward dwellings' near Bath. They were accompanied as far as Wiveliscombe by two Minehead Quakers, William Bond and William Thorne. Here at a meeting in William Ward's house, Katherine Evans was giving her testimony, when a justice of the peace, Major Robert Hawley, burst in upon them, flourishing his sword above his head. Most of those attending the meeting were fined £5, but Katherine and Sarah were sent back to prison to be charged with being present at a conventicle 'preaching and infesting the people with heresy and sedition.'

Quaker marriages were strictly controlled. The quarterly meeting had to give its approval before a marriage could take place and a church wedding was forbidden. Joseph Alloway, who in Queen Anne's reign finished the work of extending the harbour head, was doubly an offender: he was married by a priest in 1687 'to one of the World', Mary Brooke, and he added to his offence by paying tithes for his wife's land. He was expelled from the Society of Friends, as were his brothers John and Benjamin, who imported poor quality tobacco in an attempt to cheat the Government of £22. Benjamin caused even more offence by his incontinence with a girl named Jane Sandiford and he was unwilling to meet her in the presence of witnesses in order to deny her accusations. The backsliding of some of his sons must have saddened old William Alloway who, however, died in 1686 before their expulsion from the Society in Minehead of which he had been such a distinguished founder member. At the beginning of the nineteenth century there were still Alloways living in Minehead. One of them, Nicholas, an innkeeper, was described by John Fownes Luttrell as 'that old scoundrel', but perhaps his offence was no worse than to be an ardent supporter of the Whig party, to which so many Minehead Quakers had belonged.

The ground near the [present] smithy in Markethouse Lane was, in 1736, the site of a Quaker meeting house and burial ground. Later the meeting house was moved back to Butts Lane and a burial ground was acquired at Alcombe where Quakers were buried from 1741 to 1771, thirty-five persons in all. This land passed to the Methodists in 1846 by which time none of the Quaker trustees was still living in Minehead.

During the century and a half following the political and religious turmoil of the Civil War very little positive evidence of Nonconformist activity, apart from the well-documented history of the Society of Friends, has so far been uncovered. A nineteenth-century list of buildings licensed for worship as a result of the Toleration Act of 1689 includes Ann Wrington's house in that year; Sara Hayman's in 1697; Thomas Peters' in 1700; and John Kirkpatrick's in 1707. Unfortunately the names of the religious sects are not given. However, from 1726 these were recorded and because of this we know that the house of Richard Evans (late Dorothy Quick) was licensed for Presbyterian worship. A much earlier reference to a Presbyterian meeting house appears on the outside of the deeds of a house at the south end of Focklands Court leased to William Saffin. The names of the witnesses were Abraham Crockford and Sarah Crockford, 'now Delbridge'. The Saffins, father and son, were buried in linen for which their executors paid a fifty-shilling fine. Some of these houses were certainly licensed for Baptist worship. The Baptists had founded a church at Stogumber as early as 1656. Through its influence a branch of this sect was active in Minehead during the eighteenth century, and vigorous enough to build its own place of worship at Periton in 1817.

John Wesley twice visited Minehead. On 18 April 1744, he rode from Crediton. He wrote in his journal:

> *Between five and six in the evening we reached Minehead. Finding a general expectation of it among the people, about seven I preached near the seashore, to almost all the inhabitants of the place. Most of the gentlemen of the town were there, and behaved with seriousness and decency.*

On 18 July a year later Wesley arrived again at Minehead. After both visits he crossed the Channel

The old workhouse, Church Steps, c.1890.

to Fonmon Castle in a sloop belonging to Richard Forrest whose widowed sister, Mrs Jones, lived at Fonmon. Just before his second visit, in June 1745, Wesley wrote to her to ask her to arrange for her brother's ship to take him across on 19 July. In spite of the good reception given to John Wesley by Minehead people, there does not seem to have been an organised Methodist society in the town during the eighteenth century.

Puritanism and Beyond

To pick up the threads of Church history we must go back to the time when the small but vigorous Quaker community was established in Minehead. Under the strict regime of the Puritan Commonwealth the Church of England experienced painful changes that must have affected deeply its many sincere communicants and in particular its ministers, who were often deprived of their livings and thus suffered real hardship. After the expulsion of Robert Knolles as a Royalist, nothing is known of our ministers until the year 1652 when Nicholas Browse, grandson of the first Nicholas, paid first -fruits on admission to the living. He officiated at a time when marriages required the authority of a justice of the peace. For instance, the marriage of Captain Nathaniel Bullocke and Jane Webber, which took place in December 1653, was witnessed by Thomas Siderfin of Luxborough.

The use of the *Book of Common Prayer* had been forbidden in 1645 and no compulsory form of service had been ordered in its place. Evidence given to Thomas Siderfin in 1651 about some suspected trouble-makers at Wootton Courtenay reported that among other things on the Sunday in question they refused to attend 'Evening Exercise' at the parish church. Public worship varied in style and content from church to church and must have seemed very strange to good Anglicans at this time.

Nicholas Browse was confirmed in his living at the Restoration of Charles II in 1660, but he did not live long to enjoy the restored authority of the clergy and the return of the old liturgy of the church. The next long-serving incumbent of St Michael's was William Moggridge. He married a lady who had twice been widowed by former vicars of Minehead, Robert Stone (1693-1702) and Tristram Chave (1702-09). Instituted in 1709 he sold the advowson of the vicarage to the Luttrells in 1718 for £230.

His successor, Leonard Herring, was presented to the living by Henry Fownes Luttrell in 1763. Like his predecessor he was active in the affairs of the Parliamentary borough and his letters to his patron, with whom for a time he was on very friendly terms, are racy in style and range in subject from cock fighting and hunting to politics. By 1773 Mr Luttrell had decided to move the Reverend Leonard Herring to a South Devon parish in order to make room for one of his own sons. Herring believed that his annual income would be reduced by £33 and his efforts to avoid this, supported ardently but not very tactfully by his wife, appear to have destroyed the good relations that had existed with his patron. Peter Woodley succeeded him in 1775, and in 1780 Alexander Fownes Luttrell, as planned by his father, became the first member of his family to be vicar of Minehead.

Earlier in this chapter we noticed that from the middle of the sixteenth century, following the Reformation, the churchwardens and overseers of the poor were being increasingly involved in the general and secular administration of the parish. By the end of the seventeenth century they were largely responsible for the day-to-day conduct of local government. With the authority of the justices of the peace behind them and with the assistance of the constables and tithingmen, they collected the poor rate, distributed alms, cared for the needy sick, gave shelter and food to destitute travellers and vagrants who had to be returned to their place of settlement, executed government orders, indentured apprentices, enforced bastardy orders, and with the help of the waywardens kept the roads and bridges in some sort of repair.

In the year 1628 the first Nicholas Browse received an order made by the Judges of Assizes for the 'Suppressing of all Ales and Revels'. These were the notorious 'Church Ales' that had been permitted on certain feast days and which often led to drunkenness and brawling. Every constable of a hundred had to deliver a copy of this order to the minister of every parish who in turn had to report back in writing to the assizes through the constables. In short, the vicar and his officers took the responsibility for executing the Government order. On this occasion Mr Browse was also required to punish 'minstrels and such other persons that usually carry up and down bulls and bears to bate' and who, no doubt, assembled rowdy crowds about them as they presented their cruel sport.

There were about thirty poor people in 1700 who were in receipt of alms from the overseers of the poor. In the same year 1s.6d. was 'paid for water for George Haines' legs', water which perhaps was brought all the way from Bath, but in 1702 the overseers were sharply reproved for spending money contrary to the law. As one reads through their accounts it is obvious that sympathy for the poorest inhabitants of the town was a strong motive with most of the overseers, who were often at loggerheads with the parishioners anxious to reduce the annual poor rate levied upon them. The overseers had to see with their own eyes the misery of the poor and to listen to their pitiable pleas for help. By 1731 the parish meeting was convinced that it would be more economical to gather the poor together in a workhouse, so they leased Punter's tenement at the foot of Church Steps at a rent of £6.5s.0d. per annum (*see page 68*). During the twenty weeks before the poor were moved into the workhouse the expenses were as follows:

	£	s	d
Weekly payments to individuals	39	12	7
Incident charges (e.g. medical care)	17	16	1½
Apparel	4	13	10
House rent (for people living at home)	2	16	0
Funeral charges	3	12	0
Binding of apprentices	3	7	6
Total for twenty weeks	71	18	0½

The workhouse master was paid a salary of £10 per annum. Joan Trott, who assisted him, was paid 1s.6d. a week. A month's purchases of food included a bushel of oats for a shilling, two pecks of beans for 1s.6d., and two bundles of pease haulm for 5d. There was a charge of 1s.6d. for killing two pigs and of 2s.7d. for baking bread. Purchases of 'garding seed' and plants show that the sturdier paupers must have grown their own vegetables. One pound of wool for 4½d and 24lbs of flocks for three shillings suggest that others were employed in woolcombing and spinning. The smallest charge in this month (February 1732) was for a chamber pot which cost 2½d. and the heaviest a sum of £1 'paid to Mary Brotherton for the order of the justice.'

Indeed, legal charges and payments for medical care seem generally to have made great demands on the poor rate. Two trials at Taunton, of which there are no details, cost £15.8s.6d., a remarkable figure. Among the many and regular payments to doctors was a payment in 1703 to William Paul of £7 for attending Widow Cousins during her last illness. Dr Jonathan Question in 1724 received £2.7s.11½d 'for the cures he hath done for the poor', a sum which had been left over after other expenses had been met. In another entry made two years later the spelling is phonetic. Only a West-Countryman could have written: 'To Doctor John Ellis, veas for meadesons and a tendance, £1.2s.0d.' In 1733 John Trout had to be helped to the workhouse after falling from the quay and for curing him and two other inmates Dr Ball received five guineas. In May 1735, there is another entry of payments to Dr Ellis: 'for curing Joan Newton's breast and legs, 17s.6d., Burges of a swelling in his belly, 3s.6d., John Vater's son of a broken arm and fracture in his scull, £1.0s.0d.' Only Jonathan Question, himself an overseer of the poor in 1746, seems to have demanded less than his full fee for treating these destitute people.

Among the overseers in 1723 was John Merrick who twelve years before had given his bond in £100 so that he could move from Dunster to Minehead in order to play the organ at St Michael's. In the same bond he is promised a:

> ... *yearly salary of ten pounds of lawful money of Great Britain for cleaning and playing on the organ* [is the order significant?] *belonging to the Church of Minehead as long as the said John Merrick shall live and is capable of playing on the said organ.*

The cost of caring for the poor continued to rise and for a few years from 1754 the workhouse was closed. In the previous year the overseers had spent just over £200, but in 1755 the total had increased to £233, so in the next year the workhouse was re-opened.

From time to time the overseers were helped by charitable gifts which, after investment, provided annually small sums of money for the relief of the poor. The oldest charitable fund was the Cow Charity, which had been financed by the seizure of cattle illegally imported from Ireland in 1668. Some of the money thus obtained was invested in a farm at Ottery St Mary, which was eventually sold by John Fownes Luttrell to the trustees of the charity in 1822 for a nominal peppercorn rent.

A memorandum in the overseers' accounts for 27 December 1761 records a bequest to the poor of £100 made in the will of George Silliven, dated 10 July 1753 and proved in 1756. Among the witnesses to the handing over of this money by George Silliven's executors was 'Richard Evans, minister', who must have been curate to the elderly vicar, William Moggridge, then living at Porlock where he died and was buried in 1763.

The demands on the time and energies of the churchwardens and overseers of the poor, combined with the increasing poor rate which had to be levied on the unwilling parishioners, no doubt explains to a great extent the neglect of the fabric of our parish churches in the eighteenth century. In 1764 the pinnacle of the tower of St Michael's was found to be so dangerous that it had to be removed. It is hard to imagine our parish church with the stair turret rising to a point at the south-east corner of the familiar square-topped tower.

In English history old ways die hard. As late as 1763 the Reverend William Moggridge was still holding a court of the manor of the vicarage of Minehead, at which leases were renewed or surrendered. The vicar had 27 acres of glebeland and his steward, Francis Bastone, the lawyer, was advising him to maintain his claim to the Hemp Garden, which was disputed by Henry Fownes Luttrell. The leaseholder was John Bowden, a sergemaker, and as a final anachronism in this survival of the medieval manorial system Bowden paid the vicar £2.12s.6d. as a fine in lieu of a heriot.

Chapter 7
Law and Order: 1500–1800

At the end of the sixteenth century the manorial courts had lost most of their powers of criminal jurisdiction except in the north of England. The decline of the feudal system and the destruction of the great baronial houses in the civil wars of York and Lancaster had begun this process, while the Tudor policy of strengthening the authority of the justices of the peace as the agents of the King's Law had completed it. The powers of the justices were extended by each of the Parliaments of Henry VII. They were required to arrest criminals; in petty sessions they were empowered to deal with a variety of misdemeanours; and in their general sessions, which were held quarterly, they could try any indictable offence except treason. It is to these men that we must look for the preservation of law and order in Minehead during the three centuries from 1500 to 1800.

By the end of the reign of Elizabeth I the whole machinery of government depended on these overworked but devoted men. They were usually chosen from the ranks of the gentry, though from 1559 until the abrogation of the Charter of Incorporation in 1607 the portreeve of Minehead was ex officio a magistrate. Remembering the heavy burden they bore, it is surprising to discover that there was never any difficulty in recruiting men for this unpaid work from among the wealthiest and most influential families in the county; added power and status were considered an adequate reward for long hours of tedious, frustrating and sometimes unpopular labour. In West Somerset the Wyndhams of Orchard and Kentsford, the Trevelyans of Nettlecombe and, of course, the Luttrells of Dunster were almost always commissioned as justices of the peace.

For the execution of the law the justices depended mainly on the constables, two of whom until 1842 were chosen annually at the Court Leet of the lord of the manor. They were generally men of little distinction or education and consequently they were often timid or submissive when their duties demanded courage and independence. The constables of Minehead relied on the no less timid tithingmen of Minehead, Alcombe and Staunton who were required to make arrests and deal with disorders or violence. It is not surprising that the constables and their subordinates served without enthusiasm. In their small communities they were often dealing with offenders who were acquaintances, even friends or relations. The lot of these part-time, unpaid policemen could be a very unhappy one.

Professor T.G. Barnes has observed:

Somerset is fortunate in having preserved from the reign of James I virtually every type of record connected with the institution of magistracy in the early-seventeenth century.

Indeed from the quarter sessions order books and the sessions rolls a very clear picture of the way the justices of the peace governed their locality emerges, enabling an understanding of the complexity of the multifarious problems for which they were responsible to the Privy Council. The quarter sessions held in Bridgwater, Wells, Ilchester and Taunton at Michaelmas, Epiphany, Easter and Midsummer:

... display a remarkable variety of business, covering criminal offences such as murder, assault, burglary, vagabondage, witchcraft, breaches of industrial laws and recusancy; the punishments inflicted ranged from fine and imprisonment to flogging, branding and hanging. But the justices were also responsible for the repair of roads, licensing of taverns, binding of apprentices, relief of the honest poor in times of inordinate distress owing to famine, fire or pestilence; fixing the wage level for the district; regulation of the price and the export of grain; and the making of provision for redeeming English sailors from Barbary pirates. With little professional help or advice, except an able clerk, the justices fulfilled the combined functions of the present-day magistrates' courts and local councils.

By far their heaviest responsibility in the late-sixteenth century and throughout most of the seventeenth century was for the operation of

The manor office from Summerland Road looking towards Blenheim Road, c.1895.
In the back ground is Clanville, designed by Piers St Aubyn for H.A. Bosanquet in 1882.

House on the corner of the Parade and Fields Lane (now Summerland Road), c.1888.
The manor office (Old Priory) on the left is where the Court Leet met.

the Elizabethan poor laws of 1598 and 1601. To summarize these briefly, a parish rate, approved by the justices of the peace, had to be collected by the churchwardens and overseers of the poor for distribution to those genuinely in need, but for 'rogues' who would not work the law provided a harsh alternative. If they were caught begging they were returned to their last place of settlement, that is their place of birth or full-time employment. Persistent 'wanderers' were whipped, branded, and sent to the house of correction at Taunton or the fetid gaol at Ilchester. Unable to beg and faced with starvation such vagrants inevitably became criminals, for thefts of food and clothing were often obligatory for survival.

On 7 July 1613, the parishioners of Minehead petitioned the justices of the peace assembled in quarter sessions at Taunton to take action about a certain Ralph Tucker whose wife, Margaret, a Minehead woman, Sir John Wyndham had sent home by pass. Her husband soon followed and it was his reputation as a troublemaker that caused this letter to be written, signed by sixteen leading inhabitants of the town and by their priest, Nicholas Browse, 'vicar theare'.

In this missive Minehead was described was 'a place fallen into great poverty by means of the late sickness, the dearth of corn, fire and other such disastrous accidents happening to the said town.' The Tuckers were said to be great nuisances to the constables and overseers of the poor:

> *... people very unfit to be suffered to wander, for their practice is nothing else but begging, stealing and with reverence be it spoken, whoring, drunkeness, quarrelling and railing.*

The Tuckers were 'young, valiant and strong', but quite unwilling to work for their living. Ralph had robbed a barn at Old Cleeve and broken into a house at Wembdon 'at time of divine service', but after a brief imprisonment he had been twice released, and for a whole year he and his large family had been brazening it out at impoverished Minehead whose parishioners pleaded with 'their good worships to take some course' with the Tuckers 'that the poor place be not troubled with them.' The problem was referred to Sir John Wyndham and the conscientious George Luttrell, but the action which they took made matters worse. Ralph Tucker was committed to Ilchester gaol whence, just six weeks later, he was writing his own petition to quarter sessions, begging the magistrates to relieve the wants of 'his wife and seven young children' who, he wrote, had sought 'assistance of the parish', adding 'they says they shall have none, but that they shall starve.' The parish officers were ordered to relieve the wants of the Tuckers in the normal way with the rest of the poor.

One of their daughters, Elizabeth, was born lame. Unfortunately for her she was also born at Westonzoyland as her mother was returning to her place of settlement at Minehead. Our churchwardens and overseers jumped at the chance to be rid of at least one member of this troublesome family. They returned Elizabeth by pass to Westonzoyland with a polite request to that parish to care for her 'according to his majesty's laws, for that she was born within your parish.' Weston sent her back again. Minehead returned her to Weston, suggesting that if their officers considered their parish had been wronged they should apply to the justices for redress. The signatories described themselves as 'your loving friends', but by this time there was obviously a great deal of ill-feeling between the parishes. To their credit the justices decided that poor little ten-year-old Elizabeth should remain with her family at Minehead, showing their exasperation with our parish elders by adding the words: 'This last order to stand.'

However, for Minehead and the justices of the peace this was not to be the end of the Tuckers. In the same year Elizabeth's sister, Margaret, was gaoled at Ilchester for breaking into a house, and in 1623 Elizabeth herself was charged with being in unlawful possession of clothes stolen by her brother, English, from a hedge near Stringston where they had been left to dry. A certain Henry Ford confessed to stealing bacon, wheat flour and hens from his master and from Constable Baker at 'the instigation of one Tucker's wife and daughter who would often persuade this examinate so to do.'

But there was worse to come. Two other sisters, Sidwell and Christabel, were involved in a serious case of housebreaking at Pitminster near Taunton. Sidwell's story was that she set out on Friday from Minehead with her mother and sister to walk to Dulverton, but some five miles out at Lypehead she separated from the others and travelled alone towards Wiveliscombe, spending the night in an old abandoned house at Brompton Ralph with an improbably-named Cornishman, Morgan Jones, and his wife. Next day, Saturday, she told Sir John Gill and George Luttrell, the three of them came to Pitminster. Mrs Jones kept watch, her husband pulled out a window to enter a house and Sidwell stood outside to receive the stolen goods - a hat lined with taffeta, a silver ring, a partlet, a 'fashion' waistcoat and so on. They separated and agreed to meet at St Decuman's Fair, but she never saw Morgan Jones and his wife again. Her mother confirmed the first part of the story and added that she had spent the whole of Saturday with Christabel at Dulverton market. On Sunday evening, she said, when she returned to Minehead, Sidwell was already there and Christabel was given some of the stolen goods by her sister.

The evidence from Pitminster was very different. Two witnesses recognised them and affirmed that they had seen both girls on the Saturday morning. The houseowner made a hue and cry and found, presumably at Minehead, a hat and a ring in their possession and furthermore he included twenty shillings in money among his losses. If they had stolen money in excess of 12d. Sidwell and Christabel had committed the capital crime of grand larceny. Also they were persistent offenders. Christabel had made two previous appearances at quarter sessions and Sidwell was facing a fifth charge. Unfortunately for these wretched girls they were on trial at a time when the King's Council had demanded from the justices sterner measures against vagrancy and crime. It is nevertheless with a sense of shock that we learn from a self-styled friend of the Tuckers, Elinor Street, who robbed their house during their absence in gaol, that Sidwell and her sister had been executed for felony.

A few years earlier, in 1607, as one of his last official acts as portreeve before the abrogation of the Charter of Incorporation, George Quirke had examined a vagrant, John Guppie of Bodmin, who with his wife Pasca and daughter, Florence, had been arrested as they came to Minehead from Porlock. Two seals were found in Pasca's possession, 'a great leaden seal which was found hidden in the hair of her head and the other - a little seal engraven in stone which, upon search made, fell from her.' Perhaps these were to be used to forge passes that would enable them to move freely from parish to parish. George Quirke was not convinced by Guppie's explanation, especially as it was only in part supported by Pasca, so he sent the two of them to Ilchester where John was found guilty and 'burned in the shoulder for a rogue.'

The problems of vagrancy in Minehead in the seventeenth century were aggravated by the numbers of unemployed, often by unemployable, Irish people, who landed at the harbour or were sent to Minehead from other towns to await transport back to Ireland. Already in 1620, shortly after the completion of the new harbour, the justices had recorded in their minute book that Minehead was being charged with the 'maintenance of divers Irish rogues and vagabonds sent there for transportation to Ireland.' They ordered the parishes where these vagrants had been arrested and the treasurer of the county hospitals to share the cost of their conveyance back to Ireland. However, these orders were often ignored by the parishes and hundreds of the county, and in 1630 an unprecedented rate to relieve the burden on Minehead required a royal proclamation and the judges' sanction to enforce it.

The case of John Laffan shows how troublesome to Minehead and to the rest of the county these unwanted Irish immigrants could be. In the early spring of 1652 the *Cherubim of the Forest* was driven by contrary winds into the river of Waterford. On board were William Cuffe of Minehead, gentleman, and John Laffan, alias Laugharne. Cuffe returned home in the *Cherubim*, but Laffan decided to remain at Waterford because, as he told Cuffe, there was a wealthy Englishwoman there whom he intended to marry. Not long afterwards the two men met again at Minehead. Laffan had with him some Irish folk, one of whom he claimed to be his wife. Since then Cuffe had encountered Laffan and his companions wandering through the counties of Somerset and Devon, using, as he believed, forged passes to enable them to hoodwink the constables of the parishes 'to the great prejudice of the inhabitants thereof.' With his so-called wife and servants about him this Irishman had now abused and insulted the officers of the town of Minehead, calling them 'turds, fools and knaves'. When Cuffe reproved him, this overweening rogue threatened to report him to William Malin, the Lord Protector Cromwell's personal secretary. This was the last straw. Appropriately enough, on St Patrick's day, 1654, William Cuffe made his formal complaint to the nearest justice of the peace, George Luttrell, who sent forward his sworn and corroborated testimony to quarter sessions at Ilchester, where Laffan was duly charged with a number of offences, including petty larceny for which he was sentenced to be whipped. Under the vagrancy laws he was given a pass to Minehead whence he was to be shipped back to Ireland.

It happens that a copy of this pass is extant. It allowed him five days for the journey and was addressed to the constables and parish officers on the most direct route from Ilchester to Minehead. To meet the expense of sending him to Ilchester the inhabitants of Minehead were allowed to sell certain articles of his clothing, no doubt garments of some value. Evidently this confidence trickster understood the importance of keeping up appearances.

Among the papers that used to be kept in the parish chest of St Michael's church and which are now in the Somerset Record Office there are numerous bonds given to insure the parish against the eventuality of a new resident of Minehead becoming a pauper and a charge on the poor rate. The churchwardens and overseers of the poor show an almost obsessive anxiety on the subject. Even Alexander Ewens, who became a pillar of society and some of whose splendid books are displayed in our church, had to find a guarantor in the sum of £40 when he and his wife and child removed into Minehead from Dunster. In 1629 Dr Paul, chirurgeon, was required to give his bond in the sum of £30 for an assistant, and his widow Christian, in 1641, was bound in £50 for John Shepherd, dyer, who with his wife and children had lately come to Minehead, 'there (by God's assistance) to inhabit and dwell.' Pauper children were apprenticed by indenture witnessed by the churchwardens and overseers and approved by two justices of the peace. So that the parish could be relieved of responsibility for these poor children as soon as possible they were bound to their master or mistress at twelve or thirteen, girls to the age of twenty-one and boys to twenty-four. Life must often have been hard for them. The indenture included a clause ensuring that they would be adequately clothed and fed, but they had few rights and in general few privileges, though all of them had in theory to be taught a trade or craft.

The efforts that were made to minimise the demands on the poor rate are understandable. The account books of the churchwardens and the overseers of the poor record steadily growing charges for the care and maintenance of the parish paupers. By the middle of the eighteenth century some thirty people were being regularly lodged in the workhouse at the foot of Church Steps. Many of the resettlement papers concern widows or orphan children that had been sent back to Minehead as the law provided. Naturally enough our officers took every opportunity to send their paupers away from the town to their place of settlement, if it could be found.

As an example of a resettlement paper we might look at the case of Elizabeth Dustin whose husband, John, was a seaman in HMS *Nemesis* during the War of American Independence. In May 1783, Elizabeth was brought by the parish officers to Dunster Castle to be examined by two justices, John Fownes Luttrell and James Bernard. The long absence at sea of her husband had left her and her three young children destitute, but unfortunately for Minehead she did not know (or did not want to know) the whereabouts of her husband's place of settlement. She thought she had heard him say that he was born at Salcombe in Devon, but it took the magistrates, churchwardens and overseers, with the assistance no doubt of the constables, a whole year to discover that the Dustins came from the village of Malborough close to Salcombe and to send Elizabeth, Mary, William and James back where they belonged.

The most time-wasting and frustrating of the burdensome tasks that faced the local justices in the performance of their duties was the settlement of the many disputes caused by one of the greatest social evils of the times, illegitimacy. Between the years 1625 and 1638 Somerset quarter sessions confirmed bastardy orders from the justices in the divisions in no less than 250 cases. No other matter took so much of their time or was so difficult to resolve. Wherever possible the parents were held responsible for the nurture of the child. The mother was compelled to take care of the baby and the putative father to provide a weekly sum of money in support. The mother's guilt was manifest, but magistrates hesitated to convict the man on her evidence alone. For this reason there were delays and frequent appeals: for the same reason, no doubt, women in Somerset were more often sentenced to corporal punishment than men, a fact which an assize order of 1638 brought to the notice of the Somerset justices, but it is to their credit that the full rigours of this harsh law were rarely enforced on either sex.

Elizabeth Praunce of Minehead gave birth to a child whose father was said to be John Blake, also of Minehead. Their case was heard at Old Cleeve in 1616 by George Luttrell and John Trevelyan. They found the charge proved against both parties and ordered Blake, who was described as 'a very poor man', to pay 6d. a week for the relief of the baby boy until the child had reached the age to be apprenticed. Failing this Blake was to go to prison. Elizabeth was ordered to use 'her uttermost endeavour' to maintain the child without recourse to the parish for assistance. If not she was to be committed to the House of Correction. For her punishment she was to be publicly whipped at the ford (probably at Puddle Bridge) 'within the said parish of Minehead tomorrow being Thursday in the afternoon.'

In 1620 Mary Ewens, a confessed mother of twins, was not whipped, but the father, Roger Maye, had also confessed and done penance at Minehead's parish church by order of the spiritual court. This probably meant that he had made a public confession in the churchyard after morning service. He was prosperous enough to contribute 16d. weekly to the overseers, a sum barely adequate, however, for the care of twins.

George Ford, an innkeeper, water-bailiff and churchwarden in 1624, and prominent citizen, was involved in a bastardy dispute in 1631 which must have caused him much embarrassment. He had a young man working for him named Allen Carr who was the father of an illegitimate child born to one of Ford's domestic servants, Mary Thomas. Carr was plainly guilty, for he ran away when Mary Thomas accused him. The justices in quarter sessions, realising that Ford 'was privy to all this', ordered him to pay 18d. a week towards the upkeep of the child as Carr himself had disappeared. At first Carr had withdrawn or been sent to the home at Selworthy of another Quay Street innkeeper, Roger Vyon of the New Inn, where, Vyon testified, Carr had a meeting with George Ford and his wife to discuss what ought to be done. 'Ford might have caused the said Carr to have been apprehended if he would,' said Vyon, and William Tapscott, a clothier, one of the overseers of the poor who gave this information to the court, added that there was a report that 'the said Ford caused his daughter to carry the said Carr's apparel to him.' Mary Thomas was sent to the House of

Correction for a year and, in January 1632, her former master gave his bond to the churchwardens and overseers in the sum of £40, accepting responsibility for the maintenance of the child. He had already been 'bound over to the good behaviour at the general sessions of the peace.' However, just a year later the church officers reported that, as their fellow citizen had given satisfactory sureties for the care of the child and behaved well, he could safely be released from the order binding him to keep the peace.

As water-bailiff George Ford held a position of considerable influence and even power. He probably counted on this to enable him to silence the church officers over this affair, but he had reckoned without the deep-felt anxieties of the parishioners and their officers about avoidable payments from the poor rate. He continued to prosper, and in 1634 he added considerably to his property at the quay, but he does not seem to have been employed again as a parish officer.

There are very many bastardy orders among the church papers and in the quarter session rolls, some of them concerning men of some importance in the district. In 1735 Joseph Alloway, son of the prosperous merchant of the same name who completed the extension to the harbour head, admitted that he was the father of a child born to Jane Scribben and gave his bond of £50. A few years later, 1743, the Reverend Mr Clare of Porlock did the same for 'a female bastard child' that had been born in Minehead to Elizabeth Vicary, a single woman, which, because of the place of its birth was the concern of the parish of Minehead. William Clare, so that the maintenance of the infant would not be a charge on our poor rate and to save himself from being exposed as the putative father, agreed to make a contribution to the overseers. Yet another clerical gentleman, the Reverend John Anthony of Minehead, was accused by Mary Boynes of being the father of a baby girl born in September 1778. His denial of the offence did not convince the justices, J.F. Luttrell and William Hayman. He was ordered to pay £3.3s.2d. at once and to contribute 1s.6d. a week towards the maintenance. Mary Boynes was directed to look after the baby herself or pay 6d. a week in maintenance, which perhaps the repentant parson paid for her.

There are almost no records extant of criminal cases which, because of the serious nature of the crimes concerned, had to be tried before judges of the Western Circuit sitting in their twice-yearly assizes. Mention is made in another chapter the assize order requiring Lewis Lashbrooke and John Baker to appear before an Admiralty court at Westminster for an unspecified offence. In 1649, another assize order, No. 79, instructed three justices of the peace, John Newton, William Ceely and Edward Ceely, to send for a woman named Anne Meare who, from information given by John Gorges, later to become Mayor of Taunton, was suspected of being a witch. They were to examine her and hear a number of witnesses. This done she was to be brought to trial at the next assizes, but there was no record of what happened to her or of the exact nature of the charges which the poor woman had to answer. She was presumably detained in the old prison in the Town Hall, near the room in which the Court Leet sat, called for some inexplicable reason 'cock moile'.

A serious felony occurred at Minehead in the summer of 1647. Joanna Vaughan and Thomazina Williams appeared at the Taunton quarter sessions accused of stealing nearly fifty yards of cloth. They were 'vehemently suspected' by George Luttrell and their case was also referred to the assizes. What happened to them is not known.

The commonest form of crime was petty larceny, thefts of food and clothing by poor people whose need was desperate. In 1609 John Laughill of Minehead, another of its many Irishmen perhaps, stole a shirt and a child's smock that had been left to dry on a hedge at Stogumber and sold them to Richard Taylor of Monksilver. Taylor had buried them in the back garden but, when he discovered that Laughill had made a full confession, he showed the constable and tithingman where they were hidden.

Two incidents that had much in common were referred to the justices in quarter sessions in 1615 and 1623. In each a servant girl stole wool from her master and attempted to sell it to someone who could spin it. In the earlier case Elizabeth Gunne took wool flocks from the house of her master, Simon Harwood, a fuller, and delivered them at about midnight on separate occasions to Joan Owen, a widow, and her sister Alice, the wife of Edmund Duggan, a sailor. In return she was to receive a smock and a waistcoat and other things that she needed, but these, she said, were never given to her. The Minehead constable made a search and found the stolen goods, but Alice put all the blame on sister Joan. In the later incident Joan Cockram confessed 'that upon Saturday last between six and seven of the clock in the evening she took a little bag' belonging to her master, John Collings, also a fuller, 'and did put into the same a pound and a half of coarse wool... there being nobody at home but herself at that time.' She delivered this to Thomas Baker's wife 'who many times before had enticed her so to do.'

During the hard times of the Civil War Elizabeth Heyman, the wife of a Minehead sailor, was accused of a theft that, if it were proved, could have had more serious consequences and may have been referred to the county assizes. In her statement to a justice of the peace, George Trevelyan, Elizabeth maintained that two rings in her possession had been bought from Christian Hill, by this time (conveniently for her) deceased and that she had paid 6s.6d. for them. However, Anna French, who thought she recognised one of them by the death's head inscribed upon it, asked Elizabeth where she had obtained it and was told by her that her husband had sent it to her from Plymouth. Anna had accepted this explanation until 'Monday last' when she had heard about another ring very much like hers that was being sent by Mistress Heyman to the West Indian island of St Christopher. She persuaded the sailor who was to carry it thither to show her the ring, positively identified it and asked the constables to search David Heyman's house where they also found the ring with the death's head on it.

Anna French stated that two years earlier there had been stolen from her four gold rings, a silver chain and a silver seal, all taken from her trunk 'which was in her mother's chamber window at Minehead.' Elizabeth Heyman appears to have been lying and, as a theft of this magnitude would have constituted a crime of grand larceny, she probably stood trial before a judge on a capital charge.

Just before the Civil War, in 1637, Peter Willis of Minehead, a petty chapman, with Elizabeth, his wife, and three small children, was returning home from St Decuman's Fair. The road from Carhampton at that time passed through the village of Dunster and 'in the highway near the house of John Norris, Esquire', they were overtaken by two horsemen who turned out to be Norris and his friend, Edward Kitner. The story as reported by Peter Willis reveals quite a lot about the relationship of poor people and the more prosperous members of the community and also about the underlying lawlessness of the times. When John Norris suddenly asked, 'What are you?' Peter Willis replied with the like question, which may have sounded impudent to the gentleman on horseback, but it was night-time on 25 August and no doubt already quite dark. However, the incensed rider 'being a little before the said Elizabeth, stopped his horse, and with his left hand laid hold on a pack of wares (to the value of twenty pounds or thereabouts) which she carried at her back and said, 'Stand, for I will have this.' In spite of the chapman's appeals and entreaties Norris insisted on taking the pack, so Willis began to unbuckle it and as he did so he recognised the two riders. 'Good Master Norris, let us alone with our goods,' he pleaded. Kitner pointed out to his companion that they had been recognised, but the high-handed and seemingly hot-tempered Norris was past caring about the consequences; 'Rogue, I will have it', he shouted. Whereupon the Willises threw down their goods in the highway 'and went away for fear of their lives.' They demanded the arrest of Norris for felony and of Kitner as accomplice. There is little doubt that Thomas Luttrell, the examining magistrate, and the magistrates' court in quarter sessions between them saw that justice was done to these humble and aggrieved subjects of King Charles I.

Violence in one form or another was never far removed from everyday life in Tudor and Stuart England. A manorial court roll of 1507 recorded that William Roche had attacked with a poniard William Lynch who had retaliated with his fists. Three other men were also accused of disturbing the peace by fighting with their fists and were each fined 6d. Such brawls, however, were not confined to the male sex. At the same court Margaret Veale was accused of attacking Catherine Kyrrie (Kerry) with a washing kettle and so furiously did she assail her that the blood flowed. By the end of the century such crimes were no longer the concern of the declining manorial courts but had become the responsibility of the justices of the peace. Minehead as a seaport, and an isolated one at that, probably had more than its fair share of violence. One troublesome character seems to have specialised in provoking it simply because he enjoyed angering and humiliating his prosperous and respectable fellow citizens.

The examination 'touching the lewd behaviour of Philip Craugh of Minehead', a tiler by trade, was taken in November, 1623, by three justices of the peace, Sir John Wyndham of Orchard, George Luttrell of Dunster and Thomas Wyndham of Kentsford. The information they were given came from the constables present and past, the churchwardens, the overseers and the vicar of the parish of Minehead. The latter, the venerable Nicholas Browse, added a note in his own hand which reveals that this man's deliberate attempts to stir up trouble were driving him to distraction; 'In my conscience I find him not worthy to live among his majesty's sober subjects,' he wrote. This ne'er-do-well was said to be 'a common haunter of ale-houses' where he wasted the money that should have been employed to 'relieve his poor children who heretofore were enforced to beg or otherwise might have perished with hunger.' In his drunken humour he railed and quarrelled without respect of person; even the vicar and his officers had been insulted in a 'most barbarous and insufferable manner.' In the quarrels that he had provoked many good citizens had been dangerously hurt or themselves provoked into retaliation, at which this trouble-maker ran whining to a justice of the peace, complaining that he stood in fear of his life. Those he had wronged, to escape the long drawn-out consequences of a dispute with such a man, quietly withdrew their complaints (and perhaps paid him hush money) in order 'to be rid of him.' The petition to quarter sessions asking that he should 'be bridled with the full censure of the law' led to his being bound over to keep the peace, but within months of this he was still behaving 'very lewdly amongst his neighbours, as well in words as in deeds.'

This early photograph shows on the right some of the seventeenth-century buildings used as warehouses by Robert Quirke and Edmond Knowles.

Although he was again bound over, his career as a public nuisance was by no means at an end. In December 1626, a very detailed catalogue of his misdemeanours was prepared by James Fugars, steward of the manor, and signed by ten of the leading inhabitants, among them Robert Quirke, the younger, who with John Bond, was a constable in that year, John Luttrell, a Minehead resident, Alexander Leakey, whose mother attained a peculiar distinction as a famous ghost, and Lewis Lashbrooke, ex-Member of Parliament and lawyer of questionable integrity. The story is the same - provocations, complaints to the justices when his victims hit back, and wasteful habits that necessitated much almsgiving to his deprived and neglected family. The individuals he had abused included Master John Luttrell, Robert Quirke, whom he assaulted with his hatchet, Richard Pearce, late constable of Minehead, Masters Bond, Escott and Lashbrooke, and many others. Finally, 'being overcome with drink', he abused James Fugars, the steward, 'in the presence of Alexander Leakey, John Paul (the surgeon) and others, in such base, vile and most outrageous manner that flesh and blood could hardly endure from beating of him.'

Such a stinging rebuke from so many prominent citizens would seem certain to move the justices to take the sternest measures to restrain this impossible man, yet only a year or two later he was again bound over 'for raising scandalous reports and abusing Edmund Knowles' a prosperous merchant of Quay Town. It was said that he had caused the death of George Barns whom he called 'shag rogue', holding a tiler's knife in his hand as he did so, and he had threatened to cripple or even kill Michael Hole. It is difficult to understand how this rascal so successfully defied the authority of the usually effective justices in their role as keepers of the peace. Presumably he must have been a cunning barrack-room lawyer who knew just how far he could go with impunity.

In part the difficulty in keeping order was due to the inadequacy of the elected constables. For example, in 1615, the constables for that year, Robert Bond and Simon Hatsell, when they ordered Robert Stephens to appear before George Luttrell to answer a minor charge, were by 'the said Stephens very peremptorily answered that he would not come before the said justice.' Another example concerns Robert Quirke who met Arthur Webber at seven o'clock on a May morning in 1624 near Minehead quay. They were engaged in argument about Webber's brother-in-law, John Baker, one of the constables for that year, who was also present, when Webber suddenly struck Quirke to the ground, punching him in the mouth with his fist. As he rose to his feet Webber offered to assault him again, so John Deake, the other constable, intervened, 'taking hold on his bosom.' Whereat the irate Webber 'thrust the constable from him, asking him what he had to do with it.' However, John Baker, his brother-in-law, persuaded him to move away, which he did very unwillingly, 'saying he cared not a turd for any of them all, with very many other terms most shameful to be spoken' and affirming, according to Edmund Duggan, a sailor, 'that he would have some of the blood out of the said Quirke before evening.' Robert Quirke, though, could give blows as well as receive them. Hugh Davis, who had covenanted to serve him for four years as a seaman, ran away after only eighteen months because his master had treated him 'with much violence in beating and hurting him in his body without any just cause.' For breaking his covenant he had been committed to Ilchester gaol and was petitioning for his release. This said, he may well have deserved his punishment, which for a young sailor in those days often took the form of a beating.

A few years earlier a somewhat similar fracas to that between Quirke and Webber occurred. It was feelingly described in 'The Humble Petition of John Easton of Minehead in the County of Somerset, sailor.' He complained that he had been 'violently and indiscretely' abused by Thomas Bryant, also a sailor, who belaboured him with a cudgel 'to his great hurt' and, when Easton's wife Dorothy intervened, 'taking unkindly those abuses and wrongs which were offered unto her said husband' and considering them to be 'untasteful', Bryant turned furiously on her 'and never left (off) before he had beaten the said cudgel in pieces.' He continued to assault her, snatching off her 'curcher' or head-scarf and twisting 'the hairs of her head about his hand to the great grievance and hurt of your poor petitioner's wife.' John Easton did not say what he was doing whilst all this was happening to Dorothy, but he attributed Bryant's contempt for the law to the fact 'that he was a man of great means' who thought that 'his purse and worth should bear him out.'

The most colourful incident of this kind occurred in January 1626. George Bond, one of Minehead's foremost citizens, had a servant named Agess Powne.

She had given birth to a child that soon died and she stoutly maintained that her master was its father. Agess was dismissed by the Bonds. She grew sickly and had to be given some support by the overseers of the poor. However, Mistress Elizabeth Brooke had taken pity on her and for nearly two years had given her a home, receiving in return only the remission of her husband's poor rate. Her reward for this act of charity was to be openly abused in the street by Bond and his wife, who reviled her as 'a filthy jade, a scurvy baggage', accusing her of keeping a whore in her house just to spite them. 'Pray give me leave to go quietly in the King's highway,' she pleaded, but, because of the ill-will and no doubt the importance of George Bond, she decided to dismiss Agess from her home.

The culmination of this disturbance was reached on a Monday evening when George Bond encountered his former servant in the street and ran towards her 'with a naked knife in his hand.' Mary Browse, the vicar's daughter-in-law, heard shouts and screams. She ran out of the house in time to grab Bond's left arm whilst Christian Little seized the hand holding the knife. She was cut by it, but the two courageous ladies held on to the struggling Bond, who 'swore by God's blood that he would kill the whore.' Mistress Little said, 'Good neighbour, remember your wife and children.' In the meantime Agess had escaped into the house of Joan Stowey who bravely stood in her doorway, holding up her hands to keep out the girl's furious assailant. 'Good Master Bond, I pray you be quiet,' she said, but he threw her to the ground 'a pretty ways from him' and she had to be rescued by her neighbours, who by this time had presumably rescued Agess too.

Bond had cooled down enough to moderate his threat to kill the poor girl; his expressed intention now was to split her nose or cut off her ears. As for Mistress Brooke, she was 'distracted out of her wits' and had sent the parish a bill for eight shillings to meet the cost of maintaining Agess during her sickness. As there was also a surgeon's bill for five shillings to settle for 'curing a wound in her head' the parish was demanding from quarter sessions not only an order to restrain George Bond's violence, but another to compel him to contribute towards the maintenance of the servant girl that he had dismissed so summarily from his service.

To judge from the examination of witnesses made by local justices of the peace, Minehead men continued to resort to violence quite often during the 1600s. For instance, in December 1679, Wilmott Beere accused Richard Chapline, a tailor, of assaulting two other Minehead tailors so viciously that one of them, William Parsons, was in danger of death. In 1694 Philip Bouchier, a Periton gentleman whose horses had strayed on to the marshes, in his search met Thomas Adams and his son, two yeomen who had leased this particular marsh. He 'desired of them to hand his horses out' and promised to pay them for any damage done. However, they assaulted him and left him unconscious. When he came round he found thirty-six pieces of broad gold and some silver to be missing from his pocket. It is perhaps hardly necessary to add that Philip Bouchier was one of the principal property owners in the town at the end of the century. Finally, in the first year of George I, John Griffiths, a Minehead clothier, was arrested by David Jones in Robert Punter's house, beaten up, slashed about the head with a 'seirrier's' knife and kept all night in custody. He was then told to go about his business. David Jones was presumably a constable or tithingman who was also an insolent bully.

Sometimes in an attempt to escape from the consequences of their actions vagrants or petty criminals invented marvellous stories which, though patently untrue, throw light on the life of the times, because the frightened lawbreaker must have considered that his tale was at least credible and might be good enough to save him from punishment. Jonas Harris told a cock-and-bull story about being a soldier returning from Buckingham's expedition to Cadiz who had landed at Barnstaple. He was arrested at Minehead carrying a forged pass, but on a second examination just two hours later he admitted that he was a Launceston shoemaker who had been unemployed for twelve months. His captors clearly believed that the suspicious looking scar on his left shoulder, which at first he described as a pike wound, was the mark left by a branding iron.

Seven or eight years before, in July 1620, Christopher Barnes, a groom from Plymouth, was brought before George Luttrell. He freely confessed he had been branded at Gloucester four years previously. He had been sent back to Plymouth and there he had joined a merchant ship, the *Diana*, bound on a voyage to the Straits which God prospered and from which he returned safely. About two months later he made a second voyage towards the same place, 'but it so fell out that the ship was unfortunately surprised and taken (being outwards bounden) by a Turkish man-of-war and carried to Tunis where 'this examinate with divers others remained in captivity and slavery about two years and a half.' Just four months previously he and one of his fellows had escaped from prison 'having nothing at that time to cover their nakedness but a piece of an old sail.' They were, so Barnes recounted at the time, 'taken aboard a Flemish ship and were landed at Westchester just sixteen days since.' He confessed that in order to make his way back to Plymouth he had to beg for his bread and it was for this that he was arrested by the constable at Minehead as he entered the town from Porlock, a strange route to South Devon which he explained by saying that he had been sent back from Porlock to Minehead there being 'a common roadway which lyeth thence into Exeter.' Such a good story deserved a better reward, but it appears that he did not convince the magistrate at Dunster Castle who, no doubt, had heard such tales countless times before.

Almost as strange a story, which is not fictional, can be pieced together from the very detailed but incomplete enquiries that William Blackford, justice of the peace, made in May 1707. Thomas Williams, a parish apprentice, had been bound to John Warre, a yeoman whose farm was in the hill country at Stoke Pero. At sheep-shearing time in the summer of 1706 he had been sent by his master into Porlock with a pair of shears that required sharpening. When he returned he had occasion to enter a room of his master's house which was not his usual workroom and he saw there a wether sheep whose throat had only recently been cut and on which he recognised the identification mark of Andrew Arnold, another yeoman farmer of Stoke Pero. 'For some days after,' he adds, 'there was great plenty of mutton in his said master's house.' At other times he had observed hanging on a door a sheepskin from the flock of a Stoke Pero husbandman named William Eame and he saw two more, which had belonged to the same man, in his master's oven. There seems to have been some malice behind this statement; perhaps young Thomas had been ill-treated by his master or mistress. However, his story received some confirmation from Roger Valentine, a 'vellmonger' (sic) of Porlock who, in December 1705, had been sent by John Warre two sheepskins from which the heads and all the wool had been removed and which the experienced fellmonger was confident had never been taken from a sheep's back by a butcher, for 'they were much haggled and abused.'

These incriminating charges fell heavily on a man who was already in trouble with the law because of the indiscretion of his wife, Agnes, who, in her husband's words to Nicholas Snow of Luccombe, 'was so simple' as to take some corn from the barn of Richard Rublin, a farmer of the same village, a deed which she herself confessed to Andrew Arnold of Stoke Pero, lifting up her hands and eyes and saying that it was very true. John Warre showed his anxiety by appealing to Robert Pearce of Luccombe to approach his brother-in-law, William Eame, and to offer him twenty shillings to let the matter drop, not, Warre hastened to add, because he was guilty 'but to avoid trouble and be quiet.' However, Warre's next action, far from avoiding trouble, had the reverse effect and plunged him even deeper into difficulty. It is not surprising to learn that Agnes Warre was a sick woman. Her doctor was William Paul of Minehead, a member of a family of 'chirurgeons' who had been practising in the town since at least the beginning of the seventeenth century. Early in 1707 he paid a visit to his patient to give her treatment for 'a malady that she had in her cheek and about her ear.' In conversation he learned about the troublesome parish apprentice, Thomas Williams, so 'very cross and perverse to both of them that he would do his own will and pleasure', yet when they reproved him he was apt to 'threaten to mischief them and list as a soldier.' Dr Paul suggested he might be able to find an army captain who would take him off their hands. At that time he was caring for a sick soldier of Captain Edward Ford and said that if the Warres wanted him to do so he would gladly mention their problem to the captain. He did as they requested and a few days later, when Captain Ford heard that Dr Paul was going again on his rounds into the hill country, he asked him to show two of his men the way to Stoke Pero. He was therefore accompanied by two soldiers, though after he had reached the farm he saw nothing more of them and left before they did. He received no money from anyone, nor, he believed did the soldiers.

William Paul obviously tried in his statement to William Blackford to play down his part in the affair, but unfortunately for him had arranged to meet Captain Ford at his lodgings at Minehead, the home of Robert Stickland, a shoemaker, who stated that in making the appointment to meet Captain Ford the doctor had told him the whole story and revealed that the Warres 'would give the Captain any money' if he would rid them of their troublesome servant. Next morning Dr Paul repeated this to Captain Ford in Stickland's presence and offered to accompany some soldiers to Stoke Pero to fetch Williams. Stickland concluded his statement by saying that the two men who were detailed for this task set out with empty pockets, but returned with 'plenty of money'.

Here our story ends. William Blackford took such detailed statements from the witnesses that he evidently believed that he was dealing with a matter of some importance. Quarter sessions probably referred the case to the assizes, but so far no other papers have come to light. The War of the Spanish Succession was at its height; the Allied army in Spain, after some initial success, had met with reverses in the autumn of 1706. Perhaps Captain Ford and his men were awaiting a ship at Minehead to take them to the Peninsula.

This chapter has allowed us to peep behind the scenes at the onerous labours of the keepers of the king's peace in the sixteenth, seventeenth and early-eighteenth centuries. As has been said, their duties did not end with the preservation of law and order for the justices of the peace were also responsible for the administration within their districts of what we today call local government. This aspect of the work of these useful if overburdened servants of the crown has been treated in other chapters.

Chapter 8
The Town and People: 1500–1800

At the end of the fifteenth century Minehead was emerging from the Middle Ages with more prosperity than might have been expected of so remote a place. The traveller to Bridgwater or Taunton, the nearest sizeable towns, had only a little over twenty miles to walk or ride, but the roads, or more properly the tracks, which he traversed were bad even by sixteenth-century standards. However, Minehead was saved by the trade of its port which for a century had been steadily expanding. Fortunately the strings of packhorses that carried goods to and from the little creek in the bay could move easily enough along the primitive ways of West Somerset and, in fact, must have done so for many centuries - to judge by the deep and narrow lanes of Exmoor.

Through the port passed the imports and exports that gave our town greater wealth than was enjoyed by other Somerset towns of like size. Through the port and into the numerous inns and taverns came the seamen with the exciting (and often exaggerated) stories of strange lands and new discoveries, for these were the times of Columbus, of Vasco da Gama and, nearer home, of the Cabots, who sailed the Severn Sea from Bristol. Minehead during the reign of Henry VIII was trading with Aveiro in Portugal; and in the next reign Vice-Admiral Wyndham of Marshwood, with his Minehead master, John Kerry, made three voyages to the tropical coast of West Africa. Through the port also came the many Irishmen, often nicknamed Teague, who settled in the town and who, because they frequently became a charge on the poor rate, were not always welcome.

Fortunately for the local historian, King Henry VIII's travelling antiquary, John Leland, visited Minehead shortly after 1540. His report on West Somerset and Minehead in particular read as follows:

Minheved has ons a weeke a praty market. The fairest part of the Toun standith in the botom of an Hille. The residew rennith stepe up a longe hille, yn the toppe where of is a fair paroche chirche. The Toune is exceeding ful of Irish menne. The peere lyeth at the North Est point of the Hille. There was a fair park by Minheved, but Sir Andrew Luterelle of late tyme destroyed it.

He estimated the distances across to Aberthaw, up-channel to Sterte point and down-channel to 'Horse-Toun' (Hurstone), Porlock and 'Combane' (Culbone). 'From Combane to the Sterte', he wrote, 'moste parte of the shore is hilly ground, and nere the shore is no store of wood: that ys al in Hegge-rowes of Enclosures.' Already Minehead had developed the triangular plan that visitors noticed as recently as the nineteenth century, but contrary to what might have been expected, the most prosperous of the three separate townships was not around the parish church of St Michael on the hill, but, according to Leland, in Lower Town around the present Parade, soon to be called Puddle Street. The houses were widely spaced to make room for the Bratton stream to flow between them as far as the manor estate Office, where it swung northwards to form a creek at the foot of Blenheim Road which somehow managed to accommodate ships of 60, 70 or even 100 tons. Protecting it was Sir Hugh Luttrell's little jetty, 'the peere' that 'lyeth at the North Est point of the Hille.' Around it clustered the simple cottages of the sailors and the warehouses of the merchants who employed them and who themselves probably lived in or near Puddle Street. There was no street along the quay, but there must have been a path along 'the chesil' or beach leading to the battery of guns that the old map of 'Defences along the Somerset' shore places where the present harbour stands.

There could have been little building north-west of the immediate vicinity of the creek because one hundred years later, when George Luttrell's new harbour had been completed, there was plenty of waste land for development around and beyond the Weir Pool. This was a large pond which was probably made or enlarged in the middle years of the sixteenth century. It was designed to collect the water from a high tide and to sluice out the pebbles that were already silting up the estuary of the creek which, in a double sense, was the key to the prosperity of Minehead. The clusters of trees that so richly adorn the landscape today were not there in Leland's time. The lower slopes of North Hill, then known as Weir Hill, appeared from the seashore as a chequerboard of hedges and small fields.

As the land was already 'in Hegge rowes of Enclosure', the open fields had evidently disappeared very early, though their descriptions, such as 'North Field', continued to be used in order to outline the situation of the many closes made within the large fields and leased to his tenants by the lord of the manor.

The lane from the quay to Lower Town must have included a gate in its length to prevent animals from the fields, through which it passed, straying on to the beach, for there was for pedestrians a lower stile near the quay and an upper one in Lower Town near Puddle Bridge, a footbridge in front of the manor estate office. Beside it was a ford over which the carts and packhorses passed on their way to or from the creek. Near this ford, it seems, stood the whipping post and probably the stocks and pillory as well. The prison was in the same building as the Town Hall. In this hall the more important manor court, the Court Leet, met in the spring and autumn of the year. The less important, but more frequent court, almost certainly used the Tudor Rose room of the manor office building. The exact situation of the old Town Hall is not known, but its seventeenth-century successor was in Friday Street, near the present Wellington Square.

At the beginning of Henry VII's reign Minehead must have had at least two grist mills, for a manor court roll of 1486 records the fine imposed on two millers, William Millard and John Ridler, for taking excessive tolls. Just over a century later, in 1590, James Quirke was granted the lease of a water grist mill that had been 'newly builded and erected at the only cost and charge of the said James Quirke.' His new mill reputedly stood on the site of two older ones; a grist mill that had been in the tenancy of Richard Crosman and a fuller's 'tucking' mill whose tenant was Thomas Crosman. Great care was taken to protect the supply of the water which gave power to the waterwheel of the new mill. James Quirke was authorised to use in any way he could the water from the Bratton stream after it had passed through the customary mills at the foot of Bampton Street and had flowed 'under Thomas Greswill's house and so along by the gardens' to the Great Stony Bridge. The exact position of this bridge is difficult to establish, but it was, by report, 'nigh the house of Thomas Crosman' which a later lease of 1632 places on or near the site of the building that by the end of that century was called The Plume of Feathers Inn. It seems likely, therefore, that the Great Stony bridge gave access to Frog Street which led by the hollow way to the Upper Town.

This mill passed later to Maud Paul, Thomas Fugars and his widow Ann, and at the end of the century to William Hosegood and son Andrew. The proximity of the mill to Puddle Bridge no doubt accounts for the fact that William Hosegood was able to inform the magistrate, Mr Ellsworth, in November, 1700:

... [that he] did see Francis Luellen of the parish of Shepton Beauchamp... pull down by his strength the public and common bridge lying in the highway leading from the Market Town of Minehead unto the Quay... so as that no person could pass that way.

No doubt Francis Luellen was a man of great strength, but even so Puddle Bridge could not have been a very substantial structure.

But we must return to the beginning of the seventeenth century. In a deed of 1604, which renewed a tenancy first granted in 1598, George Luttrell leased to George Quirke, merchant, and Simon Hatsell, clothier, the chamber called 'the Town Hawle of Mynhed' with the room below it, 'and also all that room or house called or known by the name of Cockmoile or the prison with the room above it.' It is not certain that the four rooms mentioned here were part of the same building or even of adjacent buildings, but it seems likely that they were one or the other. As part of this agreement the right of the lord of the manor and his steward to use the Town Hall for 'their courts of the said manor, leets and lawdays' was reserved. It has not so far been possible to establish with certainty the exact position of this old Town Hall or the prison. By 1632 the New Hall, with newly erected buildings at the back, was leased to John Spurrier and these premises were situated in Friday Street, where they remained until the disastrous fire of 1791. John Spurrier also purchased from Thomas Luttrell the right to collect such dues as were normally paid by merchants at the Town Hall. It was agreed that no other house could be used 'as a common hall for the keeping or weighing of wool, flox, butter, tallow or any other merchandise whatsoever brought to the port or town of Minehead.' Three years earlier, in 1629, the market place was on the west side of the present Market House Lane where stands the market cross which can still be seen today. Later the market place was moved a little nearer to the Town Hall in the wide space between Friday Street and Frog Street with the Plume of Feathers and other houses to the west of it and Dauter's Island House to the east. It seems likely that the original Town Hall was close to this old market place. When the Town Hall was moved to Friday Street, the market place, for convenience, was soon moved as well.

Apart from the cross, the site of the old market place is confirmed by the lease to a Periton blacksmith of some land in and around it. The ground let to him included the area known as 'the shambles' where the cattle were slaughtered and the stalls of the butchers and provision merchants stood.

During the years just before the outbreak of the Civil War during the reign of Charles I many refugees from the savage religious conflict in Ireland landed at Minehead. Such a visitor, who had not been to the town within the previous twenty years, would surely have been surprised and impressed by what he saw.

George Luttrell's new pier, finished in 1616, had worked wonders for our trade. In the harbour our traveller could have seen a dozen or more ocean-going ships berthed three or four abreast along the pier side. Noise and bustle were everywhere. Loading and unloading occupied a great many men both on the ships and ashore. At the entrance to the harbour were the dwelling houses and stores of the prosperous merchant, Edmond Knowles, and the 'two inner cellars' of Robert Quirke the younger, which in his will were 'to be let for rent to him that will give most money for them to provide an annual income to support the almshouses' - which he had built for the poor in 1630 (*see pages 60 and 78*). Next to them and nearer to Compass Hill, as it was called, was the New Inn that in 1634 had been leased to Roger Vyon for a fine (or down-payment) of £100. His signpost stood outside inviting travellers to enter his great chamber, below which was the great cellar. Behind the inn was a hanging cellar terraced out of the hill, 'where the beer now standeth.' Also he had land on the chesil or beach where the modern lifeboat house was built. West of this the shipwright, Tobias Bailey, had his house, yard and launching slip. Beyond here was the 'Rowlinge Rock' or quarry at the western end of the Northwood and land further to the west 'known by the name of Greenaley, being not yet enclosed.'

Following the road into the town the traveller would have had no difficulty in finding accommodation. Just beyond the New Inn stood the Red Lyon, whose innkeeper, George Ford, was the first water-bailiff of the new harbour. Almost next door was widow Terrill's tavern, the Three Crowns. Grouped around the Weir Pool were a number of new houses, placed irregularly to use up the wider space available for building at that point. William Hatsell's lease refers to 'the way which goeth up into the said hill.' Near to him were the houses of Robert Smith, Thomas Harwood, Robert Seagar, Henry Giles (the gunsmith) and Thomas Williams (a weaver), whose house was said to be between two rocks.

All these places were newly built in the two decades after the completion of the harbour in 1616. To our traveller Quay Street with its many new houses must have provided an impressive introduction to the town. However, around the estuary of the creek with its abandoned jetty there were, no doubt, many older houses, some of them already dilapidated.

Beyond the lower quay stile was the footpath to the town. Wheeled traffic used a lane which followed the lower contours of North Hill, probably beginning at the entrance to the present Quay Lane. Both footpath and lane were re-united at Puddle Bridge, the former by way of the upper quay stile. Near the bridge to the left was the mill which has already been mentioned. In the middle of Puddle Street was Dauter's Island House and in the wide space beyond it the market.

Turning to the right along what was soon to be named Frog Street, we arrive at the hollow way which led to Middle Street where there were some large houses. There were two ways to the church: one by 'the lane from Middle Street [Church Street] the other by New Street [The Ball].' The former reached the church by Church Steps, the latter by the cross, where it met Fisher's Lane, the path from the quay. Near the churchyard was the Church House, the equivalent of the parish hall. There were also many houses around the Vicarage gate and above it, including the present Lower Moor Farm.

In Lower Town stood Minehead's largest and most important inn which by 1686 had been named The Plume of Feathers. At that time it belonged to Deborah Bullocke, a granddaughter of Edmond Knowles, the prosperous merchant of the Civil War period. Early in the eighteenth century it passed to her son-in-law, Hugh Payne, and it continued as the foremost hostelry in Minehead, the scene of much political banqueting. An advertisement in the *Sherborne Mercury* of 1756 reads:

To be let. Plume of Feathers Inn or Tavern in Minehead - large and commodious, in Market Place - spacious dining room, sashed in front, 6 rooms on a floor, large walled garden, stabling for 150 horses - enquire of Mr Thomas Leigh, attorney, Dunster.

Friday Street was a narrow but busy lane, with John Spurrier's New Hall on the left as we turn into it from Puddle Street. At the top, connecting it with Bampton Street was Butts Lane, beyond which was the open space where the archers, until the sixteenth century, used to practise their craft. At the foot of this lane was Townsend House, a sixteenth-century building that has survived the ravages of time and the passion for modernisation. During the reign of Charles I this fine house was probably the home of Lewis Lashbrooke and the wall enclosing its garden may be the same one for which he paid George Luttrell an annual rent of 12d. Bampton Street was often described as 'the highway' and it led over Oway to Timberscombe and so to Bampton and Tiverton, an important route for the strings of packhorses from the harbour laden with Welsh or Irish wool. Just above the junction with Butts Lane was the pound where stray or distrained animals were kept. Below the many large houses near Court Green was the mill belonging to the lord of the manor which many of his tenants were contracted to use in their leases of property or land. Park Street had not yet been built.

The Feathers Inn and Frog Street, c.1885.

Nineteenth-century Friday Street still had some seventeenth-century buildings standing.

The old house called 'Sea View' at the junction of Blenheim Road and the Avenue, c.1910. It was demolished in 1921.

Frog Street leading to the hollow way. Note the steps leading to the higher road.

Water Lane, now the Avenue, c.1860.

On its site were gardens and small fields, but there was a continuation of 'the highway' which was linked to Frog Street by Tything's Court.

Every one of the seventeenth-century houses from Frog Street to Puddle Bridge have now disappeared except Robert Quirke's almshouses, but facing the old manor office on the Avenue side of Blenheim Road one old house survived until 1921, when it was demolished to make way for the building that is now used as a restaurant. The old house had the date 1569 over the front door and was in its later years called 'Sea View', a name that was justified before the houses were built along the sea front. Opposite this house, over Puddle Bridge, was Field Lane. This followed the line of the west wall of the manor office. It had only a few houses built beside it, but it gave access to a number of fields enclosed from the old medieval open fields. Along the present Avenue ran a very old lane (*above*) that led to the Warren of the lord of the manor. Here he kept certain game birds and large fish which were reserved for his own use. At the Warren, in 1636, lived Philip Evans, Thomas Luttrell's fowler, perhaps in the second cottage from the Dunster side which has a splendidly proportioned upper room, open to the roof, and a fine stone doorway at the eastern end which in earlier times led through an ancient gothic arch to an exterior stairway. In this upper room, perhaps, the Luttrells and their friends dined on their duck-shooting and fishing expeditions to the Warren. There is a similar arched doorway on the ground floor and clearly this unusual building was something more than a poor man's cottage. About 50 yards to the north there is a deep pool which may well have been the fish weir in the seventeenth century.

In each generation the details change but the triangular pattern of Minehead with its quay, Lower Town and Higher Town, remains unaltered until the coming of the railway. From the many leases, manorial surveys and political canvassers' books it would be possible to reconstruct the town with fair accuracy for almost any generation after the Civil War. Unfortunately an Elizabethan survey that once existed has been lost, but by the end of the eighteenth century the houses are listed in order in each street and the names of the householders are given. Further work on the old town and its inhabitants would be a fruitful subject of research for a local historian interested in such matters.

It has often been necessary to refer to members of the Quirke family both in this chapter and elsewhere. From the late-fifteenth century to the Restoration of Charles II they were generally to be found in the forefront of affairs in Minehead. As early as 1461 a John Quirke was mentioned in a manor court roll. In 1498 Morys Quirke was one of a twelve-man jury called to settle a dispute about the ownership of a small vessel. Robert, who was probably his son, owned, in 1543, one of Minehead's largest ships and he (or another Robert) was one of the principal burgesses chosen for the Common Council under the charter of 1559. James Quirke, the miller, attached his seal to the lease referred to earlier in this chapter. On it was embossed an acorn, the Latin for which is 'quercus', a pun on his name. He represented Minehead in Parliament in 1592. George Quirke was a constable in 1582 and portreeve (or mayor) in 1607, at the end of the period when Minehead was incorporated as a borough.

There are two Roberts in the early-seventeenth century, sometimes, but not always, differentiated as the elder and the younger. At times it is not possible to distinguish between them with certainty but on the whole Robert the younger seems to have been the more active. He was the son of James and it was he who, in 1630, gave the almshouses to the town and conscientiously provided for their upkeep in his will. It was he who erected in the parish church the painted boards with the Commandments and the Lord's Prayer inscribed upon them. The information that he laid against Lewis Lashbrooke as a Royalist sympathiser, which led to the arrest of that devious lawyer in the last years of the Civil War, shows that Robert was a Parliamentarian and probably a Puritan, as he was elected churchwarden in 1643 when the church was about to expel its Royalist vicar.

His son, also Robert, was very influential during the republican Interregnum. He assaulted Captain Nathaniel Bullocke who in his petition to the justices sought protection. He described him as a man of great influence in Minehead, 'being there very potent and [an] owner of shipping' who 'hath many sailors and servants under his command.' At this time the Quirkes had arrived at the zenith of their power.

Robert, the younger, died in 1649 and in his will he left to his son his houses and property in Minehead, Periton and Dunster and also made him and his heirs responsible for the upkeep and management of the almshouses.

As time went by, the Quirkes gradually gave way in importance to another family, the Haymans, who had connections with the port of Youghal near Cork in southern Ireland They are first mentioned in

Minehead documents in 1618 when John Hayman leased from George Luttrell a large property for which he paid £340, an exceptional amount for that century. By a deed in the same year he leased a tenement near Butts Green, with a reversion to his brothers, George and William, and his sister, Joan.

Their father was a Robert Hayman who was described as a clothier of Minehead and who must have been living here some years before 1618. He died in 1655 and in his will he shared his considerable fortune among his many descendants. His chief inheritor was George, John having presumably predeceased his father. Robert had at least twenty-two grandchildren, all of whom were given legacies by their wealthy grandfather. Even the ten children of Joan Giles received forty shillings each to remember him by. The poor and the church were given thirty shillings each and the old merchant clothier's servants, Christian Cobly and Elizabeth Jenkins, both received £1.

The inventory of his goods and property amounted in value to £290.8s.0d. The lease of his dwelling house was valued at £100 and his second house at the quay at £40. Other items listed included clothes, plate, bedding and furniture, brass and pewter vessels, tableboards, forms, chairs, stools, cupboards, chests and coffers. There was also 'his lynnynge' and a very special 'brass kittle', mentioned separately and valued at £2, which was twice the value of his beams, scales and weights, so essential to his commercial undertakings. There was a surprisingly large sum of money due from his trading ventures - an estimated £100. As an afterthought a sum of £1 was added at the bottom of the list for 'some things omitted.'

The Haymans continued to prosper, both in West Somerset and in southern Ireland. In 1683 George's son, Samuel, leased from Colonel Francis Luttrell a tenement in Friday Street described as a good dwelling house having a large court with a planked storehouse and two lofts above, a bakehouse and a stable, with other property and land in or near Bampton Street. His cousin, Robert, leased in the last-named street an old inn called the Limerick - more evidence of the close links between Minehead and Ireland. However, he used it as a dwelling house.

By 1696 George Hayman, William's son, had acquired an estate at Bye in the parish of Old Cleeve. A few years later, in Minehead, Nicholas leased for £25 and two broad pieces of gold the lands and property of Samuel Crockford. The old dispute between the Stewkleys and the Luttrells about the ownership of Minehead Parks was revived when Samuel Hayman, at the end of Queen Anne's reign, tried to buy these lands from Sir Hugh Stewkley of Hinton Ampner. In 1717 Samuel was advised by his lawyer, Nicholas Hooper, that he could safely pay the residue of the money that he owed because Sir Hugh's title to the Parks was good.

In the early years of the eighteenth century the Hayman family must have been far and away the biggest property owners in and around Minehead, except, of course, for the Luttrells. William Hayman had moved to Gloucester. His land and property were purchased in 1727 for £200 by Robert Deake, a shoemaker, who had been appointed administrator for the will of Samuel Hayman. A part of Samuel's farm was leased by Deake to John Hensley and one of the conditions required him to sow four acres of this land with 'colver' (clover). It seems that West Somerset was not behindhand in its acceptance of the new theories of husbandry, but this need not surprise us for the long-established enclosures, noticed by Leland as far back as the sixteenth century, gave liberty for changes that were still unattainable in the great open fields that covered so much of the rest of England.

By the middle of the eighteenth century William Hayman of Bye had become a most influential man in Minehead politics. He gave shrewd advice to the young Henry Fownes Luttrell and some of his racy descriptions of electioneering may be read in the chapter on the Parliamentary borough. Earlier he had been one of the two constables who served as returning officers in the election of 1741. He was a justice of the peace, a prominent member of the trustees of the Minehead Turnpike Company, a trustee of the harbour, and his name appeared first in the list of guests invited to the Grand Ball at Dunster Castle in 1775.

Little evidence of social or cultural life in Minehead in the sixteenth or seventeenth centuries has survived. Men worked long hours and rose very early in the morning. Their women-folk must have spent most of their time in and around the home, spinning or sewing when the housework was finished and passing such leisure time as they had in gossip with their neighbours. Alexander Ewens' gift of books to the church and to his friends at his death in 1675 shows that some Minehead men by some means had obtained sufficient education to be able to read good literature, such as, for example, *Plutarch's Lives* which Ewens left to his 'loving friend, Francis Pearce of Marsh.' During the reign of George II there was a school in the old Quaker meeting house on the north side of Market House Lane near the almshouses kept by a Mr John Thomas, but this seems to have been closed down by 1753. During the next few years the promise to open a free school was held out by the politicians as a tempting bait to the voters of Minehead. In 1767 Charles Whitworth of Blackford undertook to open a school if he was returned to Parliament. This perhaps forced the hand of Henry Fownes Luttrell, for at about this time he drew up a memorandum entitled: 'Articles for Instituting a Free School at Minehead.' A school house was to be provided in which twenty poor boys were to have pens, ink and copybooks so that they could be taught writing and arithmetic. A master was to be appointed by the founders who was to be allowed to add to his endowment of £20 a year by taking in as many fee-paying scholars as he was able. Mr Luttrell had estates at Nethway in South Devon and the first master was a Mr Henry Dugdale who was an usher (assistant master) at Brixham School. The handwriting of his letter of acceptance, dated 6 April 1769, is an excellent specimen of the copperplate taught to children at that time. Mr Dugdale writes that he is 'very well pleased with the conditions of the school.' A Henry Dugdale was still its master at the end of the century, when there were a number of girls among his pupils, presumably fee-payers who were admitted in order to keep up the numbers and maintain his income during the lean years when the wealth and population of Minehead had declined so disastrously. A Dunster Castle map of 1822 shows the school room on the site of the present Further Education Centre at the foot of The Ball, and the Free School was probably established there in 1769.

Almost no references to concerts or plays have been found, but considerable expenses incurred at various times for the purchase and repair of the organ and on the salary of the organist are evidence of the importance of music in the church services. The burial register tells us that 'Walter the Fiddler' was buried in 1614. That he was so described suggests that Walter was a familiar and popular figure in the town. In the eighteenth century four fiddlers and a drummer were employed to march in the procession for the election of 1774.

A letter from a Mrs Blake at Nethway to George Gale, the steward of Dunster Castle, shows what sort of entertainment found its way into the provinces, though as the Princess Royal was in the audience it was, no doubt, a rather special show. It took place in an old barn. There was a puppet show; a drama, *The Prodigal's Return to his Father*, some opera airs, both vocal and instrumental; and a famous 'Balance Master'. This was a long programme which detained them from home until one o'clock in the morning, which the old lady feared Mr Gale might consider 'a little rakeish'. The only reference that has appeared so far to a theatre in Minehead in these early times is an obscure advertisement of 1802 with a half-crown ticket to the 'Theatre, Minehead'. It seems to be a ponderous piece of political satire. The programme included 'a favourite comedy' called *Monkey Face Imitations*, a song, 'Paddy's Ramble', and a farce with the intriguing title: *Lady Wanton*.

Politics in Minehead during the eighteenth and early-nineteenth-centuries was both a secondary source of income to its inhabitants and a primary excuse for fun and games. The voters expected sports like those arranged in Collins' field and there were at least two bowling greens, one north-west of the harbour and the other on The Ball, which seem to have been maintained partly for political reasons.

Minehead, until late in the eighteenth century, was a very isolated town, cut off from London, and even from Bristol, by appallingly bad roads. A journey by sea was sufficiently dangerous and uncomfortable to be avoided if possible, but at least it was swifter than one which traversed the so-called highways. The footpost, who in 1663 carried the letters from Taunton to Sherborne to hand them on to the mounted postboy for delivery in London, could make the journey of 50 miles each way just once a week. At the end of the eighteenth century in a letter to his attorney, J.F. Luttrell noted that for one of his men to ride post-haste to Taunton and back took at least seven or eight hours. The earthen surfaces of the tracks that served as roads were cut into great ruts by the vehicles that used them and were virtually impassable during the winter. Even in September, in 1642, when Sir Ralph Hopton was marching his force of Cavaliers from Sherborne to Minehead, he objected to the route chosen because it was unsuitable for wagons and in describing the journey he particularly mentioned the bad roads.

That the roads he traversed were so bad should not surprise us, for they were the responsibility of the parish through which they passed and had to be repaired by a corvée of the able-bodied inhabitants imposed on them by the churchwardens and enforced by the local justices of the peace. For example, in 1673, the parishioners of Timberscombe petitioned quarter sessions to release them from the court order that had been found necessary to compel them to work on the highway through the village. Believing that the road was now 'sufficiently repaired' (a modest claim), they sent William Thorne to Ilchester with a petition requesting their release from the court order. Their request was granted and he returned with a small subsidy of thirteen shillings towards the costs they had incurred. For more serious repair work, like the collapse of New Bridge between Allerford and Porlock in 1632, the parish of Luccombe was assisted by a subsidy levied on the hundreds of the western division of the county, and to ensure that the money was well used the work was supervised by George Luttrell and his son, Thomas.

The Turnpike Act of 1663 opened up a way by which road improvements could be financed, but for a private Turnpike Bill to pass through Parliament the support of local landowners was essential, and their interests were often at variance. A later Act of 1751 made it easier to set up a turnpike trust, but it took yet another Act of 1773 to clear the way for real progress.

Before this Act was passed the gentlemen of West Somerset had decided to initiate a Minehead Turnpike Bill. Their action was triggered off by the merchants of Minehead who in 1762 petitioned Henry Fownes Luttrell for permission to make a new road from 'Puddle bridge in Lower town to the Strand near the entrance to Quay Street.' They had already raised more than half of the £87 which it was estimated this new road would cost; and a toll house near Lamb Cottage would, they believed, collect from strangers a sufficient income to repay in time the capital which they would have to borrow. Blenheim House had to be removed, but otherwise the way was clear for the new road and it was soon finished. Encouraged by this success, Minehead, Dunster and Carhampton set about improving the roads in their immediate vicinity. Stimulated by the enthusiasm of the local people, Sir Thomas Dyke Acland of Holnicote and Mr Luttrell promoted a private petition to Parliament in 1764, seeking permission to set up a Minehead Turnpike Trust. Their first proposals were coldly received by the justices of the peace assembled at Williton in January 1765; but the people of Watchet and the Wyndham family, who feared that their port would be isolated and its trade suffocated if Watchet should be by-passed by the new roads, were won over by the promise that one of the seven roads in the final plan would run from Watchet harbour to Bampton.

The oddly chosen engineer for this enterprise was Samuel Kingdon, a sergemaker of Milverton, who had set up as the master of a writing school and had become a part-time surveyor. He was instructed by Mr Luttrell to work closely with George Gale, the steward of Dunster Castle, and together they produced the preliminary plans which were piloted through the House of Commons by a Somerset lawyer, John Popham, with chambers at New Inn in the City. On St George's day, 1765, the Minehead Turnpike Act became law. Nearly one hundred trustees were chosen: among them Lord Thomond, a Wyndham and MP for Minehead, a privy councillor, Lord Percy of Enmore, Sir William Wyndham, Sir George Trevelyan and, of course, Sir Thomas Dyke Acland and Henry Fownes Luttrell, the chief promoters of the Bill. Among the Minehead representatives were William Hayman and Robert Blake.

The overall plan provided for seven linked roads. The first was from Minehead to Dunster and on to Timberscombe, with a tollhouse and gate at Cowbridge, and a stop-gate near Knowle to prevent teams of packhorses from crossing Oway and avoiding the toll-keepers. This route continued through the village of Timberscombe and up the hill to Beazley and Lype on its way to Bampton. There was secondly a short linking road connecting the first road to Brushford Green, Washfield and Worth. A third road was to run from Minehead to Loxhole Bridge past a tollgate at Paradise and on to Carhampton. From here it was routed through Sandhill, Bilbrook, Torre and Monksilver to Hartrow Gate. The fourth road branched away at Carhampton and passed through Blue Anchor, where there was a tollhouse, on its way to Watchet; the fifth connected Watchet to Tower Hill in Williton, where a fine tollhouse has survived; the sixth route took the Doniford road out of Watchet and was planned to connect eventually with the Bridgwater turnpike at Nether Stowey. The last of the seven routes was, of course, the contentious road out of Watchet by Five Bells over the Brendons to Bampton, which was not expected to pay for its upkeep but was said to be essential in order to preserve the failing trade of Watchet.

Before the work on these roads could begin an acrimonious dispute about legal costs and management decisions had to be settled. Some of the trustees accused John Popham, the solicitor, of incompetence and of charging exorbitant fees. Poyntz, a Parliamentary clerk, they said had done all the work. Kingdon, the sergemaker turned surveyor, was, so they claimed, 'very little acquainted at that time with surveying roads.' Gale, the Dunster steward, had started life as a carpenter which was no sort of preparation for the presentation of a turnpike Bill to Parliament. As for his master, Squire Luttrell, he, they hinted, had forced the plan through by employing his own servants and being extravagant with their money. The sub-committee appointed to examine the accounts was presided over by the erratic Thomas Carew of Crowcombe who described Popham's Bill as that of a 'twopenny solicitor' and abused him mercilessly at a meeting of the trustees. Popham attributed Carew's 'dirty insinuations to the product of a distempered brain which has been continually on the rack for these seven years last past' in studying nothing but mischief. As for the rest of the sub-committee, he believed 'they would have signed our death warrants for a piece of roast beef and a pitcher of good October.'

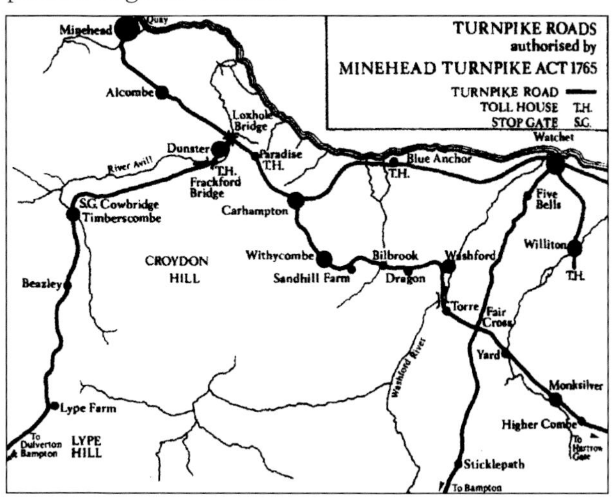

Henry Fownes Luttrell was very thorough in his approach to the Minehead Turnpike Bill. Before any irrevocable decisions had been taken he ascertained that the tolls would provide an adequate income. From a trial period lasting one week he discovered that a tollkeeper at Dunster, at a time when there happened to be a very small market there and when there was no carriage of culm or coals, would have collected £3.11s.1d. This sum was made up of charges for 811 horses at 1d. each, four carts with three horses at 9d. and one cart with two horses at 6d. At Exbridge it was estimated that there would be an income of £250 a year to set against expenses of £50 which included the toll-keeper's wages of five shillings a week. To reduce damage to road surfaces heavy vehicles were to be fitted with broad wheels. For the actual work of construction some parish labour would be requisitioned or money in lieu of it. The latter seems to have been preferred by both the roadmakers and the parishes. The initial enthusiasm for the new roads was maintained and already by 1778 a proposal to extend them had been formulated, though work on the original plan could hardly have been completed.

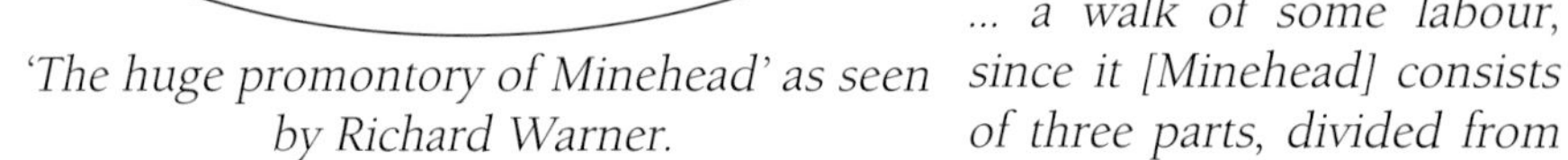

'The huge promontory of Minehead' as seen by Richard Warner.

In spite of this brave attempt to improve communications between Minehead and her neighbours, the trade of the town continued to decline. The harbour deteriorated; the Industrial Revolution, which re-animated so many depressed areas of England, passed by the impoverished 'inhabitants of the borough and ancient port of Minehead.' Nevertheless there was still hope. A notice advertising building land for sale at Alcombe in 1796 reads:

The country about Minehead cannot be surpassed in beauty and natural conveniences by any part of Great Britain... It is also much resorted to by company in the bathing season for which purpose it is presumed that the building [of] some lodging-houses would be a good speculation.

And so in the long run it proved to be, but unhappily Minehead had first to sink into the slough of despond before its fortunes were to revive with the coming of the railway in the second half of the nineteenth century. Even the 'company' that had resorted to it in the bathing season had apparently deserted the town by the turn of the century.

The Revd Richard Warner of Bath described a visit to Minehead in the year 1800 in *A Walk through some of the Western Counties of England.* From the hill above Watchet he observed 'the huge promontory of Minehead' and descending to the seashore he spent that night at a 'neat little inn called the Blue Anchor' which had accommodation for lodgers and a good bathing machine. Next day he crossed the sands to the Warren, making on his way a diversion to Dunster Castle. He reached Minehead in the evening and found accommodation at The Plume of Feathers, which he described as a 'comfortable caravansery'. While a chicken was being prepared for his dinner he set out to explore the town, but found this involved him in:

... a walk of some labour, since it [Minehead] consists of three parts, divided from each other by fatiguing heights. The Bottom, or Quay Town, by far the most considerable of the three stretches along the shore under the menacing head of that vast promontory called Minehead-Point, a rugged steep rising to the height of eight hundred feet, and beetling over the houses that crouch at its roots. Its chief boast is a convenient harbour, accommodated with an excellent quay and pier, the animated scene, formerly of a busy coasting and foreign trade. But, like Watchet, Minehead can only now refer to its quondam importance; for though the pride of extinguished greatness be sufficiently visible here, yet the extensive commerce and proportionate affluence, which in times of yore inspired this inflation, and gave it some sort of consistency, have long since become the mere shadow of a shade.

The Middle Town he described as running 'along the declivity of an hill, over a quarter of a mile from the Quay-Town' and having 'the conveniences of a post-office, shops and lodging-houses.' The Upper Town disappointed him. He saw 'nothing to recommend its shabby, irregular lanes, but the extensive prospect necessarily given to it by its elevation.' He reported that although Minehead had

... long since deplored the loss of its extensive trade, some appearance of cheerfulness and animation has been given it... by the company which resorted thither in the summer season for... bathing.

Richard Warner was thus anticipating the town's future role as a seaside resort.

Chapter 9
Poverty and Agriculture: 1791–1851

The Great Fire of Minehead

On 5 July 1791, a fire broke out in the yard of Mr Edward May's mill at the foot of Bampton Street. An eye-witness in a letter to a friend written the next day described the outbreak and its consequences:

> *Report says that Mr May, a considerable miller, who lived in Bampton Street, yesterday noon had occasion for some pitch which was in a barrel near his back door, and with a hot iron or poker he meant to take some, but it unfortunately caught in a flame and he rolled it into a small stream of water near at hand where it blazed much more; near the spot stood a wood or wallet rick of immense size, to which it immediately communicated and from thence to the adjoining houses... that side of the street.*

The fire spread rapidly through the town and 'about 70 good dwellings, with a number of warehouses, store rooms and outhouses, were entirely destroyed.' 'Most of the sufferers', the writer continued, 'were reputable shop-keepers and supported large families.' He concluded: Between 400 and 500, who were yesterday morning in prosperous circumstances, are now rendered destitute.' Among those who hurried to help were the town's two main property-owners:

> *Much praise is due to Sir Thomas Dyke Acland for his kind assistance during the fire and also to J.F. Luttrell, our Representative, for directing his servants and the populace to give every possible assistance to the sufferers. Many were dreadfully scorched. Mr Luttrell appeared much more distressed to see the valuable effects of his tenantry destroyed and hear the cries of their wives and children, than for the loss of his property, which must have been very considerable. Both gentlemen stayed till a late hour and did not leave the awful scene till they thought the remaining houses in some safety.*

Many good houses were lost but the only casualty of the fire was a 'Mr D. Price, a maniac, locked up and forgotten in the confusion.' The consequences of this fire were varied and long-lasting, They affected not only those whose homes and property had been lost but also the political and social life of the town. An appeal was quickly made to the public and a relief fund begun, but what happened to the money that poured into Minehead from elsewhere remains a mystery. Perhaps it was distributed to those made destitute and was used to cope with their immediate needs, but the discontent of the townspeople in the years following makes this seem very unlikely. Most of the property destroyed belonged to Mr Luttrell and it was expected that he would immediately set in hand a rebuilding programme. Yet when Parson Swete visited Minehead on a walking tour in 1796 he described the distressing appearance of a 'vast number of houses in a state of blackened ruin and utter dilapidation presenting a scene of melancholy confusion, a result of a fire of a few years before.' He considered that the damage should have been repaired by then, particularly since 'to relieve the immediate distress of the poor sufferers, a very large contribution... had been levied on the generosity of the public.' Certainly he had not heard of any distribution of money. A statement made in the *Bath Chronicle* of August 1791 denied that the fund would be used to help in Mr Luttrell's re-building programme as if this had already been rumoured. Yet, if the money was not distributed amongst the fire victims, it was certainly not used by Mr Luttrell for new buildings either, for these just did not materialise.

Soon after the fire a report was published stating that Minehead was soon to be rebuilt in such a manner that it would 'be raised to a state of elegance and repute' at the expense of its liberal benefactor, Mr Luttrell. This article, which raised the hopes of the people of Minehead for a brief while, soon brought a reply describing the plan as 'a chimera only of groundless fancy... totally void of foundation.' Only one cottage had been rebuilt by then and Luttrell papers of the period show few signs of any house repairs or rebuilding at this time. Mr Luttrell's failure to provide a basic need for his tenants, that of houses to live in, probably contributed to the new climate of critical opinion that swamped Minehead in the 1790s. Parson Swete records that 'Mr Luttrell, for the want of a good policy and liberal treatment, had rendered the major part of his constituents disaffected,' thus provoking the turbulent and angry election campaign of 1796. The opposing candidate, Mr Langston, recognized the need and had forty small houses constructed. This stood him in good stead in 1796; nevertheless in 1802 the electorate rejected him and he left Minehead, but before leaving he disposed of all his property in the town to Mr Luttrell who by this time had realized that he needed to provide more for his tenants if he was to expect their support.

From the point of view of ordinary Minehead townspeople, the fire and the subsequent years must have marked an all-time low point in the affairs of the town. From its maritime supremacy in the early part of the eighteenth century Minehead's fortunes had deteriorated drastically. As we have seen, her trade had fallen off, employment had become scarce and as a result her population had declined steadily throughout the second part of the century. The fire, which destroyed the central part of the town, rendered many homeless and without work. It is recorded that seventy-three houses and other buildings were destroyed. Some of these in Friday Street and Bampton Street belonged to fairly well-off merchants and tradesmen while in Puddle Street (now the Parade) many smaller homes of labouring men were lost. The lack of rebuilding meant that these men and their families had to look elsewhere for accommodation and, in some cases, for fresh work. Some must have been compelled to leave Minehead to seek work, while others may have shared housing.

Certainly the population continued to fall. In 1796 there were 175 electors as against 228 in 1780.

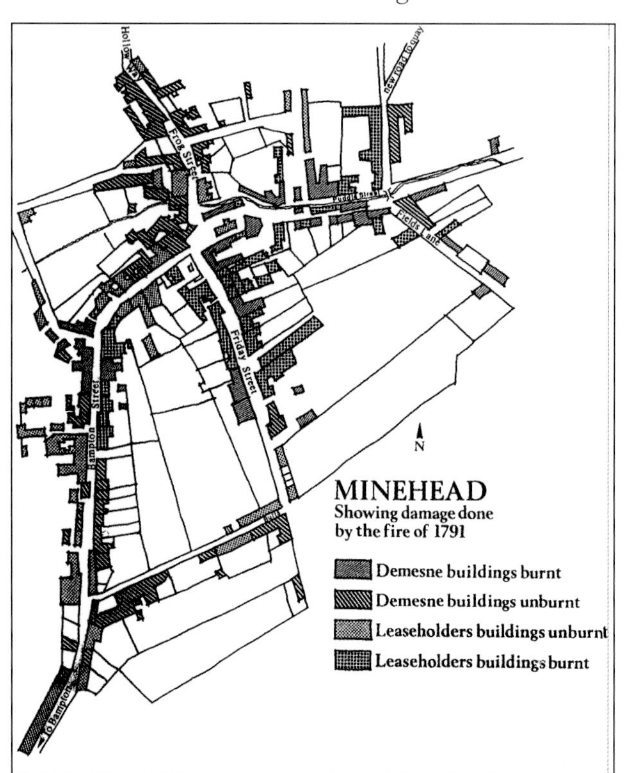

Although this reflects a number who had left the parish completely, it may also hide the fact that some who previously held the vote still lived in shared accommodation in the town so that they no longer held a property, the qualification for an elector in the borough. In spite of these depressing circumstances few, if any, of those affected by the fire became really destitute or were compelled to fall back on parish relief. This was, perhaps, because the fire hit many of the wealthier townsfolk, who had more than one financial interest and whose investments were scattered throughout the town.

The only reference to the fire in the overseers' accounts are in the lists of rate arrears for 1791, and the years following when several of the Friday Street and Bampton Street properties which were burnt were 'allowed' - meaning that payment was waived - because they were no longer tenantable. Most of these properties, including the Town Hall which was near the foot of Friday Street, were never rebuilt and remained on the list of arrears until a new assessment was made It was not until the 1820s that any substantial rebuilding and development began.

POVERTY AND ITS RELIEF

In Minehead the pattern of poverty and its relief from 1791 seems to have followed that generally found in the south of England in the last decade of the eighteenth century and the first third of the new century. The poor rate account books for the town give a fairly full, if sometimes annoyingly enigmatic, picture of poverty in Minehead, and they are augmented by details in the Luttrell estate accounts and various letters.

Up until 1834 the poor were the responsibility of the parish, represented by the churchwardens and by the overseers of the poor who generally had a thankless task. On more than one occasion they found themselves paying the outstanding bills of the poor account and recouping their losses only months later. The overseers were elected by the Vestry meeting each Easter, from the more substantial farmers and tradespeople of the town. Money for the relief of the poor was raised by the poor rate levied on every property in the town. This rate could be levied whenever it was required so that in a normal year four rates would be raised, while in bad years the ratepayer would be liable to contribute his share of the poor rate as many times as it was needed. Thus, in 1795-6, eight rates were levied while in the exceptional year of 1801-2, the rates were levied as many as eighteen times; and the sum of £904.7s.10d. was collected from the ratepayers. One can imagine the unpopularity of the overseers, compelled by circumstances to collect the rates every three weeks instead of every three months. It is not surprising that the property owners, equally affected by the adverse economic situation, were frequently unable to meet the rate demands and found themselves in arrears. Often the most substantial farmers were among the slowest payers. As these men were also those from whom the officials were chosen it was not unusual for deadlock to be reached, and for the vicious circle of non-payment and arrears to be broken only with difficulty.

In 1790 the relief of the poor was centred on the workhouse rented for £6 a year. The building can almost certainly be identified as a contemporary private house at the foot of Church Steps. By tradition this building was once the town gaol, but this cannot be substantiated by any written evidence. The stone building, with small square wooden-frame windows, rambles backwards. Now tiled, part of the building in the 1790s was thatched since reed was purchased presumably to patch the roof. Inside, a troublesome furnace, stoked with either turfs or coal, provided heat and cooking facilities in the kitchen of the house. Food at this time seems to have been fairly cheap and plentiful. Meat and vegetables were bought from local farmers. Corn was ground into flour at the Town Mills. The flour made a coarse brown bread and oatmeal was used for porridge. Veal, beef and mutton featured frequently in the accounts together with cheese, milk, potatoes and green beans. A large garden was cultivated in some years. In April 1795, 600 cabbage plants were bought for 3 shillings and 3½d. was paid for other seeds. Lime was used to improve the soil. In 1797 two pigs were bought and these would have been fattened and killed to provide bacon. Perhaps a cow was kept and cream made since a 'sceamer' was in use. Water was obtained from a well, a new well rope costing £1.6s.8d. being purchased in 1811. (Perhaps it was made in the town in the rope-walk now known as Parks Lane.) Clearly a fairly balanced diet was provided within the workhouse though it is not possible to work out the quantity of food supplied per head. At times of illness the ordinary fare was augmented by more beef, white bread and wine.

The workhouse was in the charge of a governess who was responsible for the administration and discipline of the institution; and the happiness of the inmates would have depended to a great extent on her attitude. We do not know exactly how many inmates there were in the early 1790s, but they must have lived in very over-crowded conditions and the close proximity of many senile, simple and handicapped people must have aggravated this situation. By 1810 twenty-three men and women were being maintained within the workhouse. In 1792, the surgeon, Phillip Ball, who was retained for six guineas a year to attend to the sick poor, inoculated seventeen persons against smallpox, perhaps the number of inmates in that year. In spite of this, a smallpox epidemic of 1799-1800 carried off at least eleven paupers whose plain coffins figure in the accounts. There would be little chance of preventing the spread of infection within the crowded workhouse.

Clothes were provided where necessary. Miss Buller was paid 2s.6d. for making two gowns in 1793. A jacket and trousers for William Morgan, cloth included, cost 10s.7½d. in 1805. Parish apprentices, when first going to their new masters, were supplied with sufficient clothing. James Phelps, apprenticed to James Merrick of Lower Woodcombe in 1812, was given two new shirts and two bedgowns. Boots and shoes were expensive items which were carefully repaired and nails for boots feature in the accounts. There is a hint of more comfort in the entry in 1808, 'For a carpet to make rugs for the workhouse: 9s.1½d.', and in the same year a quilt was bought for 9s.6d.; but generally life in the workhouse would have been austere and fairly comfortless.

Whenever possible, work was provided for the able-bodied pauper and the income used to supplement the poor rate. There is little to show what work was available but the purchase of hand cards is mentioned more than once, indicating that wool was being carded and therefore probably spun, within the workhouse. Later in 1804-5 when the financial situation was particularly acute, we find that large quantities of wool were being put out to the poor. William Lewry, the schoolmaster, who lived in the house opposite the workhouse at the foot of Church Steps, provided a room where this transaction could take place. Raw wool was bought by the overseers, who supplied it to the poor for carding and spinning. The finished yarn was returned to be sold to local merchants who would then have put it out for weaving. In 1792 there is a record of cash being received for the poor's labour. The able-bodied would also have been employed at busy times by the local farmers and the wages earned would have offset the costs of their accommodation.

Besides the workhouse inmates, there were people living in their own homes receiving 'outpayments'. These were generally widows, often with young children to support, and at the beginning of our survey they were paid roughly one shilling per head per week. The number varied slightly but in the early 1790s was between fifteen and twenty. These people were given work as already specified when it was available, but the basic weekly payment would generally have been their sole means of support. From 1797 the number of the outpayments began to increase steadily, until in 1808 they averaged around fifty-three a week, about three times the number in 1791.

The causes of this increase in the number of people needing poor relief were national rather than local. England was at war with France from 1793 until 1815, with only a brief respite in 1802. She was compelled to rely on her own food resources; and the

Top: *This was almost certainly the old workhouse. William Lewry, the parish clerk, lived opposite.*
Above: *The Middle Street workhouse opened in 1821.*

shortages coupled with bad harvests brought high food prices in the first years of the nineteenth century. As a result the numbers forced on to poor relief rose dramatically and from 1802 onwards the overseers fought a losing battle against the increasing demands of those needing poor relief. Unfortunately for us a new clerk, William Lewry, took over in 1802 and he, though most conscientious, no longer made a clear distinction between the various bills presented for payment Weights of food-stuffs were no longer noted. In spite of this it is clear that the overseers not only had to cope with larger numbers but also with the increasing prices of essentials. In 1801-2 they were compelled to call for eighteen rates and in the next year for fourteen. As a result, many ratepayers fell into arrears of payment which were to accumulate, in some cases, for years. Francis Pearse, Lord King's agent at Bratton Court, the most substantial farmer in the parish and not living on Luttrell property, at the time of the 1806 election was involved in the movement against the Luttrells' interest using high poor rates as a plank in his platform of attack. In some way that is not very obvious, Luttrells in the past had subsidised the poor rate, but at this critical time when the charges had become exorbitant, this support had been withdrawn and the full burden laid on the ratepayers. Francis Pearse was among those who in 1810, after continual warnings, was summoned for non-payment of the poor rate and it is possible that he deliberately withheld his contributions as part of his protest. Others, however, must have found the rates impossible to pay and only after several years were able to meet their arrears. In 1811, Mr Pearse paid four years' arrears and then in 1812 became a churchwarden, perhaps a conciliatory move. At the same time several particularly poor people were excused back payment.

In spite of the increased income the charges on the poor rate continued to soar so that the overseers still found it difficult to make ends meet. In the exceptional year of 1802, bills had had to be held over and at the Vestry Meeting at Easter 1808 the accounts were declared to be in an 'unsettled state' and the meeting adjourned. The number of inmates of the workhouse rose to twenty-three in 1810. Because of the economic depression and the war there was a larger number of vagrants passing through the town. These people, beggars, wounded soldiers and others forced to move through circumstances, were usually given temporary help, but in 1813 it was decided that no more assistance would be paid to vagrants. A further charge was the support paid to the families of those men who had joined the army and were unable to maintain their families while away. The salary of the surgeon was raised to twelve guineas in 1808, but his duties were also qualified by being made exclusive of midwifery cases, fractures and smallpox and of visits to paupers outside the parish. A yet more drastic increase in charges on the poor rate was made as a result of a meeting held in November 1812 to inspect the pay of out-paupers and the condition of pauper apprentices. There had been no attempt to develop the Speenhamland system by which outpayments were related to the cost of bread. Payments remained steady based on the size and need of the family. The outcome of this meeting was to raise each outpayment by roughly 6d. per week, adding round about

£70 to each year's outpayments. The attempts to provide work for the paupers, either agricultural work or spinning, made little difference to the soaring costs.

It was probably with some idea of saving money that the administration of the workhouse was altered in 1811. For the twenty years from 1791, the workhouse had been ordered by a governess; first Ann Sealey and then, from 1800, Ann Wicklan, who was paid a small salary of £5 per year. Now the workhouse was to be leased and the lessee was to be responsible for the maintenance of its pauper inmates, being paid four shillings per head per week. It seems likely that affairs were muddled at this time since for a few months in 1810 John Powell, the overseer, took matters into his own hands and set them to rights. Then Thomas King took over. It is probable that his administration was not always efficient or humane, perhaps through no fault of his, but because of the small sum allowed for the maintenance of each pauper. In 1819 a note in the accounts states that wholesome and sufficient victuals were to be provided in the workhouse and clothes to be made by those who were capable. Earlier it was said that bedclothes were to be mended at Thomas King's own expense. Thomas King was replaced as guardian of the workhouse in 1822, this time by Thomas Graddon, who supervised the new workhouse in Middle Street.

This building was put up at Mr Luttrell's expense and the third and last instalment of the costs, £160.10s.8d., was paid to William Horn, the builder, on 19 November 1821. A cash payment was made to him on account of extra work done earlier in the month, and since the old workhouse was let as a dwelling house in 1822 it seems that the move must have taken place in the latter part of 1821. Almost certainly overcrowding was the reason behind the new building project since by 1820 the house above the Church Steps workhouse was being used to provide extra accommodation for the poor.

The building of the Middle Street workhouse coincided with a new assessment of the poor rate, fixed at 5d. in the pound in 1821. The uninhabitable premises were excluded from the survey at last. These included not only those burnt in the 1791 fire but also buildings burnt in later fires - Middle Street in 1811 and later New Street. New premises were also rated as were the occupations of the tradesmen and shopkeepers At this point the accounts became less detailed, but outpayments and the supply of clothes continued until 1836 when responsibility for the poor was transferred to the Williton Board of Guardians under the 1834 Poor Law.

Those who administered poor relief in Minehead found it a trying and demanding task. For those who lived in near poverty there can have been little respite from the never-ending struggle to make ends meet. Not only did they have to feed and clothe their families on their inadequate wages but also pay rent for their homes, and, if not a pauper, contribute themselves to the poor rate. There was little distinction between these and the others at the bottom of the scale, who in a bad year might be unable to pay their debts and have to turn for help to the parish. The rent books of the Luttrell estates have many examples of poor people who in certain years were unable to pay their debts. Each was treated on his merits. Some of the poorest would have been assisted by privately ordered charities. The almshouses in Market House Lane, founded in 1630 by Robert Quirke, accommodated eleven needy people of the town while the Cow Charity supplemented the incomes of a number of poor parishioners who were not on weekly relief. In 1831 a report showed that the income from the fund was being used annually to provide coats for fifteen poor men, cloaks for fifteen poor married women or widows, a pair of blankets for each of ten other persons and small money-payments to the remainder in need. The income from Sillivan's Charity, founded with a gift to the poor of £100 by George Sillivan in 1753, was also distributed among 'sixteen aged weak people of this parish not receiving alms' each year. These small payments must have been very welcome, particularly in the years of exceptionally high prices and food scarcity.

More light is thrown on the situation of the poor and the attitude of the rich by certain papers in the Dunster Castle records. In 1816, when John Fownes Luttrell inherited the Dunster estates from his father, concern was expressed over the inability of several tenants to pay outstanding rents and repair bills. In a letter to Mr Luttrell twenty-one people were listed and described as very poor; and the hardship that would exist if they were compelled to pay their debts was recognised. However, this concern was tempered with a more basic hope, that by showing mercy the Luttrells would hold the support of the people of the town. Mr Searle, the agent, thought that if distress were levied for non-payment this might injure the Castle interest at the next election, but the reply from John Fownes Luttrell showed a more generous attitude in allowing leniency to those owing money. In another note Mr Searle also appeared to show a slightly more humane approach:

In the case of Henry Cave it appears that he was in arrears up to Last Christmas £1.18.7½.... In the present year and before the death of Mr Luttrell he had disbursed £3.19.6. By an after arrangement I am informed that all Disbursements made up to the time of Mr Luttrell's death are to be allowed out of his estate, so that a balance of £2.0.10½. is owing from the Trustees. His extreme distress requires early payment. This poor fellow is thoroughly honest - to meet his payment of rent he has sold his only bed, has pawned his watch and has borrowed of a poor but kind sister all she had - 25s. He has a wife and several children who all sleep upon straw. He and his family have constantly been friends of the Castle interest from which they cannot easily be detached.

Perhaps the last sentence illuminates Mr Searle's concern. There seems to have been little real care for the condition of the poor which could over-ride the promotion of the Castle interests. At an earlier election it is clear that if people were not prepared to support the Luttrell interest then they could not expect to continue living in Luttrell property. Those who did not vote for Mr Luttrell were given notice to quit at the next quarter day. Both squire and tenants had their duty to perform. It is no coincidence that the Victorian hymn, 'All things bright and beautiful', is said to have been written with Dunster in mind.

'The rich man in his castle, The poor man at his gate, God made them high and lowly, And ordered their estate' - this rhyme is a complete reflection of the relationship between the Luttrells and their tenants in the late-eighteenth and early-nineteenth centuries. To those who were loyal and deserving, consideration was shown. Poor tenants were allowed to run their rent into arrears and, if circumstances deserved it, forgiven their debts. Thomas Morgan was forgiven his arrears because of a serious accident met with when he was tithingman. In 1849 William Burgess, a pauper lunatic in an asylum and Joseph Sutton who was a very old tenant and had suffered a long illness, were also 'forgiven', as was Thomas Williams whose labour was done and Thomas Graddon who was very poor, with a long family. On the other hand William Tucker, a very bad character, was to quit or pay his debt in full! Several who found themselves faced with the bailiffs ran away leaving the miserable contents of their homes behind them, while others were faced with the sale of their belongings in order to pay the arrears.

During the early 1830s several fields were taken in hand by Mr Luttrell and let as allotments to poor persons. In 1833 the Timber Fields were divided into ten 20-yard-long plots, and let for five shillings a year. In 1834 Frank's Field was also divided and in 1835 Crosslands was taken out of Higher Woodcombe Farm and divided. In a deplorable state, the return after the first year for this field was so poor that the new tenants only paid half-rent for this first season while they cultivated the land. New gardens were also enclosed. All this points to an attempt to help the very poor to maintain themselves and avoid new and fearful workhouse opened in Williton in 1838.

As the century progressed Minehead was to become more prosperous, so that the situation at the beginning of the 1800s, when so many were below the poverty level, was not to be repeated. There is no evidence of exceptional hardship during 1831 when agricultural labourers in other parts of the country were in revolt. Yet even the desperate situation of the early part of the century was not without pathos and humour. Crammed in with the pages of overseers' bills, outpayments and arrears are the odd compassionate entries. In March 1803, old Hulett, being sick, was provided with a pair of shoes and a neck of mutton. And Nathaniel Alloway, farmer, butcher and one-time overseer, did not hesitate to claim for 'is apprentice towards curing is scruff head.'

Farming

A survey of Minehead's farms made for an assessment of the vicarial tithe in 1822 gives a full picture of the parish's farms, fields, and the use to which the land was put at that time. The table on page 98 gives a breakdown of all the holdings over 20 acres, together with details of crops and stock as shown in the assessment.

In many cases these holdings can be identified with holdings named in a survey of the manor made in 1753. Three things stand out about the period between 1753 and 1822. First, the smaller holdings were still fairly fluid. Fields were added and taken away and holdings were amalgamated. This was particularly easy with the decline in population in the later eighteenth century. In 1753 smallholdings, held either by lease or copy on three lives, had their fields scattered over the town, perhaps as they were first distributed after the enclosure of the demesne land in the 1400s. A tenement near Moor for example included a field by the Pound, a field by West Field and two fields in Skinhouse Lane, a landscore in Gybb Taylor. The indentification of these smallholdings with later holdings is sometimes possible, but difficult, since it depends very much on names which are not always specified in the earlier survey and which are liable to alter with changes of tenant. [Recently maps linking with the 1753 survey have come to light endorsing these findings and making identification of properties easier.]

Secondly, the period marks the final delineation of the fields in the town area. At the time that the demesne land was let in the 1400s, it seemed that the one- or two-acre fields were probably marked out and then enclosed. The question now arises as to the scope of enclosure since, in the 1753 survey, there is still reference to the West Field and the North Field and to landscores or landshares or simply acres within these and other fields. For instance William Stote held 'two landscores in the little field' and another in Upper Town, Abraham Clothier one acre in West Fields, two acres at Quay Stile and Nicholas Sillyvan one acre in North Field. Certain map extracts dating from the period of this survey show boundaries within Gybb Tayler and within the North Field as dotted lines, compared with the continuous line around the perimeter of the fields. In the later tithe map of 1842 these semi-permanent boundaries have become permanent boundaries and the sub-divisions have specific names. It therefore seems that some fields were not permanently established as fully enclosed units until the later eighteenth century and before this were perhaps divided only by low banks. Besides this many fields in the 1753 survey were not specifically named but referred to in general terms. Examples include the divisions such as those described above; John Bowden, Francis Cridland and William Clark between them held 'two pieces of ground called the Clift, Ground on the banks, a landscore in Churfield, part of Smith's Tenement.' By 1822 each field had its own name firmly established although many were rather basically Two Acres or Marsh Meadow. Between 1756 and 1822 a new survey must have been made and each field measured and its name recorded.

The third factor deserving comment at this period is the beginning of a tendency for the larger holdings to increase in size while the smaller, scattered ones were split up. The more economic farms drew land to themselves at the expense of the poorer or less well-defined holdings. Already by 1822 the valley farm of Hindon had been enlarged with land from West Myne on the hill, and at Periton, Siderfin's and Davis' holdings had been amalgamated under Robert Ward who also held land at Middlecombe and Bratton. Land was also being enclosed from the common in the few places where it was feasible. John Atkins at Higher Woodcombe had 21 acres newly enclosed by 1822, while Richard Taylor at Oway had also tried to improve his poor hill farm by enclosing more land for sheep pasture. This tendency to enlarge holdings continued and was an important feature of mid-century farming in Minehead.

By 1822, every substantial farm in the parish was well established. Most of the country farms were of ancient or medieval origin. Bratton Court and East Myne were once independent Domesday manors; Hindon and Wydon were named in documents by the 1200s together with Periton, now split into smaller units. Combeshead, Woodcombe and Lynch were named by the mid-fourteenth century. Nearer to the town the holdings were generally smaller and often more scattered. Lower Hopcott was just over 61 acres, but several of the other town holdings were between 20 and 30 acres. A group of farms was situated around the church on North Hill. This included James Edbrooke's farm at Bond's (Postboy), David Rawle's farm at Higher Moor, Robert Moreman at Stoates, Charles Coles' holding, Ellis', and Nathaniel Alloway's holding near Higher Moor named Blackfords. Stoates, incidentally, is named here after previous owners but its real name was Shute Farm and this probably means that it was a farm developed on a block of strips or a shot, at the edge of the open North Field. This may mean that it originated in the 1400s when demesne land was let for a money-rent and could be held in a block with other strips. (Another use of the word 'shute' is in Shute Close at West Myne which raises the possibility of some form of strip-farming in the manor of Mene.) There were other smaller, more scattered holdings in and around the town and these included Saffins, Hillards, and John Hake's and James Taylor's farms.

At Periton there were three main holdings: Robert Ward's Siderfin's and Davis', already mentioned, John Williams' holdings known as Balls and Kents and John Rew's farm, Greenslades. It was a common practice for any holding to be known by the name of its previous tenant and this sometimes can prove helpful in identifying holdings, but can also be very confusing when several tenancies held the same name and when the names were altered at the death of another tenant.

Much smaller acreages were leased by many who were not strictly farmers. These included gentlemen such as Murdoch Mackenzie who lived in Bampton Street and held 8½ acres on which he could run and feed his horses. Innkeepers also used their land for keeping horses and, in some cases, for growing barley to be made into malt for beer-making. Ann Jones who kept the Plume of Feathers Inn for more than thirty years held 51 acres scattered about the town, from which she was able to provide summer grazing and winter fodder and bedding for the horses stabled behind the inn. These horses drew coaches to Taunton and to Lynton, carried the post-boy and were also available for hire. Tradespeople such as coal merchants, lime-burners, tanners and millers again all rented a few fields to support their horses and doubtless kept a cow, pigs and poultry as well if their acreage was sufficiently large.

Every farm in the parish was mixed, although the hill farms inclined particularly towards sheep. Wheat and barley were grown on every farm in 1822 except Oway and attempts were made to grow grain even there in the 1830s and 1840s. The higher farms such as East and West Myne found sheltered spots lying between 700 feet and 800 feet for their corn crops. Oats were grown at only a few of the larger farms and with pease would have provided winter fodder for the large number of working horses that were kept. Wheat was ground into flour either at the Town Mills at the foot of Bampton Street or at Bratton Mill. Barley was processed into malt for making beer at one of several malthouses in the parish. In 1842

Changes in ownership of farms 1822–51

	1822	1824	1842	1851	Acreage	Men employed	
Bratton Court	Francis Pearse		Francis and William Pearse	Francis Pearse	225*	12	
Hindon	Thomas Paramore				230*	14	1 in
East Myne	Robert Moreman	Thomas Moreman	William Rawle	Lived in Church Street	110	3	1 boy
Part Knowl Farm	John Snook		James Hole		From Wootton Courtenay		
Part Lynch	William Clarke				From Selworthy		
Wydon	John Cavill	John Kent	Thomas Kent	Thomas Kent	71	2 + 2 boys	2 in
Higher Woodcombe	John Atkins	Holding split between James Atkins and Francis Pearse					
Oway	Richard Taylor	Thomas Copp	John Nurcombe				
West Myne	William Stoate		James Stoate	(Living in Bampton Street and described as Landed Proprietor)			
Part Lower Hopcott	Lewis Taylor		Daniel Sayer	Elizabeth Sayer	110*	4 + 1 boy	2 in
Greenslades	John Rew		William Siderfin	Diana Siderfin	56	1	1 in
Plume of Feathers	Ann Jones			Ann Greensill			
Siderfin's and Davis's	Robert Ward		Charles Protheroe	John Ridler	180*	5	1 in
Bratton and Deakes	Robert Ward	Holding split	Middlecombe James Stoate Bratton. *Broken up*				
Rawles	Jos Rawle		Thomas Paramore Amalgamated with Hindon				
Higher Moor	David Rawle	David Willmotts	Jane Rawle	Samuel Moorman	32	1	
Lower Woodcombe	Francis Merrick		Thomas Merrick		32	2	
Combeshead Overland	Robert Moreman	Thomas Moreman Thomas Pearman	Thomas Paramore Amalgamated with Hindon				
Greenaleigh	John Rawle			John Rawle	96*	2	1 in
Kents	John Williams			John Williams Jun.		5	1 in
Bonds	James Edbrooke		Thomas Edbrooke	?	35	1 + 1 boy	1 in
Balls	John Williams		*Broken up* in 1844				
Ellis's	Charles Coles		Robert Powell	?			
Deakes, Stoates, Jenkins	John Hake		James Hake	John Hake	30	2	2 in
Hillards	James Newcombe	*Broken up*					
Stoates	Robert Moreman Jun.			Robert Hake	30	1	
Jones's, Griffiths, Husseys	John Tapscott	*Broken up*					
Middle Moor	Nathaniel Alloway						

Sources: 1822 Tithe Accounts; 1824 Poor Rate Assessment; 1842 Tithe Map; 1851 Census.
Notes: Acreage is that in 1851. An asterisk indicates a much increased acreage. The number of men employed is taken from the Census. 'In' refers to living-in.

Farms over 24 acres in 1822

Details taken from the Tithe Accounts for that year

Holding	Farmer	Acreage	New inclosures	Crops: Wheat	Crops: Barley	Crops: Potatoes	Crops: Other	Stock: Cattle	Stock: Sheep	Stock: Lambs	Stock: Wool	Stock: Horses
Bratton Court	Francis Pearce	215–1–18		39–1–24	17–1–9	2–1–4 40 bags	Turnips 27–0–13	6 Cows 25 Bullocks		100	1000 lbs	12
Hynham (Hindon)	Thomas Parramore	178–2–36		24–2–29	27–1–22	1–1–32 60 bags	Turnips, oats, peas, ley	5 Cows	200 old sheep	90	600 lbs	
East Myne	Robert Moreman Sen.	109–1–35	*After 1822	8–3–22	14–2–11		Turnips, oats	4 small cows	250 old sheep	60	500 lbs	3/4
Part Knowl Farm	John Snook	71–1–33		12–1–36			Turnips					
Part Lynch	William Clarke	70–2–06		16–3–30		4–0–37	Turnips					
Waydon (Wydon)	John Cavill	69–1–35		13–0–23	9–3–2	30 bags	Turnips	3 cows	160 small sheep	40	400 lbs	5
Higher Woodcombe	John Atkins	65–1–07	20–3–25	5–3–30	5–0–22	c. 1 acre 20 bags	Turnips, pease	2 small cows		30	260 lbs	2
Oway	Richard Tayler	64–3–12	*After 1822									
West Myne	William Stoate	62–2–27		3–2–29		3–1–30	Oats, turnips	2 cows				6
Part Lower Hopcott	Lewis Tayler	61–3–09		15–3–17	0–2–03		Turnips	4 cows				4
Greenslades	John Rew	55–2–21		5–1–15	12–1–10	2–3–07 100 bags	Turnips, pease	3 cows		30	150 lbs	4
Plume of Feathers	Ann Jones	51–2–12		3–3–33	8–0–27							
Siderfins' and Davis	Robert Ward	50–0–11		6–0–03	5–3–33	2–2–0 40 bags		6 cows	200 old sheep	60	500 lbs	3/4
Bratton and Deakes	Robert Ward	49–2–36		13–1–01	2–0–28		Preparing for turnips					
Rawles	Jos Rawles	45–1–34		7–0–22	16–3–05							
Higher Moor	David Rawle	42–0–08		2–1–08	3–3–28			3 small cows		20	120 lbs	
Lower Woodcombe	James Merrick	40–1–14		1–1–10	6–2–03	0–3–29 30 bags	Pease	2 cows		40	260 lbs	3
Combeshead Overland	Robert Moreman Sen.	40–1–10		3–1–32		3–0–03 40 bags						
Greenaleigh	John Rawle	39–1–12		4–2–13	9–1–24					25	200 lbs	3
Kents	John Williams	37–1–30		4–2–28	8–0–28		Pease					
Bonds	James Edbrook	35–2–25		1–1–20	5–4–06	20 bags	Turnips	1 cow		15	90 lbs	5/6
Balls	John Williams	34–0–27		5–0–03	3–1–15							10
Ellis's	Charles Coles			6–2–35	7–0–26	3–1–10 60 bags		2 cows		25	180 lbs	3
Deakes, Stoates, Jenkins	John Hake	31–0–06		7–2–10	3–1–01	3–7–36 250 bags	Pease	2 cows				2
Hillards	James Newcombe	27–1–32		8–1–16	4–3–0			2 cows		15		
Stoates	Robert Moreman Jun.	26–3–02		4–1–12	6–0–13	30 bags		2 cows		20	100 lbs	2
Jones's, Griffiths, Husseys	John Tapscott	25–3–19		7–0–37	10–0–34	1–2–01						
Middle Moor	Nathaniel Alloway	24–1–32		5–2–35	3–2–30	30 bags	Turnips	1 cow		20	10 lbs	

Above and left: *Traditional cider-making at Highermoor on North Hill, c.1965. On the left is Sid Iles who was always very proud of his strong cider!; The cheese; a straw and pulped apple sandwich ready for pressing.*

Harvesting corn with a reaper and binder. On the left men are 'stitching' - standing bundles in stooks.

there were at least four in the town itself; one near the Black Boy in Bampton Street and one part of the Plume of Feathers. Yet another was near Puddle Bridge and the last in Quay Street near the Red Lion. Turnips were widely grown as winter feed and this may have been a relatively recent innovation since, in 1822, Robert Ward was introducing turnips on his holding. Water meadows were constructed and the water channels can still be seen at Wydon. Potatoes were grown on a large scale and must have been an important part of everyday diet. There certainly must have been a good market for them since John Hake was prepared to plant about 3½ acres of his land with potatoes in 1822 perhaps incidentally to clear the ground. However, the 250 bags of potatoes produced such an exceptional income and incurred so high a tithe that a special assessment had to be made.

Sheep were the mainstay of all the larger farms and the production of wool for sale the chief source of income to the commercial farmer. The usual breed kept was probably the Porlock, small with short horns and with a tendency to leap about. (They were the ancestors of today's Exmoor Horns.) East Myne, Hindon, Wydon and Siderfin's and Davis' at Periton each produced large quantities of wool but where this wool was destined is not clear. A local woollen industry centred on Dunster flourished until the 1800s but the extent of the industry in Minehead can only be surmised. There are certainly signs that the industry did still exist in the town in the early part of the century. We have seen how the work of carding was put out to paupers in the town on more than one occasion. Furthermore, on the site of the present Methodist Church in the Avenue there was a tucking mill mentioned in documents as early as Elizabeth's reign and until 1842. However, no evidence of it working in this later period has yet come to light. Rack Meadow and Rack Close show where the tenting frames had been kept earlier on for the woven cloth to be stretched and dried after the fulling or tucking. It seems probable that at the beginning of the century some of the Minehead wool was still processed locally. Some would have been sold direct to merchants putting out in other villages in West Somerset and some would have still been spun and woven into cloth for immediate local use. However, the whole West Country woollen industry was feeling the competition from the north of England and very soon all raw wool was being sold out of the area.

The number of cattle recorded for each farm in the tithe assessment is very small and there seems to have been little or no commercial dairying. A supply of milk, butter and cheese for the farm and its labourers was obtained from the farm cows. In the town several smallholders also kept a house cow to supply their own needs and presumably there was enough surplus from these sources to meet the needs of townsfolk. Of beef cattle only one mention is made. A herd of twenty-five bullocks was kept at Bratton Court but, as meat was certainly obtained locally as we saw in the overseers' accounts, it seems probable that there were more cattle for both beef and milk, and that in some way they were exempt from tithing and so are not recorded.

Details of pigs kept are not given but, included for many holdings is a general list of tithable assets which included pigs, poultry, gardens and apples. Smallholders would generally have kept a pig to be killed at Christmas and also a few chickens. Nearly every house in Minehead had a garden where this was possible. In August 1884 there were complaints of the smell of pigs being kept in the back yards of Bampton Street. No mention is made of horses in the tithe return, but a pencilled note added at a later date gives the number of horses at several farms. Unfortunately we do not know whether these were working horses or the total number kept, so the figures are not very helpful. Horses were used at this time for farm work as well as the more usual oxen: ox shoes are still being turned up on occasion today by the plough. At Wydon there was a round house where the circling horse provided the power for threshing. Cider was produced on every farm and a cider supplement was an integral part of each man's wages. It is still made at Bratton today [1977], though it was discontinued at Wydon when the tractor was introduced, the two things not being considered compatible.

We have then a fairly accurate, if static, picture of Minehead farms in 1822. Many were little more than smallholdings where subsistence farming was carried on. Wool, potatoes and other excess produce in a good year would have been sold, but the farm was not viable as a commercial venture. Some were too small, others too poorly situated. The next twenty years were to see an amalgamation of holdings in which such farms were annexed to larger ones or broken up between several tenants. By 1842 (see page 99) Thomas Paramore at Hindon had added Combeshead and Rawles at Bratton to his farm, Francis and William Pearse at Bratton Court had annexed most of Higher Woodcombe and several fields from broken holdings at Bratton. Thomas Edbrooke at Bonds also held James Taylor's farm known in 1822 as 'late Griffiths'. James Stoate had added the low-lying Deakes at Middlecombe to his main holding of West Myne, and it was perhaps here that he kept his hounds to hunt fox and hare. Several of the smaller farms had been enlarged by the addition of one or two fields from holdings like Saffins or Hillards which were broken up. In this way the wealthier farmers holding the most economically viable units were able to develop their farms as profitably as possible. However, several 30-acre farms were still kept up nearer the town.

There was little more enclosure of moorland, but it was generally easier for a farmer to enlarge his holding by annexation rather than by reclamation. Nevertheless between 1824 and 1842 the farmers at East Myne and Wydon did reclaim adjacent fields on North Hill. At East Myne the 50-acre newly-enclosed Mene Allotment stretched east of the medieval boundary bank and represented a tremendous act of faith. The work involved in reclaiming this huge, sloping field, even with the help of horses, must have been back-breaking, and rewarding only in so far as it fulfilled the vision of the hill farmer looking with longing eyes at the rich farms in the valley below.

With these valley farms there was some success, though not every farmer was rewarded. Robert Moreman (junior) who farmed at Stoates, twice found himself insolvent. His farmhouse, named in these documents Herring Shute Farm, was in 1822 completely renovated. William Thorne was the builder, William Baines the carpenter, while Henry Reed rethatched the roof. Three bushels of hair were used in remaking the cob walls. The completed house consisted of a kitchen, parlour and three bedrooms, with a dairy, cellar, brewhouse, cider house and furze/turf house. Perhaps this restoration of the house brought an increase in rent, but whether or not this was so, Robert Moreman fell behind in payments, and so in February 1823 his property was seized and sold to defray outstanding debts. Then in 1829, yet another sale of Moreman's effects took place under 'distress for non-payment of rent which he was wholly unable to pay' Whether this ill-fortune was due to Robert's lack of ability as a farmer or perhaps to some illness or other handicap, we do not know. It is more likely that the the small size of Stoates, only about 27 acres, meant that it was no longer an efficient, economic, farming unit at this time of improving methods. Similarly at East Myne, the thin soil and relatively high altitude made it difficult to farm profitably. Robert Moreman (senior) seemed to have managed with fair success but when the farm passed to Thomas Moreman soon after 1822 he quickly found himself in difficulties. A pencilled note in the tithe book limits the tithe payment to £3.10s.0d. 'for the present till times rise.' In 1829 Thomas, whose annual rent was £77.10s.0d. was in arrears of £188.1s.1½d. Described as 'a very poor man' Thomas had to give up East Myne and Combeshead and in 1834 was on parish relief. A similar farm was Richard Taylor's at Oway on Grabbist of which Josiah Easton, the clerk, wrote in 1822: 'This is a very coarse farm and no tithe will arise to the Vicar but from the depasturage of sheep' - this, in spite of the recent additional enclosure of some 20 acres to provide extra grazing for the sheep. In 1839 a note in the estate accounts stated that there was no corn again at Oway. Clearly attempts were being made to improve the farm but with little success.

After the amalgamations between 1822 and 1842 there was little change in holdings until land began to be sold for building purposes from about 1850 onwards. One exception was the holding developed by John Ridler, who settled at Periton in 1844 and who, by 1851, was farming 180 acres.

The decennial Agricultural Returns for Minehead for the years 1866 to 1906 show a steady, though slow, decline in agricultural activity in the parish. There was a marked fall in the amount of wheat and barley grown, although the acreage given over to oats increased, presumably because of the number of horses being kept. Conversely, the acreage devoted to root crops was reduced by 39 per cent over the last forty years of the century. The number of cattle kept decreased over all by 20.6 per cent in the same period although the number of milk cows rose from 91 in 1866 to 130 in 1906, an increase necessary for the provision of dairy products in the developing holiday resort. The real decline in agriculture is seen in the reduction by nearly 50 per cent in the same forty years of the number of sheep kept in the parish. Although the larger farms were maintained, the smaller holdings with fields in and around the town itself were gradually sold up as new houses were built to cater for the growing population, and this loss of land eventually resulted in lower agricultural output. Although some land would by then have been farmed more intensively the poor quality of much of the higher ground limited this possibility. The national depression in agriculture in the 1870s must also have aided this decline if only through the low prices for farm products, but this was masked in Minehead where provision for the holiday-maker was rapidly outweighing agriculture as the chief source of employment and income in the town. In 1851 agriculture and allied crafts provided the largest single source of occupations. By 1901 the emphasis was on the service industries, catering for the visitor. Agriculture had served to keep the community going between the eighteenth century when Minehead declined as a port, and the end of the nineteenth when she emerged fully as a holiday resort.

Chapter 10
Holiday Resort: 1794–1901

Minehead's modern role as a holiday centre originated in the second half of the eighteenth century. In 1794 the *Universal British Directory of Trade, Commerce and Manufacture* spoke of Minehead in this way:

> *The port trade and wool industry in which the place was largely engaged has hitherto gone much into decay, but on account of the pleasantness of the situation and salubrity of the air, a number of persons of fashion have been induced to visit it as a bathing place in the summer season.*

Sea bathing became very popular as a health treatment during the mid-eighteenth century with the fashionable sector of society who had previously enjoyed 'taking the waters' at spas such as Bath, Cheltenham and Tunbridge Wells. Their popularity led to the discovery and exploitation of springs of healing water in many smaller places, including Glastonbury and Edington on the Poldens where pump-houses were built. One Minehead person who claimed to be entirely cured of 'a continual running in her leg' by the efficacious powers of the Glastonbury waters was Elizabeth Moggridge, wife of William Moggridge, Vicar of Minehead for 53 years in the first half of the eighteenth century.

The use of sea water for medical treatment, already a fairly widespread practice, was given added encouragement by the publication in 1752 of the physician, Richard Russell's dissertation on the benefits of sea water. He not only advocated immersion but also the drinking of sea water as being beneficial for various ailments. This medical stimulus was enough to popularise the practice of sea bathing among a section of fashionable society, and foster the development of seaside resorts such as Brighton, Weymouth and Scarborough.

The reasons for Minehead's development along similar lines are not obvious since the town was so far from any other centre of fashion. The laying down of a system of turnpike roads had, of course, opened up the way to Minehead and made the journey there as comfortable as was possible at that time. By 1830 a coach ran from the Plume of Feathers to Bridgwater three days a week, returning on alternate days, and a mail coach had recently started running from the Wellington Inn to Taunton every day. There was as yet little or no competition from nearby places that were later to become very popular as coastal resorts. Burnham-on-Sea had a population of only 653 in 1801, compared with Minehead's 1168, while Clevedon and Weston-super-Mare were little more than villages in the 1700s. Minehead was not only an established port with some accommodation for travellers but, as the harbour declined in the eighteenth century, there was plenty of opportunity for its inhabitants to look to new occupations which catered for the visitor. Minehead, too, had a mild and salubrious climate, but her real advantage was the town's position so close to Exmoor, yet beside the sea.

The scenery of mountain and water was eulogised by the poets of the Romantic Revival, interested not only in Nature itself but in its spiritual influence on life. Wordsworth and Coleridge, Shelley and Southey all visited and walked on Exmoor on a route that seems to have been well-known before the 1790s when war with France put a stop to European travel for a while. Their poetry was influenced by their love of the region. As the popularity of their poetry grew so did the desire to visit the scenes that had influenced the poets themselves.

Minehead, then, was ideally placed as a centre for visitors who wished to combine the enjoyment of Nature with beneficial sea bathing. The Revd Richard Warner of Bath who stayed a night at the Plume of Feathers in 1799 during a walking tour of the West Country wrote:

> *...though Minehead has long since deplored the loss of its extensive trade, some appearance of cheerfulness and animation has been given it ... by the company which resorted hither in the summer season for the purpose of bathing... The shore is hard and fine; the machines* [right] *commodious; the lodgings reasonable;*

Seaside Resort and Rural Escape

Above: *Looking across the Parks, c.1885.*

Right: *Quay Street from North Hill, c.1896. The Beach and the Metropole Hotels can be seen in the distance.*

Below: *The Beach and North Hill, c.1890. In the centre of the picture is Lamb Cottage which provided commodious accommodation. It was later demolished as part of a road-widening scheme.*

Below right: *The Wellington Hotel, c.1880.*

Bottom right: *On North Hill.*

provisions cheap and plenty; and though its access be rendered easy by an excellent turnpike road which runs to Bristol, yet its distance from the metropolis and the populous parts of England is sufficiently great to prevent those felicity hunters, the teasing insects of fashion, from disturbing with their impertinent buzzings the pensive or rational pleasures of them who choose to enjoy Nature at Minehead during the summer season.

From the start Minehead developed as an exclusive resort, chosen by those who wished for peace and quiet within easy access of beautiful scenery rather than a fashionable social centre. In spite of the 1791 fire, also noted by Richard Warner, Minehead continued to grow in favour with sea bathers. James Savage, in his *Hundred of Carhampton* written about 1830, says:

To a certain class who wish to visit the seaside, Minehead offers many advantages; lodgings are low, provisions are good and cheap; there is a fine sandy beach, and they will not be annoyed by the company of the frivolous part of the fashionable world of whom so many are to be found in some of our watering places at particular seasons of the year.

A cosier view of the town is seen in a few lines of doggerel written by an anonymous resident between the years 1823 and 1828. They are entitled 'Lines Descriptive of Minehead, its Trade, Visitors and a few of its Principal Characters.' The verses begin:

Whoever visits Minehead a welcome will find,
Provided their purses with cash are well-lined.
The views are extensive, both the sea and the land
From the top of the hills and likewise the strand.

They describe Minehead's development as a favoured seaside resort and continue:

A post-coach thrice a week from Bridgwater
Often invalids brings to bathe in salt water.

In the summer season this place quickly fills
With persons in hopes to cure all their ills.
Some are cured, some are better, few ever died
By making a trial of our famed air and tide.

Convenient for bathing, machines there are three
Drawn by a horse down and up from the sea,
And in attendance there's always a guide,
Who charges a shilling for each dip in the tide.

The shillings went to John Fownes Luttrell, who, with others who profited from the visitors, must have been delighted at Minehead's developing popularity.

At first Minehead must inevitably have been exclusive since suitable accommodation for visitors was very limited. Among the inns was the old established Plume of Feathers, which was the posting-house and main centre for travellers although it deteriorated during the 1840s. According to the proprietress, Mrs Ann Greensill, the cause was the competition provided by the Duke of Wellington Inn, built opposite the Feathers in 1820, which also acted as a posting-inn servicing the 'opposition coach'.

Thomas Warden, Mr Luttrell's agent, said that the real reason for the decline in trade at the Feathers was that Mrs Greensill was 'entirely unfit for the business and never could make it profitable.' Fortunately, the poor lady handed in her notice to quit before these truths could be brought home to her.

Other inns in the town in 1824 included the Queen's Head in Frog Street, the Castle Inn in Puddle Street, the Ship Aground and the Queen's Head in Quay Street, and the Black Boy in Bampton Street. However, these may well not have provided the type of hospitality required by the wealthier visitor. Lodging houses, too, were limited in number. By 1851 only eight people described themselves as lodging-house keepers and only one had a lodger. In that year, a painter and his wife and young family were staying at an inn in Frog Street where all the other lodgers were Irish beggars. Since the census was taken on 30 March when few visitors would be in the town, this does not give a very clear picture of the types of accommodation available. In 1861 only five lodging houses were named and there was no real increase until the 1880s. It therefore seems that most visitors must have taken rooms in private houses and of these we have little or no knowledge. A letter written by John Hake in 1851 and quoted on page 133 certainly implies this practice.

Besides those who came to Minehead for a holiday, there were those wealthier people living on private means who were also attracted to the town. A hand-bill of 1838 advertises several houses to be let by Mr Luttrell in the 'salubrious and beautiful watering-place of Minehead.' Three of these were unfinished while three others with walled gardens would form 'suitable Residences for respectable families.' These latter were perhaps in the Parks where building began about this time or alternatively in the Parade where several elegant houses were soon to be built. By 1851 there were twenty-five people of independent means living in the centre of the town around the foot of Bampton Street, Friday Street, the Parade and the Parks where new housing was gradually replacing property damaged in the fires some fifty years earlier. Most of these people are described as annuitants, fund-holders, or, less frequently, landed proprietors, and most kept at least two servants. Although a few came from a distance, most were born in Somerset, usually within twenty-five miles of Minehead and evidently the town was already thought of as a suitable place for retirement. In the second part of the century more people began to be attracted to Minehead from further afield. The most important influence in this accelerating development was the coming of the railway.

As early as the 1840s Mr John Luttrell had, with his brother Francis, enthusiastically supported the idea of bringing the 'iron horse' to Minehead. At a time when most landowners were vehemently opposing the development of the railway across their land, the Luttrells seem to have foreseen the benefits of a rail link to Minehead. A Bill concerned with the provision of such a railway was introduced in the House of Commons but did not get past the first reading. After this defeat the inhabitants of Minehead wrote to Mr Luttrell expressing their disappointment that the railway scheme had not come to fruition, and agitation for a railway continued in West Somerset for a decade. Then in 1862, a line from Taunton to Watchet was opened and a coach service begun which connected Minehead with Williton, the nearest station.

In the summer of 1866 the Defiance coach left Williton station after the arrival of the 11a.m. train from Taunton for Dunster and Minehead and returned in time to catch the 6.21p.m. up train. The Royal Mail Coach, the Prince of Wales, similarly linked Williton and Lynton, the journey taking about $4\frac{1}{2}$ hours. Sometimes these coaches must have been filled to bursting point with excited passengers and luggage. In 1874 a report in the *West Somerset Free Press* stated that:

> *Minehead is reached by GWR to Williton, whence a drive of some eight miles carries the daring discoverer to Minehead, but by next Spring to the town itself, thus sparing the father of many children and owner of innumerable trunks the trouble and expense of coaching.*

The growth of traffic on the line showed the West Somerset Company that it would be worth while extending the line to Minehead. In 1865 the extension was authorised and the Minehead Railway Company founded. However, financial difficulties prevented the fulfilment of the project and the Company was dissolved in 1870. Nevertheless, the perseverance of several local people led by Mr Thomas Ponsford, Mr Luttrell's agent, was rewarded by an Act of Parliament passed the next year which re-formed the Company, this time with successful results.

In December 1871, the first sod of the extension to Minehead was cut by Master Alexander Fownes Luttrell, the eldest son of the squire, who 'loaded the

Top: *The Beach Hotel, c.1900.*
Second from top: *Friday Street, c.1912.*
Third from top: *The Parade, c.1875.*
Bottom: *Quay Street looking towards the harbour, c.1880.*

barrow and wheeled it away in a workmanlike manner.' A similar act was performed by Mr G.F. Luttrell and others. The wheelbarrow and spade were later presented to Master Luttrell as mementoes. In celebration, 'Loud cheers were given, volleys were fired in the town, the band played at intervals, several tar barrels were ignited and rolled up and down, and the church bells were rung.'

The eight miles of broad gauge track took two-and-a-half years to lay, the project being hindered by poor weather, labour scarcity and the problem of obtaining certain pieces of land, but on 16 July 1874 the line was opened. It was worked and maintained by the Bristol and Exeter Company at a rent of half the net receipts with a guaranteed minimum of £2000 a year, until 1897 when the Minehead Company was absorbed by the Great Western Railway. In October 1882 the broad gauge track was converted to standard gauge, the whole length from Taunton to Minehead being completed in one day. Correspondence shows that the use of the line increased steadily, but that even as early as 1879 a train had to be taken off because it did not pay.

The extension of the railway to Minehead brought immediate results. Excursionists had already come by steamer to Minehead and by train to Williton and then on by coach. Now the regular arrival of trains - not hindered by any tide - brought day trippers to Minehead in their hundreds. People flocked to the town, some taking advantage of a combined steamer/rail trip, but they were not always welcome. Soon after the opening of the railway 800 persons from the Bristol Waggon Works visited Minehead. The following complaint was printed in the *Free Press* on 1 August 1874:

> *Their conduct was most discreditable. Gardens were despoiled, people were insulted, goods openly abstracted from shops without payment. People were actually lying down in roads and fields... Drunk! The little town methinks, would rather have their room than their company.*

Fortunately most visitors to the town who stayed longer still expected a quiet and exclusive holiday, and as they also began to arrive in greater numbers Minehead turned its attention to providing the kind of holiday and facilities that were in demand. The Beach Hotel was built in 1875 for Mr Luttrell as a necessary adjunct to the new railway. In 1879 Bond's *A Guide to Minehead and its Neighbourhood* claimed that lodgings could be obtained at nearly all the houses at the quay, one of the most commodious being Lamb Cottage, but these old properties were not sufficient for the needs of the new holiday-makers. The number of apartments available increased steadily during the 1880s and 1890s and many of the new houses built in Summerland Street (now Summerland Road) advertised apartments to let. In one week early in May 1885 there were forty visitors staying in The Avenue. The new Visitors List published each Tuesday in summer from 1881 gave details of visitors and where they were staying - a handy guide for the young men who watched the young female arrivals with avid interest and, having noted where they were staying, ascertained their names in the list. It was then not difficult to scrape an acquaintance with an attractive young lady: a raised cap and the use of her name gave immediate advantage in the slightly freer atmosphere of a holiday town.

Mr George Luttrell, in conjunction with Thomas Ponsford, now took a series of steps which led to a real improvement in the town's facilities Already a company had been formed to provide a gas supply for the town and by 1869 Minehead was lit by gas. Soon after, and in anticipation of the railway, the Avenue was laid out as a main thoroughfare to replace the very wet lane which previously led to the beach. In 1874 a company was formed to provide a water supply for Minehead. Water was brought into Minehead from Periton and from Woodcombe where a 120000-gallon reservoir had been constructed. The works were completed by July 1875, after which date inhabitants could 'avail themselves of the opportunity thus offered to them of obtaining for their own houses a plentiful and constant supply of excellent water', and this 'under sufficient pressure for all domestic requirements.' Finally, in 1878, George Luttrell built a network of sewers at his own expense and most of the 300 existing houses were connected to it as were new houses constructed afterwards. All these improvements came within a very short space of time and quickly made the town a much more attractive place to visit.

There was at the same time a growth in the number of houses being built. The Parade began to

Beach & Pier

Left: *The Opening of Minehead Pier by Mr G.F. Luttrell in 1901. In the centre one can see reporters from the* Free Press *recording Mr Luttrell's speech.*

Below: *The Pier from an early postcard.*

PIER HOTEL, MINEHEAD.

THIS New Hotel is built with every convenience for Visitors. Hot and Cold Baths and Sanitary Arrangements perfect. It is situated close to Minehead Harbour and Pier, and has a fine expanse of scenery embracing the Quantock Hills and various others. A large room (capable of accommodating 250, with sea-view and overlooking new Pier, for Pleasure Parties, where TEAS and LUNCHEONS will be PROVIDED.

GOOD STABLING. LOOSE BOXES, &c.

H. CHIDGEY, Proprietor.

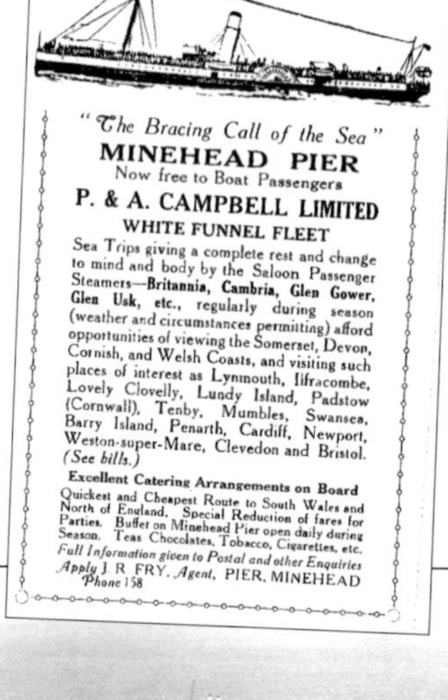

"The Bracing Call of the Sea"

MINEHEAD PIER

Now free to Boat Passengers

P. & A. CAMPBELL LIMITED

WHITE FUNNEL FLEET

Sea Trips giving a complete rest and change to mind and body by the Saloon Passenger Steamers—**Britannia, Cambria, Glen Gower, Glen Usk, etc.,** regularly during season (weather and circumstances permitting) afford opportunities of viewing the Somerset, Devon, Cornish, and Welsh Coasts, and visiting such places of interest as Lynmouth, Ilfracombe, Lovely Clovelly, Lundy Island, Padstow (Cornwall), Tenby, Mumbles, Swansea, Barry Island, Penarth, Cardiff, Newport, Weston-super-Mare, Clevedon and Bristol. *(See bills.)*

Excellent Catering Arrangements on Board

Quickest and Cheapest Route to South Wales and North of England. Special Reduction of fares for Parties. Buffet on Minehead Pier open daily during Season. Teas Chocolates, Tobacco, Cigarettes, etc.

Full Information given to Postal and other Enquiries

Apply J. R. FRY, *Agent*, PIER, MINEHEAD

Phone 158

Centre left: *People throng to watch a performance by the pierrots at the original stand on the Green Spot opposite the Hotel Metropole, c.1905.*

FOR SPORT AND PLEASURE IN HOURS OF LEISURE

VISIT THE—

WARREN PROMENADE

MINEHEAD

Safe Sea Bathing. Up-to-date Bathing Huts. Miniature Golf Course. Putting Greens. Commodious Rest Huts, for Hire by Week or Month. Glorious Views of Sea and Land, and other Attractions . . . .

For further particulars and terms apply—

THE DUNSTER TRADING CO.

DUNSTER, Som.

Above: *Women and children could bathe from the beach but boys had to undress at Warren Point.*

Right: *The Pier, 1924.*

be redesigned, the first new building, Stuckey's Bank, being in existence by 1870. The terraces in Blenheim Road were begun and by the 1890s Friday Street and Frog Street were being re-built and Summerland Street and Tregonwell Road laid out. Only the state of the roads themselves seems to have left something to be desired. These were still unsurfaced and in many places easily flooded by the Bratton Stream which ran through the town, in spite of Mr Luttrell's drainage system. The *Free Press* is full of letters complaining about the state of the streets. Dissatisfaction with the amenities, and the feeling that they could only be dealt with by a central body representative of the town, encouraged many local inhabitants, foremost being Thomas Ponsford, to agitate for a Local Board of Health. As a result a petition was made through the churchwardens and overseers to the Local Government Board that Minehead should become a Local Board District. After the usual enquiry which saw only benefit to the town if it became a District, the application was approved in November 1890, and in May 1891 the first Board was elected with Thomas Ponsford as Chairman and Robert Hole of Alcombe, clerk. The Board appointed a surveyor, a medical officer of health, and a rate collector, each at an annual salary of £10, and an inspector of nuisances who was paid £5 a year.

The Board adopted the design of a ship in full sail with a woolpack beneath it for their seal. Whether or not the Board were responsible at first for much municipal improvement is a moot point if *Free Press* correspondents are to be believed, but three years later in 1894 the Board became an Urban District Council and the town began to go ahead rapidly under the guidance of men of progress and enterprise. While the inhabitants of Minehead were much concerned about the improvement (or lack of it) of the town's facilities, visitors seemed very satisfied and many wrote to the local paper praising the town. A letter to the *Free Press* of 11 July 1885, was addressed to those who were seeking a semi-rural holiday:

Above and left: *The Forman family at Mentone in the Parks, c.1904; Rosamond Forman, later wife of Geoffrey Fisher, sometime Archbishop of Canterbury.*

When she was 95 Lady Fisher, born in 1890, remembered happy holidays at Minehead. 'Before 1890 my Father, who was a schoolmaster at Repton in Derbyshire, used to rent a house in the Avenue for the summer holiday. We were a family of twelve of which I came No. 7. In the fairly early '90s he rented unfurnished Mentone in the Parks, furnished it from Sales, and let it all the year to the same tenants; we had it for six or seven weeks only in August and September. We used to bring down a small staff of Domestics. The whole family came, plus dogs and a canary! Of course we had no vehicle with us, though we had three ponies and carts at home, and later on a donkey too. But we brought bicycles. Every day my mother would charter two of the beach donkeys to help us on our walk home for lunch. In those days our brothers had to undress for bathing on the shingle along towards the point. We had a tent for Mother (a keen bather) and the girls. Two very weather-faced Quay ladies ran the bathing huts and machines.'

Left and inset: *Minehead Station in broad guage days and the seal adopted by the Board.*

Left and below: *Carriages waiting for passengers off the train outside the station and on the Promenade, early 1900s.*

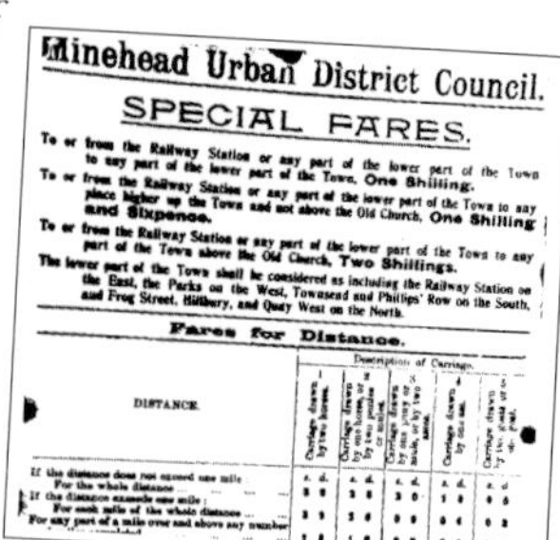

Minehead Urban District Council.

SPECIAL FARES.

To or from the Railway Station or any part of the lower part of the Town to any part of the lower part of the Town, **One Shilling.**

To or from the Railway Station or any part of the lower part of the Town to any place higher up the Town and not above the Old Church, **One Shilling and Sixpence.**

To or from the Railway Station or any part of the lower part of the Town to any part of the Town above the Old Church, **Two Shillings.**

The lower part of the Town shall be considered as including the Railway Station on the East, the Parks on the West, Townsend and Phillips' Row on the South, and Frog Street, Hillbury, and Quay West on the North.

Fares for Distance.

DISTANCE	Carriage drawn by two horses.	Carriage drawn by one horse, or by two ponies or mules.	Carriage drawn by one pony or mule, or by two asses.	Carriage drawn by one ass.	Carriage drawn [illegible]
	s. d.	s. d.	s. d.	s. d.	s. d.
If the distance does not exceed one mile: For the whole distance	[illegible]	[illegible]	[illegible]	[illegible]	[illegible]
If the distance exceeds one mile: For each mile of the whole distance	[illegible]	[illegible]	[illegible]	[illegible]	[illegible]
For any part of a mile over and above any number [illegible]	[illegible]	[illegible]	[illegible]	[illegible]	[illegible]

Above: *An early motor car outside the Town Hall.*

Below: *The Minehead to Lynton stagecoach, c.1910.*

Right: *During the 1920s, most of the town's supplies were carried by rail.*

To those who seek such a resort I venture to recommend one from which I have returned today. Minehead, a little place for which tourist tickets are issued by the GWR, is delightfully situated, with an extensive and firm sand beach for children A small harbour is formed by an ancient pier, and good boating and sea-fishing can be had. Capital arrangements are made for bathing, there being machines for ladies and children at a small charge, while gentlemen can 'dip' from an unfrequented part of the sands. The water is almost as clear as at Ilfracombe. The town is quaint and rural, the landscape essentially 'English'. The walks are simply enchanting, Selworthy Woods, Bossington Point, Dunkery Beacon, Cloutsham, Culbone, Periton Combe, Fern Hollow, Dunster Castle, Cleeve Abbey, Blue Anchor Bay and St. Audries, while the Doone Valley, Porlock, Exford and Lynton can be reached by carriage or the four-horse coach.

The drainage of the town was recently completed under the supervision of Mr Walton, the well-known sanitary engineer; a pure supply of water is brought from the neighbouring hills, the houses are commodious and the charge for lodgings moderate, the postal arrangements are excellent (letters posted in Bristol in the morning are delivered the same day) and there are two churches and a Wesleyan and a Baptist chapel...

Playtime in Bampton Street. Children lived healthier lives in the new houses in the town. (Harold Lomas)

The arrangements for bathing were clearly superior to those thirty years earlier that caused ladies to complain of the 'indecently public exposure of men and boys bathing at the entrance to the beach and dressing and undressing on the breakwater' - a state of affairs which, it was claimed, 'entirely prohibits ladies from the enjoyment of bathing on the sands whenever the tide is in.'

By now many beautiful walks were laid out on North Hill at Mr Luttrell's expense, a popular one being the Marine Walk leading eventually to Greenaleigh Farm where a luscious cream tea and exceptionally good junket could be obtained (*see page 6*). Refreshment rooms abounded and these catered particularly for the day visitor. Some 1000 of these trippers were 'expected' on Whit-Monday 1894; and for them, special ranges of novelties such as dress materials, flowers, feathers, and other trimmings were advertised in the *Free Press* in the weeks before the bank holiday. Many of the day trippers came by steamers which had been calling regularly since the early part of the century when the *Lady Rodney* made the first recorded landing at Minehead. By the 1890s the White Funnel Fleet provided a regular service between Minehead and other Bristol Channel ports, and in order to extend the times when passengers could embark and disembark at Minehead, Mr G.F. Luttrell initiated a scheme to build a pier. First mooted in 1895, the project went ahead in 1900, and on 25 May 1901 the 700-foot pier was opened by Mr Luttrell. One aim was to encourage people from across the Channel to visit Minehead and this they certainly did although some were not very welcome. One *Free Press* correspondent complained that 'when the steamers arrived from Wales there were drunken men in the streets at noon and filthy language at nearly every corner.' Another proposed a recreation ground to accommodate the Welsh trippers.

Such occasions were doubtless exceptional and the influx of visitors, both day and for a longer stay, indirectly brought rapid improvement to Minehead, not only in the material ways we have seen already. The visitors brought increased revenue to the town and many people were now able to augment their incomes by taking lodgers thus improving their living standards. The new terraced houses being built in Tregonwell Road and Summerland Street were a vast improvement on the dark overcrowded cottages where most Minehead children had been brought up in the older parts of the town. Employment opportunities also increased. By 1901 many people were involved in service occupations, working in shops or providing accommodation or refreshment for visitors. Banking and insurance services had also developed.

With the influx of wealthier residents who lived in imposing dwellings on the slopes of North Hill, many girls continued to go into service, while a greater number of men and boys were now working with horses, both for hire and for private families. Private dressmakers, tailors and milliners abounded. With the rapid growth of the town opportunities in the building trades also multiplied. Such increases in employment and income helped to turn Minehead into a thriving town where new shops and other amenities reflected an improved standard of living.

Pupils at Minehead at the Middle Street School, c.1896. Murray Hill who provided our glimpse at shopping, c.1900 is second from the right in the front row with his sister Evie immediately behind him

Belvedere Girls School, 1919/1920. Left to right, back: Elsie Cooksley, ?, ? Wanson, Gwen Nicholas, ?, Mary Stickland, ? Stevens, ?, ?, ? Passmore, Marjory James, Phyllis Besley; second and third rows include: Molly Burgess, Miss Badger, Mrs Stansfield, Phyllis Young, Edna Boddy; Greta Crocker, Agnes Tudball, L. Nethercott, Ned Crocker, Phyllis Holliday, Jessie Godfrey; left to right, front: Gwen Pugsley, Sheila Hardy, ?, ? Crocker, ?, ?, Phyl Holcombe, Norman Batchelor, ?, ?, Hilda Barsby, M. Derrick, D. Johnson, Nellie Hodgson.

Chapter 11
Education: 1767–1998

One influence in the rapidly developing town which must not be neglected is that of the growth of education for all children. To understand the development of the education system in Minehead over the last hundred years, it is necessary to have some idea of the historical and national aspects. It is obvious from the accounts, bills and inventories surviving from medieval days that there was at that time some teaching of basic reading, writing and arithmetic. This teaching was often done initially by the parish priest, and then by either monasteries or schools associated with cathedrals, churches, or chantries and guilds or hospitals. Girls of wealthy families, if educated, were either taught at home or in nunneries. As there were two communities of landowning monks in Minehead in medieval times, it seems probable that they were responsible for some form of education. The convent run by Benedictine nuns at Cannington was available nearby for the education of the wealthy girl. Until the coming of the printing press, books were rare and precious objects. This invention certainly helped in the spread of education by making books more easily available.

During the Reformation many of the schools were closed as endowments were absorbed with other Church property; and the mass of the population, particularly in small towns, once more became illiterate with little opportunity for formal education. Those who could afford it could still obtain private tuition, but for the rest they received oral instruction in religious doctrines from whichever church or chapel they attended.

During the 1700s there was a gradual awakening of interest in the plight of poor children. One of the first societies formed to help these children was the Society for the Promotion of Christian Knowledge (SPCK) while Robert Raikes was instrumental in starting the Sunday School movement in England in 1780.

Looking at Minehead during this period of awakening interest in education we find that a free school was established by Mr Luttrell in 1767 with the support of Charles Whitworth, then MP for Minehead. A school house was provided for the first schoolmaster, a Mr Henry Dugdale from Brixham, and the school had places for twenty poor children. For many years the lord of the manor was responsible for supporting these children, and in 1793 we find Mr Luttrell paying Mr Dugdale's salary of £20 a year - a state of affairs which continued until 1827.

A little later a school was being run by Mr William Lewry, the parish clerk, who lived in the house opposite the workhouse at the foot of Church Steps, and who died in 1864 after sixty-six years as schoolmaster and sixty as parish clerk. William Lewry was paralysed in some way but led a full and active life. He drove about in a donkey chaise and had to be carried to his seat in church in a chair. When he was married (for the second time) he was carried into church on a man's back. He conducted his classes from a chair and if any boy misbehaved he threw a heavy ruler at him. From methods in use at the time we can assume the children were taught mainly by rote, and that subjects were limited to the basic three Rs. This school was, incidentally, where Thomas Ponsford received his early education.

Throughout the later half of the eighteenth, and the entire nineteenth century, the demand for education was such that private establishments like dame schools proliferated along with charity and Sunday schools. Two societies in particular aided the formation and foundation of both charity and Sunday schools, the National Society for Promoting the Education of the Poor in the Principles of the Established Church (NSPEPPEC) and the British and Foreign Bible Society (BFBS) for the Nonconformists. In 1818 each parish was asked to submit a list of all schools and their details in the education returns to Parliament. Minehead reported that there was a free school for twenty children of the poor which only one child from each family could attend at any one time, and that no child could be kept after fifteen years of age. There was no endowed school. There was a Sunday school supported by private subscription at which fifty children were instructed, and several day schools attended by a hundred children. A need for more facilities was expressed. Certainly the number of children described as 'scholar' in the 1851 census implied a real concern for education.

In 1833 the government had made a small building grant to these two societies (the NSPEPPEC

School play at the Grammar School, c.1932.
Left to right, back: ?, ?, Eileen Perry, Patsy Fulston, Jeanne Floyd, Margaret Johnston and Bunty Harrison (tall hats), ? Hurford, Audrie Baker, Mary Hopping, Eric Short, Jack Richards, ? Stoate, ?, ? Hurford;
third row: John Hill, Cecil Hobbs, Doreen Somers (?), Joe Bodely, ?, Margery Sadler, Joy Mansell (tall hat), ? Loveridge, Neil Prance (crowned), Peggy Burt, Chris Ridler, ? Taylor;
seated: Peggy Keith, Margaret Hill, Joan Perry, Freda Johnston, ? Fulston, Olive Stevens, ? Sage, Gladys Yeandle;
front: Michael Floyd, Peter Barron, Verena Yeandle, ? Cornish, Trevor Rowarth.

Maypole dancing on the Recreation Ground, the culmination of the practices on the Mentone field (see page 5). The juniors in the centre kept going in the same direction while the outer ring were weaving in and out.

and BFBS), and six years later the idea was extended when a committee of the Privy Council was set up to administer grants and to arrange inspections, the first step in the 'nationalisation' of education. Owing to the shortage of money the Government found ways to ensure reasonable standards of education and building in aided schools by routine annual inspections and examinations. If either fell short of the standard required the annual grant was withheld, i.e. a system of payment by results was used. School Boards were set up to administer the schools, and as most of the money still came from religious organisations, religious education was a major part of the curriculum, the schools being regularly examined by diocesan inspectors. To help improve the standards of teachers, maintenance grants were introduced in 1846 for pupil teachers in the form of a stipend, and in 1853 a system of capitation grants was introduced ranging from three shillings to six shillings per head, payable if three-quarters of the children attending passed a specified standard of educational testing for that age. In 1862 the grants were made payable on the result of individual examination, resulting in a large saving for the Government.

Evacuees from London arriving outside the Regal Cinema, 1939.

Despite all these advances much of the education of children remained in private hands but purpose-built schools were increasing in number as their advantages were appreciated. A final spurt to the building programme was given in 1870 when Forster's Elementary Education Bill was passed. This enabled the School Boards to pay fees of needy children out of the rates and to pass by-laws making school attendance compulsory. Minehead Parochial School was built just before this, opening in 1867. The building is now the upper part of the Middle Street Community Education Centre. It was split into two departments, Infants and Junior. The fees for attending were 1d. per week per child. The principal infant teacher was Miss Mary Jane Rawle and the two monitresses were Caroline Hill and Fanny Groves.

Private schools were still plentiful at this time and the demand from the poor for secondary education was growing. In 1880 elementary education finally became compulsory, but was still not free and was not made so in Minehead until 1891 at the start of the September term. The numbers in school in Minehead then were such that a new building was required, and in 1898 a new infant department was being built on the other side of the road from the old school. The infants moved in on 28 August 1899 when school re-opened after the summer holiday, with 145 pupils. There was a little more freedom for the teachers now; time was allowed to be spent on physical education, as well as games, some music and singing, and practical subjects for both boys and girls.

The next major step forward came in 1902 with Arthur Balfour's Education Act. This established a comprehensive local government system for both elementary and secondary education. It abolished individual School Boards and replaced them with Local Education Authorities administering all of the Government-aided schools in a county or county borough. Pupils at the Minehead schools continued to grow in numbers until a new school was needed. Sited in Watery Lane, it took boys only in 1914 from the age of seven upwards. The infant department stayed where it was and the girls remained in what had been the junior department. The junior schools were re-named Minehead Council Schools for Girls or Boys. In 1918 the school leaving age was raised from thirteen to fourteen, increasing numbers still further. In 1929 a County Grammar School was built in Ponsford Road originally for boys only from Minehead and the surrounding area, although it was soon made coeducational.

At the outbreak of war in 1939 many children from London were evacuated to this area and a double shift system was tried at all of the schools, the local children attending school from 8.30a.m. to 12.30p.m. and the evacuees from 12.45p.m. to 4.45p.m., but this simple system didn't work - there were far too many children. One of the schools that came to Minehead was from West Ham in the charge of Mr Roy Chenappa. Overcrowding was so bad at Watery Lane that West Ham pupils had to be taught at Alcombe Village Hall. At the girls' school in Middle Street it was so cramped that the older Minehead girls were sent to Bancks Street to be taught in the old Victoria Reading Rooms. Violet Jones recalls that little real teaching was done there.

Little change took place in school buildings after the war for several years although numbers increased, the school leaving age was raised to fifteen and the curriculum greatly widened. At last in 1958 the secondary pupils moved into a new building at Alcombe on 1 April. It was officially opened in September of that year. The Junior School moved into the Watery Lane buildings and the Infant Department became a separate school, taking over all the buildings in Middle Street. However, with the growth of population, the raising of the school age to sixteen and the move towards comprehensive education, Minehead schools were again reorganised from 1968 over several years The secondary modern school was taken over and greatly expanded to become Minehead Upper, and then the West Somerset School, taking children from thirteen from three contributing middle schools at Minehead, Dulverton and Williton. Today it is the West Somerset Community College. The Grammar School building expanded to become Minehead Middle School, taking children from nine to thirteen, while the Junior and Infant Schools combined to form two First Schools, one in Watery Lane and the other in the former Roman Catholic St Theresa's School buildings in Townsend Road.

Because of its climate and position Minehead was always a popular centre for small private boarding schools. In 1851 there was a boarding school in Bampton Street run by Whiston Bristow and his sister Maria for fifteen boys between the ages of eight and fifteen. The schoolmaster's daughter, Isabella, was also taught at home, which perhaps accounts for the presence of one other girl scholar among the boys. In the 1880s there were at least three boarding schools in the town, and by 1901 there was a high school for boys in Townsend House, a boarding schools for girls in the Parks, and a private school in the Avenue. There were also private schools in Alcombe. Several schools of this type, including Llanberis in Blenheim Road, and Belvedere in Irnham Road, together with the High School, remained until the 1920s and '30s when their function was taken over by the new Grammar School.

From the mid-nineteenth century there was also some attempt to provide educational opportunity for adults. By 1861 there was a free reading room on the quay where daily papers, periodicals and a collection of books was provided. In 1874 a number of businessmen petitioned Mr Luttrell that a building known as the Old Schoolroom in Market House Lane - in use then as an assembly room and for concerts - might be turned into a reading room but it only survived for a few years. Perhaps the numerous rules and relatively high charges - between six and twelve shillings a year - put it out of business. In 1884 a similar sort of reading room was opened at the Wellington Inn - now a Temperance House - specifically for the working classes where, besides books, there were games such as bagatelle available. Various series of open lectures were given, frequently, though not always, connected with the church or the temperance movement. In 1885 a series of lectures took place on the 'Manners and Customs of North American Indians' while in 1894 'English Church History' was studied under the auspices of the Minehead Branch of the Diocesan Society for Promoting Higher Religious Education. At the same time the Williton and District Technical Instruction Committee arranged popular classes in the study of dressmaking, carving, health and sanitation, cookery, farm stock and soils, plants and animals, at Minehead and the villages round about. Oxford University Extension Lectures were also given in Minehead.

Yet another influence in education, particularly of the poor, was the founding of the *West Somerset Free Press* by Mr Samuel Cox, printer, bookseller and stationer of Williton in 1860. Many local influential people regarded the venture as dangerous since it might give ordinary folk ideas above their station in life, and threatened to boycott not only the paper but Mr Cox's whole business. Believing firmly that such a local paper could only benefit the working man, Samuel Cox went ahead with his project and on 27 July 1860 the first issue appeared. Since then the *Free Press* has disseminated ideas and reported news throughout West Somerset.

Top: Girls from the Middle Street school, 1940s. Left to right, back: ?, Margaret Axon, Eileen Cane, Doreen Willis, Mary Commings, Freda Binding; middle: Peggy Heard, Betty Heard, Lillian Jordan, Violet Land, Margaret Male; front: Audrey Gough, Josie Young, Audrey Dyer, Barbara Young, Peggy Winter, Jean Warr, Winnie Thresher, Pam Baker. Bottom: Minehead Evening Institute Dramatic Society in J.B. Priestley's Now we are Married, *1951. Left to right: Fred Hunt, Dawn Goostrey, Irene Jones, Herbert Sutton, Walter Heppel, James Perks, Molly Ridler, Margaret Sutton, Olive Russell. Missing from the photograph: Mabel Wharton, Audrey Ponting-Baker, Mike Hine.*

Chapter 12
Religion: 1800–1900

The nineteenth century saw a revival of religious activity in Minehead marked by building and restoration projects in the churches, and the firm acceptance of Nonconformist groups in the town. At the beginning of the century opposition to both the Methodist and the Baptist causes is recorded. In 1810, a Methodist preacher, the Revd John Henley, was driven out of Minehead by an angry mob, symbolically shaking the dust from his shoes as a testimony against the wicked place. At the same time the Baptists were finding it impossible to buy land for a chapel, and not until 1817 were they able to lease land at Periton from Lord King of Bratton Court, where their first place of worship was built and opened on 18 May that year. At first it was served by visiting preachers including Mr Samuel Gill who 'undertook pastoral responsibility in a sphere of usefulness that was very extensive.' In 1825 the chapel had its first resident minister, the Revd J. Cocks, and in 1831 a new chapel in the Parks was built on land reluctantly leased by Sir Thomas Dyke Acland. A house for the minister was also built for 'the house was as needful as the chapel, there being no possibility of a Dissenting Minister getting a house in the town.' Periton Chapel continued to be used for Sunday afternoon services and other meetings for another fifty years before the tenancy was given up. The chapel in the Parks was enlarged in 1902 at a cost of £1153 and there have been many useful additions and alterations made since.

Not until 1871 was a nineteenth-century Luttrell prepared to lease land which would be used for a chapel for Nonconformist worship, although there are records of Quaker Meeting Houses on Luttrell land including one in the Butts next to Townsend House and in Alcombe. In that year the Avenue site was leased to the Methodists who erected a sizeable church which was enlarged in 1886 to seat 500. The Congregational Church in Bancks Street was built and opened in 1904.

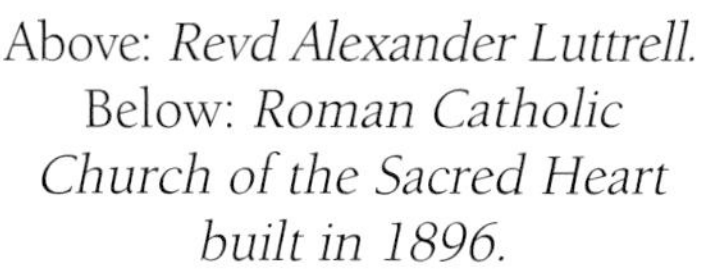

Above: *Revd Alexander Luttrell.*
Below: *Roman Catholic Church of the Sacred Heart built in 1896.*

Minehead Methodist Sunday School, Primary Department, 1919.
Left to right, back row: Miss Cranmer, Miss Selwyn (behind), Miss Rawle, Douglas Stevens, Miss Passmore, ?, P. Venn, L. Hardy, F. Wilkins, M. Rawle, D. Winkworth, M. Burgess (Kievill), Miss Francis, Miss Bale (Scott), Miss F. Baker (behind), ?; middle row: Gladys Coles, ?, ?, ? Staddon, P. Staddon, Eric Brown, S. Hardy, ? Court, Iris Corney, G. Burgess; seated: G.H. Ridler, ?, O. Cheek, F. Cheek, M. Hardy, E. Hardy, Edith Wilkins, ? Wilkins, Jack Ridler.

Erecting the statue of Queen Anne in Wellington Square in May 1894.
Note the Wellington Hotel in the process of being rebuilt.

Roman Catholics from as far away as Taunton had worshipped in a low thatched building in the Butts for many years, but in 1896 they were able to move to the present church of the Sacred Heart in Townsend Road, built with the generous aid of Belgian refugees.

Similar activity had taken place within the Church of England. The enlargement of the Lower Town, becoming, as it was, the new residential and commercial centre of Minehead, made the parish church on the hill seem distant and irrelevant. It was also becoming unsafe. In 1880 St Andrew's Church was built in Wellington Square, the gift of Mrs Charlotte Luttrell, wife of the vicar, to serve this new and prosperous area. Once built, a full-scale restoration of St Michael's Church began. In spite of heavy supporting buttresses the walls of nave and aisle were bulging out of perpendicular by as much as eighteen inches and it had become necessary to rebuild the main body of the church, adding a new pine roof. Only the old chantry chapel was left untouched. Queen Anne's statue, given to the town by Sir Jacob Bancks, was removed from the church and stored, the intention being to place it in the new Town Hall. However, it was eventually erected in Wellington Square where it was unveiled by Mrs Luttrell at 4p.m. on 16 May 1894.

This flurry of building and restoration towards the end of the century reflected a revival in religious activity. How much of this was directed towards the labouring classes we do not know. Certainly religion seems to have been more the prerogative of the wealthy and the middle and artisan classes. Many of the names of those involved in the extension of the Methodist church such as Floyd, Shrives, Preddy and Phillips are of families involved in commerce and thus of some financial standing. The influx of respectable retired people must also have contributed to this expansion, and it is difficult not to attribute some of the enthusiastic activity to the fact that religion was, in the late-Victorian period, the correct and socially acceptable thing. By identifying with a specific church group, one could identify with a particular social stratum, and find a satisfying position within it. This is not to discount true religious devotion and piety but these qualities seemed rarely to appear at the time untinged by more worldly influences. Most churches continued to have rented pews, unfortunately a necessity to help pay for the new buildings but not an encouragement to the poorest to go to church. In the enlarged Methodist church only four rows at the back and two in the front were free, and if more than one person desired the same pew it could go to the highest bidder.

Nonetheless by 1890 the worshipper in Minehead was well accommodated and details of services and clubs show an active and dedicated church life. That the societies could be as duplicated as they were - for example, five temperance organisations - shows that there was considerable interest in matters of religion and morals although, of course, it is not possible to measure spiritual involvement. The churches continued to provide much of the variety in life for many of their members as had the medieval church. And yet, a contemporary postcard still manages to cast a cynical eye at the worshippers who slept through the 'soothing sermons at Minehead' *(see top of page)*.

Old Roman Catholic Church, demolished 1901.

Tannery wagon, late 1890s, loaded with skins to be taken to the railway station for transportation.

Workforce of John Burgess, builder, preparing for a works outing. Seated (starting third from the left) are Sidney Burgess, Molly Burgess, Archie Burgess and John Burgess.

Chapter 13
Industry: 1750–1950

In 1890 John Ll. W. Page in his *Exploration of Exmoor* wrote about Minehead in a way which makes us think again before eulogising the developing holiday resort of Minehead. Looking down from St Michael's Church he notes the intrusive presence of the railway heralding the spirit of change:

> *The town gathers unto itself stark regiments of brick and mortar called 'streets', and detached boxes of like material, called 'villas'; perhaps a tall, unsightly factory chimney overshadows the landscape, or a brickfield poisons the air with odours stifling as those of the bottomless pit. At all events, dark lines of metal rule the face of the land with unerring precision, bearing the noisy train and still noisier excursionist to the once peaceful and still beautiful country.*

So speaks the conservationist of every age! The building development Mr Page refers to was aided by the local brick which had provided material for new building since before 1800. During the previous two centuries there were two areas in the locality where the clay had been found suitable for the manufacture of bricks, tiles and similar products. Hence two works once flourished, both originally located in the parish of Dunster and on land owned by the Luttrell family.

Warren Brick and Tile Works

This yard, at Warren Point, which covered about seven acres and is now the holiday camp, was under the control of the Luttrells who exercised their power through a local agent. It is uncertain when the blue clay was first excavated at this site but production had started by the 1750s. The key figure in a small brickworks such as the Warren was the manager who would have had the many skills necessary for the production of the goods. He had to dig and prepare the clay, make the bricks and tiles, and, most important of all, pack or set the kiln and ensure its correct firing. The Luttrells had to search for their brickmakers throughout Somerset. One of the first recorded was John Mogg, a potter of Bristol, who came to the Warren in 1759. Among the tasks that he undertook were '2 days work for himself and wife in Sorting, Chiping, Stoping Cracks and packing away each Kiln of Goods at 2s.3d per day for 14 days.' Not all employees were able to carry out these jobs satisfactorily. Jonathan Southan was asked to furnish character references to show his honesty and sobriety since during his work at Warren in 1771 he neglected a kiln for 24 hours during the firing of some goods.

Early bills or vouchers indicate that earthenware vessels, in the form of kitchen utensils, were once made at the yard on the Warren or at the kiln at Dunster that stands behind the Luttrell Arms Hotel. But for commercial reasons there was a concentration on brick and tile production. Accounts for the 1780s list plain tiles, a traditional clay tile since medieval times; 'pantyles' (pantiles), gutter bricks (for drainage channels), bars for malthouse kilns, and ridge tiles.

Wooden moulds were needed to enable the maker to form the shapes of the objects. In 1765 an inventory was compiled of the tools in the Pantyle House (the shed where the goods were made). Included in the inventory were '2 pantyle molds and stock, 1 Clay cutter, 1 Brickmold & 24 pallet bords, 1 Seeve and 2 box wheelebarrows.' Sales and numbers of items made at the Warren were carefully recorded. In 1786, 7776 bricks were made for general sale and 1550 for use on the Dunster Estate. By modern standards the yearly output was small: the combined total of bricks made in 1786, for example, would only be sufficient to construct about six garages. A check was also made on goods by the Customs and Excise Officers under the powers of an Act of Parliament passed in 1784 which stated that rates would be '... raised, levied, collected, and paid, throughout the Kingdom of Great Britain... upon all Bricks and Tiles.' Bricks were taxed at 2s.6d. per 1000 with tiles at various rates depending on design or usage. Receipts for the payment of the brick duty survive and the tax itself was increased in later years. It was terminated in 1850.

In the operation of the yard the Luttrells were conscious of the large-scale manufacture of clay goods taking place at Bridgwater. In 1813, William Turner, who had previous experience at both Castle Cary and Bridgwater, was contracted. Earlier in the

1700s the need for competition was recognised in a letter from an agent to a prospective brickmaker:

You will fix your lowest prices as the Goods will be for Sale and must be rended as low as at Bridgwater in order to be enabled to export at the same prices they do...

A brief description of the works is given in an entry dated 1 July 1819: '... one Yard containing one Workhouse, one Shed, four Hacks and one Kiln.' The hacks mentioned were bricks and tiles which had been stacked in rows, of up to 100 yards in length, in the open before being fired in the kiln.

A significant development which took place in the nineteenth century was the arrival of Samuel Cornish who, with his family, served as brickmaker at the Warren until the closure of the yard in about 1919. The 1851 census return shows that he was born at Taunton where there were also brickmakers of the same name. An account for the year 1882 sheds some light on the working of the yard in the period of Samuel Cornish. Coal to fire the kiln was shipped to the Warren via Minehead by a Captain H. Pulsford. Various craftsmen effected repairs at the yard including blacksmiths, carpenters and masons. Also in that year bricks were made for use at Dunster Railway Station and in innumerable tied cottages on the Dunster Estate, particularly for new floors. Field drainpipes from the Warren were now replacing and supplementing stone land drains on local farms. Some curious survivals from the Victorian era are bricks bearing dates from 1869 to 1879. A number have been found in the locality although it is not known why they were stamped with a date.

Victoria Brick and Tile Works

On the Dunster Tithe Award Map of 1843 there is a field in the vicinity of Alcombe named 'Brickland'. This suggests that the clay in the area was known to be suitable for making bricks long before the opening of the Victoria Works in 1897. Built by John B. Marley the works were a response to the Victorian demand for substantial quantities of bricks and tiles for the expanding resort of Minehead. Products from the works also found their way to towns in Ireland, Cornwall and the south coast of England through the development of a thriving coastal trade.

The scale of operations at the Victoria Works was reflected in its layout. The clay pit extended over ten acres to the south of the Minehead-Porlock road and the clay was transported on a tramway, the trucks moving on a counterbalance principle. The taller of the two chimney stacks which serviced the works on the north side of the road was completed by William Court of Minehead. It was reported that upon completion Mr Court stood on his head on top of the stack in celebration!

The history of the works follows a similar pattern to other brick and tile works during the twentieth century. Although producing some 60000 bricks per week, operations were subjected to the economic upheavals of the inter-war years and the two wars themselves. After 1945 cement and sand tiles and concrete blocks became popular alternatives to their clay counterparts in contemporary architecture. The Victoria Works closed in 1947 and the site has been built over. Only the name Marley Close serves as a reminder of the former industry.

Top: *The site of Marley's brickworks at Alcombe. Brick kilns can be seen in the background.*
Centre: *The Avenue tannery just before demolition. In the foreground are the pits for holding tannin.*
Bottom: *Fleshing a skin inside the old tannery.*

Other Industries

Another industry carried on in Minehead was that of tanning. The tannery, which stood until the 1930s on the present site of the Regal Theatre and car park, celebrated its centenary in 1894, but was probably older still. In 1813 the tanyard was leased by a Mr Berry, probably the same Samuel Berry who was there in 1826. At the time there were no guards on machinery and little attention if any was paid to safety on industrial premises. On 8 March, 1831, it was reported in the *Western Flying Post* that a girl surnamed Culme, about sixteen years of age 'was attending the bark mill of Mr Berry, tanner, when she was unfortunately caught in the wheel and her head and arms literally torn to pieces.'

Prince, who drew one of Burgess' carts.

By 1843 the tannery had been taken over by the Siderfin family and over the next forty years developed steadily with its main markets being the industrial towns of South Wales. Then in March 1893 Mr W. L. Evans took over and rapidly increased the efficiency and turnover of the business. At that time the tannery produced butts (sole leather), from ox-hides imported largely from South America. Local oak bark, together with other foreign woods, was used in the process which took fifteen months from start to finish. Coal to drive the steam pumping engine, hides and other raw materials were imported by sea while the railway carried many of the high quality finished skins.

Behind Haywards Bars on the corner of the Parade and Bancks Street was the Parade Aerated Water Manufactory which, started in 1888 by George Hayward, produced 10 000 dozen bottles of 'pop' annually. The bottling plant was powered by a $3^1/_2$ hp gas engine; and two 100-gallon water tanks held the raw material which was processed day and night during the season. Codd's patent bottles with pinched necks and a marble 'stopper' held the finished product.

At the far end of the sea front beyond the gasometer was a chemical works which produced artificial fertilisers but little is known about it. Its high chimney stack can be seen in some old photographs which means that the power must have been provided by a steam engine. Lime was also produced near the quay. The limestone was mined in the vicinity and also imported. It was burnt in several kilns, one was near the harbour and another at the present junction of Blenheim Road and Northfield Road. There were also kilns in Alcombe where local limestone may have been built. Limestone and culm, the fuel used in the process, featured prominently in the cargoes carried to Minehead during the second part of the nineteenth century.

The important timber business of the Ridler family was centred at their timber yard near the beach at the bottom of Blenheim Road which existed prior to 1843, and was concerned with the export of locally-grown hardwoods and the import of Canadian softwoods.

Perhaps because of its deceptive name, mining has often been thought to be associated with the town of Minehead but there is little evidence to show that any large-scale exploration for minerals has ever taken place within the parish. However, the survey made of the town in 1753 specifies at the end in a hand-written note that there were mines within the manor which were formerly of great advantage. Although indications of iron-working have been found at Alcombe no signs have been found in Minehead, but in spite of this some exploration for minerals must have taken place in the mid-nineteenth century In a letter to Mr Luttrell dated 4 January 1853, Mr W. Tibbits of Island Cottage, Dunster, wrote that he had not been able to meet with iron ore in sufficient quantity at Periton and wanted to try the unenclosed part of the hill near the quay at Minehead. Mr Tibbits was also exploring for ore on Sir Thomas Acland's land at Porlock and on Earl Lovelace's property. In 1854 a letter from Mr Luttrell's agent, Thomas Warden, to Mr Philip Harris of the Wootton Courtenay Iron Works mentioned unsuccessful attempts to find iron ore at Hopcott. Some iron was certainly brought to and shipped from Minehead, perhaps from Wootton Courtenay, Luccombe or Luxborough, for problems were found in accommodating more than 200 tons at the quay at a time, and the rumbling of the carts was sometimes an annoyance to the townspeople. In March 1854, James Hake, who lived next to the Red Lion Inn in Quay Street, wrote to Mr Luttrell saying that he wished to quit the house he occupied 'in consequence of the great disadvantage of the Iron Ore carts and others constantly passing the house' which caused it 'to shake so much that no gentlefolks will lodge in the house.' Almost certainly these mining searches had negative results, the quality of the ore holding out little hope of profit.

Martlet Road, c. 1905. This road leading towards North Hill was developed between 1890 and 1914 with many houses designed by leading architects. The girls are looking across a meadow where Herbert Harrison built a pair of houses, Dalkeith and Avondale, in 1911.

Industry on a large scale was not to find a natural home at Minehead. Local resources and local demands led to industrial activity in the later part of the nineteenth century, but it was to be relatively short-lived and after the closing of the tannery in the 1930s there was no industry until the opening of Clark's Vennland factory in 1954, a response to the real need for such a concern to provide employment in the town. Its closure in the 1970s was a blow to the town from which it took some time to recover.

Prebendary Hancock in his indispensable *History of Minehead* wrote in 1903:

> *Minehead now is rapidly changing. New houses are springing up everywhere and new streets being formed. We can find a sentimental sigh for the low, old houses, myrtle clad to their over-hanging roofs which until recently were to be seen even in the heart of the town... such alterations are the necessary concomitants of that increasing prosperity... which seems to be coming upon [Minehead] with rapid strides.*

In this prosperity Minehead enjoyed her heyday of popularity as an Edwardian watering-place. Page had regretted the changes; Hancock, more wisely, could see their benefits.

Postal Services

A postal service existed in Minehead by 1669. The Post Office was formed on 24 June 1673:

> *Placed in charge of Mr Vicary of Minehead.*
> *You will receive from Mr John Smith of Taunton ye letters from London to Mynehead and places Ajacent, to whom alsoe you are to deliver all you can collect and Receive from those Pts to bee retorned to London, keepeing the Letter office there, and P forming ye service according to your late agreement with my Agent Mr Sawtell, wherein I pray be very Carefull and diligent for ye good of our Office & Satisfaccon of ye people whereby you will much oblige*
>
> *Your very etc.*

In the eighteenth century Minehead was issued with its own handstamp to be applied to all outgoing mail. In 1809 'Minehead was made a permanent establishment and the ride being done at £6 per mile plus an addition of one shilling per day or £15.12s.0d. per annum.' After much consideration Minehead was given a Penny Post service in 1829. Various handstamps were used, one showing the distance from Minehead to the Post Office in London. After 1844 a numerical obliterator was used incorporating the number 779 (*below*) and this number is still [1977] used for special hand cancellations. Other cancellations in Minehead include the 'squared circle' and the 'double circle'. The latter was used generally until 1930 when machine cancellations came into use. An interesting special handstamp was issued in 1907 for use at the Army summer camp which was held on North Hill. Minehead postal authorities have used slogan cancellations to help in the holiday trade, one being 'Minehead, Gateway to Exmoor' in 1966 and the other 'Centenary of Lorna Doone' in '69.

Part of the building in Wellington Square, which now houses the Midland Bank, was the Post Office for some years until 1913 when the building in the Parks was opened. It was enlarged in 1934. Today the sorting office is still at the rear of the Parks buildings but counter services have been transferred to the Avenue Post Office.

Chapter 14
Shopping, c.1900

In 1900 the Parade, Friday Street and Parks Street boasted most of Minehead's shops as they still do today. The 1870s and '80s had seen the opening of many new businesses which included several shops which have traded under their original names until very recently. In 1884 came the early-closing movement when most local shops agreed to close early on one day a week. Messrs I. Floyd and Co., E.J. Foy, W. Passmore, Samuel Cox, and Palmer and Tarr, among others, agreed to close on Wednesday at 5p.m., presumably continuing business on other days until 8p.m.

Floyds itself was opened in 1877 in a shop in Friday Street. Mr Isaac Floyd expanded his business by hiring a pony and trap to carry merchandise out to neighbouring villages and hamlets, but with the development of the town trade increased and soon he acquired the corner premises formerly occupied by Mr J. Bond, Chemist and Draper. At first the shop, like many others, was dark and lit only by candles. Customers carried the goods to the door to examine them in the daylight. Later gas lighting was to be installed which even in the 1970s served Floyds in good stead during electrical power cuts. Primarily a drapers, Floyds in 1889 supplied a wide range of goods from mob caps and Champion corsets through velvets, faille, damask and calico to fur boas and women's cork sox. The business continued to expand and the premises extended to include shops in both Friday Street and the Parade. New ventures were introduced so that the slogan 'At Floyds you can dress the whole family and furnish the whole house' soon described the comprehensive service on offer.

The following is a description of the Parade c.1900 through the eyes of Mr Murray Hill:

Henry Wood's shop and workshops [now W.H. Smith] were owned and occupied by Mr W. Tarr, but the present shop fronts were put in after the premises were acquired by Mr Henry Wood. The only shop windows were those facing the Parade as, in common with most other businesses in the town, the owners lived on the premises, and the entrance door in Summerland Road was where the entrance door to the house had been sited. All the first and upper floors were living quarters of the family. They also owned a large hardware and ironmongery shop in Friday Street, where Gateway's premises are now located. Their premises there extended back to Bancks Street, where Floyd's shop is now situated. Mr Henry Wood came to Minehead from Penzance about 1905 and carried on the business as furniture showrooms and removal service. He was joined later by Mr Andrews who came from the same district, and on Mr Wood's death Mr Andrews carried on the business which was formed into a private company. Mr Wood built the premises now occupied by their second-hand shop in Bancks Street, but it was originally a small cinema called the Cozy Cinema.

Wellington Square before 1893. H. Bridger's music warehouse occupies the present HSBC premises. This shop was soon to become the Post Office run at first by Mrs Catherine Kinnersley who also let furnished apartments. On the right are the first buildings in Park Street.

A.J. Baker's butcher's shop [Hartgen] was occupied by a Mr George Brown, butcher, who moved to No. 1 Holloway Street when the shop adjoining the old Plume of Feathers premises was built. This was later acquired by Mr Eli Harding, just before the 1914 war.

Mr Walter Holloway owned the next shop, a drapery emporium, where the entrance to the International Stores [Boots] is situated. Mr Holloway had a powerful voice, and if one happened to be anywhere within fifty yards of the

The Parade & Around

Top left: In 1920 Lillie Slade (left) and Lily Sully established a Ladies' Outfitters and Milliners' business when Rose House in Friday Street was altered to accommodate Slade's old-established Monumental Masons business, which moved from Higher Town, as well as the dress shop.

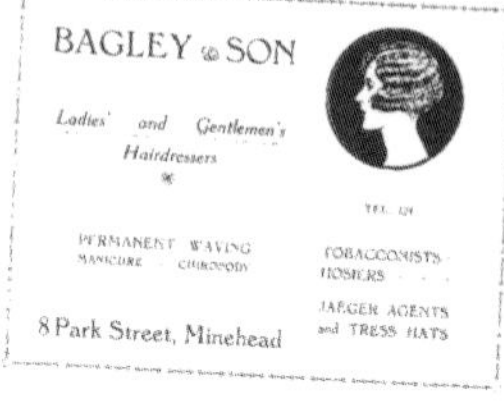

Above: Friday Street c. 1925. Note Slade's Monumental Masons on the left and Bradbeer's Garage on the right.

Above: Holloway Street, c.1905.

BATCHELOR'S CENTRAL STORES TEA WAREHOUSE.

Teas of Sterling Value, and Blendid to suit the waters of this Neighbourhood. Certain to please the most fastidious.

'DUNKERY 2/6 BLEND,'
A delicious Afternoon Tea.

OUR FAMOUS . . .
'EXMOOR BLEND,'
(Awarded Gold Medal at Foods Exhibition),
1/10 lb., 1/8 by the 3lb., 1/7 by the 20lb. Chest.

'MINEHEAD BLEND.'
The Popular Economical Household Tea.
Exceptional Value, 1/6 lb., 1/5 by the 3lb., 1/4½ 20lb. Chest, also 1/4 and 1/2.

COFFEES.
In Tins or Fresh Roasted and Ground to order, from 10d. to 1/10.

COCOAS AND CHOCOLATES
Of the Best Makers.

W.E. BATCHELOR. THE CENTRAL STORES
SEVILLE ORANGE MARMALADE
TEAS

Wiltshire Bacon, Hams & Sausages, Farmhouse and Danish Butters, New Laid Eggs.

Primost English and Canadian Cheddars. Jars Cream and Cream Cheese in Good Variety.

Preserved Provisions.

Tongues, Brawns, and Patés in tins & Glasses by the Best Packers only.

LARGE VARIETY OF ENGLISH AND FOREIGN FRUITS.

Bananas, Oranges, Grapes, Tomatoes, and Cucumbers.

Mineral Waters in Syphons and Bottles.

Kop's Ale.

Pickles, Biscuits, Preserves and Bottled Fruits, by Lazenby's, Huntley & Palmers', Gray Dunn's, Beaches', Cairns & Keiller's.

ALL GOODS AT STORE PRICES. STRICTLY CASH.

Wholesale Prices for Hotels and Boarding Houses for Cash Orders.

THE CORNER PREMISES, Holloway Street, MINEHEAD.

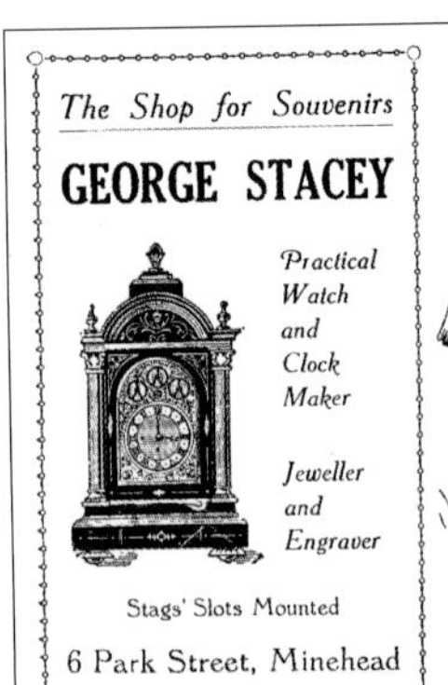

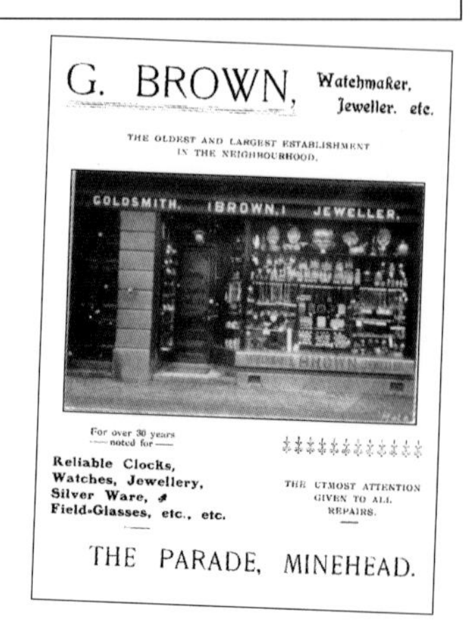

The funeral cortège of Station Officer Teddy Capron, Minehead Fire Brigade, coming up King Edward Road towards St Andrew's church, 1952. Bearers: F.M. George Bushen, Reg Palk and Mike Hine. Geoff Harrison is undertaker. G.K. Croote is the new Station Officer beside the driver.

Baptist Chapel in Park Lane on a Sunday during service time, one could always hear him above all others.

A Mr Robert Hunt, grocer, owned and occupied the next shop where the International Stores have their wine counter. He had a son, Wally, rather a rip-roaring character, often to the fore in activities such as torchlight carnivals, sports days, etc. which in the days before radio and television were the highspots of life in a small town like Minehead. Next came a plumber and sanitary engineer's shop, owned by Mr Mark Capron, where Peter Dominic's [Threshers] shop now is. He was also what was known as a 'turn cock', i.e. he was in charge of the local water supply system. He also captained the local fire brigade, equipped with an old hand-pump engine. Mr John Croote (who was also a plumber and had workshops and a shop at the top of Bancks Street) followed him for a number of years as Fire Brigade captain; and he in turn was succeeded by Mr Ted Capron until the fire service became a national organisation, when his son Fred took over. Fred is now chief fire officer of one of the midland counties, and holds a high position in the service, having recently been decorated with an honour at Buckingham Palace.

Haywards' premises came next, the owner being Mr George Hayward, a man of the hunting, shooting and fishing type, as were many traders in country districts, and who sent their children to public schools. He had a daughter with a fine voice much in demand at local concerts. The premises now occupied by Hedley Rendell & Co were built by Stuckey's Bank, one of the old county banks of that period, later absorbed by the Westminster Bank who moved across the road when the latter's premises were built in the early 1900s. A firm of antique dealers from Taunton named Halliday took over around 1910, and did a very good trade with visiting Americans and visitors to Minehead.

Next came a block of property, originally one building but since divided into three shops. In the early 1900s this was a glass and china shop owned by Mr George Tarr, a local character, who spent a

The Parade, c.1950.

lot of time standing on the steps leading up to his front entrance. His well-bearded and corpulent figure was a familiar landmark, which disappeared regularly about mid-morning into the Feathers Hotel. There was a chemist's shop between here and Floyds, but earlier it had been a superior tailoring establishment, a branch of a Bristol firm named Popperwell, which sported an elaborate coat of arms on its window, 'By appointment to the Duke of Beaufort.' Floyds occupied the corner site with living premises for the family and staff over...

The Parade, North Side. *The corner site now occupied by Smith's jewellery shop [bakery] was owned by a family named Preddy, harness makers. Preddy also had the contract to carry the mail daily to Taunton, and the departure of the large pair horsed van from the Square each evening was always a matter of interest to us youngsters. Miss Preddy ran a young ladies' school for the tradesmen's daughters who were, in their parents' eyes, a 'cut above' going to the Church School on top of the Holloway. The premises were converted about 1910 and occupied by Messrs Copp of Watchet, as a dress shop, Mrs Copp being a Miss Preddy before she married.*

Passmore's shop came next, until 1975 little changed during the previous seventy years or so except for the back premises, a later addition. Mr Joe Passmore's grandfather was a noted shot, and spent a good part of his leisure time shooting rabbits. Browns the jewellers were next, where Barclay's Bank stands today. One of their two sons was drowned when a cruise ship, the Egypt, *went down after striking a rock in the Mediterranean, and Mr Sidney Phillips also died in hospital of injuries sustained when leaving the ship.*

Next was Boddys, bakers and confectioners, where Boots [Bastins] is now. Mr William Boddy, son of the founder of the business, was another splendid shot and a first-class billiards player in spite of losing his left forearm in a shooting accident. The old market house occupied the site of the present one - a picturesque building set back from the road - and replaced in 1904.

Next to the old market house was a pretty little dwelling aptly named 'Rose Cottage', with roses growing over the front porch. I can only faintly remember these two, so they must have been demolished some time before the present market house and Westminster Bank were built.

On the opposite side of Market House Lane was Shrives' greengrocery shop. The present sports shop [Jones' bakery] was then a greenhouse for the exhibition of indoor plants, etc. Old Mr Shrives was a most imposing figure with a long beard, and the family were very staunch nonconformists. The old gentleman wore a round black hat, as favoured in those days by the clergy. Next, where Horlicks and Francis James have their shops, was a combined draper's and grocer's establishment, owned by Mr W.C. Rawie, who looked after the grocery side while his sister Mrs Godfrey was in charge of the drapery. He also owned the grocer's shop in Bampton Street, the County Stores. He was sidesman and one of the stalwarts of St Andrew's Church, immaculate on a Sunday with his pale bluey-grey striped trousers and black frock coat.

Hawkins's shop, formerly Culverwell's, has been there as long as I can remember. The small part of the shop (through the arch on the left) has only been opened up in later years, the entrance being around the corner at the back. It was locally known as the Torture Chamber as old Mr Culverwell was something of a dentist, and I, on more than one occasion in my youth, suffered from his ministrations.

Fox Fowler's Bank occupied the site where Lloyds Bank is now. This was another of the old county banks, originally in Park Street, where the optician's premises are situated. The corner premises to Blenheim Road were occupied by Mrs Sarah Beckett as a high class gown shop. She was a Miss Perkins from Porlock Weir, whose brother kept the Ship Inn, and I believe his father before him; Mrs Beckett's husband was secretary of the original Minehead Gas Company.

Across the road on the corner, where Stenners have their cafeteria [now books], was a whitewashed house with a sweet shop on the ground floor, and a guest house occupying the remainder. It was entered at the side where the 'Do It Yourself' is now situated, and had a small lawned garden.

Next down the Avenue was a photographer's shop, a branch of Hole's of Williton, with a fairly large studio building extending to the entrance of the Old Town Hall. Until the latter was taken over as a VAD hospital during the First World War, it had been the centre of community life in the town with concerts, dances, flower shows, bazaars, and so forth. The building was later taken over by the Council who used the ground floor as offices. Part of the premises also served as a bank, probably the West Somerset Bank, later absorbed by Lloyds.

At the time of writing (1977) change seems more rapid than ever. Houses are being built on every spare scrap of land. Old-established family firms are being forced to sell out to huge national concerns. The re-opening of the railway in 1976 may seem merely a nostalgic gesture, but the patience and persistence involved in its re-opening typify the hard work of generations of Minehead townsfolk who have each contributed in some way to the town's history.

Chapter 15
Alcombe: 1086–1953

Alcombe is situated a mile to the east of Minehead. Today it is no longer possible to tell when you pass from Minehead into Alcombe for the two run together but this is a really recent development. Seventy-five years ago the two places were quite separate as they had been from Saxon times. Alcombe, meaning the narrow valley of alders, has always been overshadowed by its thriving neighbours. On one side, Dunster with its castle, lord of the manor and important woollen trade and on the other, Minehead, a port and commercial centre for West Somerset, Parliamentary borough and eventually tourist centre. Alcombe remained small, agriculturally self-sufficient but dependent for its spiritual welfare on Dunster and on Minehead for a wider view of the world. In the nineteenth century it developed as a residential area and today is too often thought of as just a suburb of Minehead. In fact, Alcombe village retains its identity, deep-rooted in the past and consolidated by its becoming a separate ecclesiastical parish in 1953.

There are few traces of prehistoric or Roman occupation either in or on the hills immediately above Alcombe. Continuity of settlement began in Saxon times. The Saxons pushed into West Somerset in the eighth and ninth centuries, King Ine building a castle at Taunton in AD710. Soon after, groups of Saxons settled in the fertile valleys of Taunton Vale and around Exmoor. The Domesday Book tells us that just before 1066, Algar was the thane in Alcombe - almost certainly the same Algar that held Minehead.

After the Battle of Hastings in 1066, Alcombe, along with Dunster, Minehead and numerous other West Somerset manors, was given to William de Mohun, one of King William's staunchest supporters and a man of some substance and importance. William made his centre at Dunster where he built a

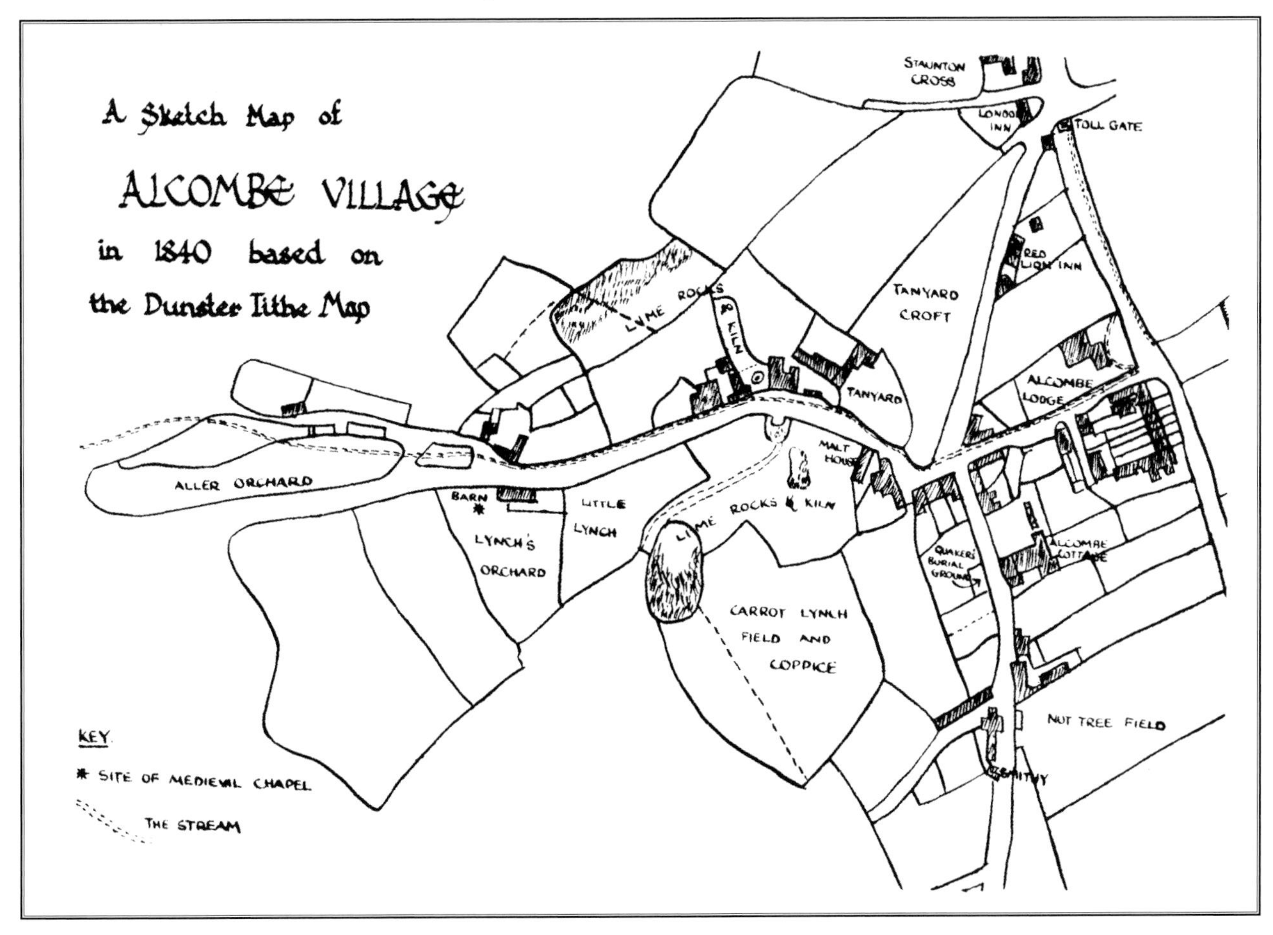

Aubrey and Florence Blackwell with baby Harold between Tregonwell Road and Townsend Road, 1921. One of the chimneys at Marley's brickworks can be seen in the background.

castle and continued to hold Alcombe himself for the time being. At Domesday, 1086, there was arable land for three ploughs in Alcombe. A third of this was demesne land held directly by the lord and worked with one ploughteam by four serfs, while the other two-thirds was worked with two ploughteams by three villagers and four smallholders. There were eight acres of meadow and three furlongs of pasture. Livestock included a riding horse, five cattle, probably oxen, and 200 sheep. The whole manor was worth 20 shillings and had not altered in value since William de Mohun took it over. It was very small and regarded primarily as a source of food for the table at the castle.

Then, some time between 1090 and 1100, William de Mohun gave the manor of Alcombe to the Benedictine monks of Bath as part of the endowment of the priory at Dunster. An undated charter concerning Dunster in the Bath Cartulary records the gift: 'et totam villam Alcume, et omnia sibi pertinetia, libere et quiete ab omni servitio... .' From then until the Reformation we may suppose that the day-to-day running of the manor was supervised by the monks at Dunster. Alcombe was in Dunster parish but the villagers were provided with a chapel-of-ease in the village so that they did not have to walk to Dunster for every service. The chapel was dedicated to St Michael and was built near 'le lynch'. A series of fields on the hill opposite Manor Farm - now partly built over - included in their names the word 'lynch' which means a cultivated field on a hillside (and these must mark the site of 'le lynch'). The foundations of an ancient building, perhaps the chapel, were visible in Lynch's Orchard when an old barn was pulled down and the site cleared for houses to be built in the 1930s.

The tiny priory at Dunster was dissolved with the general dissolution of small religious houses in 1536 and its lands, including Alcombe, passed to the Crown. Sir H.C. Maxwell Lyte tells us that in 1561 the manor was sold to Sir George Speke of Whitelackington. His first wife was a daughter of Andrew Luttrell whose family was by then the owner of the Dunster estates. Some years later a member of the Speke family wrote feelingly of their inheritance by marriage of the 'manner of Alcombe'.

Notes made by George Gale in 1778 after conversations with Farmer Tom Edmonds, who was then over eighty, and with others, show that the Spekes held meetings of the manorial court and received certain customary payments from free tenants so that in buying the property at Alcombe they had clearly purchased the lordship of the manor as well.

The Speke family had become involved in 'great trouble' through their support, and that of their relatives, of the Duke of Monmouth in the rebellion of 1685 and had been fined a crippling sum. In order to raise this the family mortgaged two manors, including Alcombe, and eventually were forced to sell the fee simple and inheritance at Alcombe to those tenants who would buy. Alcombe, dismembered as it was, then passed to Col George Speke on his marriage with Madam Brooking but they, finding that it 'lay remote' and provided only a small quit-rent, thought it best to sell the reversion of the remainder of the estate to tenants who wanted it, including Mr Richard Escott of Rodhuish. In about 1720 Mr Aldred Escott purchased the lordship of the manor. Fifty years later in 1778 there were still disputes concerning manorial rights. The lynchs, site of the medieval chapel, were said to have never been part of the manor but priory or abbey property, although certain trees opposite these fields did belong to the lord of the manor.

Throughout this period of changing landlords farming went on, perhaps with a shift to more large-scale sheep farming in order to provide raw wool for the Dunster woollen industry. Arable land and gardens would have provided much of the villagers' food. The practice of using lime to improve the land, and also for building, was known and the limerocks on either side of the combe had probably been quarried for centuries. The abundant supply of limestone and number of kilns in such a small place indicate some trade in lime. Red sandstone for building was also quarried locally and provided the main building material for the village from at least the sixteenth century.

Then, in 1707, a licence was granted enabling a search to be made in Alcombe for copper, tin, lead and coal. John Speke had mentioned searches for minerals in Queen Elizabeth I's reign, so this was not the first attempt at mining. On this occasion five men were employed to sink exploratory shafts. There is no mention of the exact site of the mines although there is one reference to the Marsh. However, an examination of the 'caves' in the Lime Rock indicates that they are man-made and are likely to have been exploratory adits dug by these miners. The search must have proved fruitless for by 1713 it had been decided to give up and accounts for the venture were drawn and balanced. One unfortunate miner was John Bryant, who broke his leg during the explorations and was paid five shillings as compensation for his injury.

In 1730 a John Bryant of Dunster - could this have been the same man? - and Thomas Trull of Selworthy made an inventory of the goods of Abraham Allen of Alcombe who had recently died. He seems to have been a fairly well-to-do farmer with two horses and three colts, a bull and various other cattle, pigs and poultry. Crops already sown included wheat, peas and beans and there was plenty of hay, and also corn, stored in the barn. Equipment included plough tackling, pack saddles and crooks and also a cart with wheels. Besides the usual contents of the farmhouse - pewter dishes, brass pans, chimney stuff, a table-board and enough chairs for all the farm servants, feather beds and a small clock - there was equipment for brewing, cider-making and making butter, cheese and cream. Which farm he lived in we do not know but the inventory is an indication of the way that relatively prosperous farmers and their employees lived at the time.

The main properties in Alcombe changed hands - both by purchase and lease - very frequently in the eighteenth century. One landholder, Mr Blyth, died at Alcombe in 1763 and his executor's papers give interesting details of the winding up of his affairs. The surgeon's account shows that Mr Blyth developed an abscess on his foot. He had a toe amputated at a cost of 10s.6d. but it seems likely that soon after this gangrene set into his leg. The surgeon, Samuel Bradley, visited him once, and later, twice a day, for several months at 3s.6d. for each journey and dressing. Despite this attention and numerous draughts, digestives and paregorics, more surgery became necessary and the date of the closing of the surgeon's account was only just before that of Mary Napcott for fifteen dozen 2d. cakes for the funeral feast. At this time anaesthetics and antiseptics were unknown - Mr Blyth must have undergone excruciating pain and the gallons of simple medicines can have done little to ease it. For the ordinary labourer who could not afford the surgeon there would not even have been this; only traditional herbal remedies.

The tithe map of the parish of Dunster gives us a detailed picture of Alcombe about 1841. There were two main farms; Staunton Cross, the property of the Luttrells, farmed by William Staddon, and Manor Farm (as we know it) belonging to Giles Edmunds. Both farmers worked a sizeable area around Alcombe. Other landowners included Thomas Hole who lived at Alcombe Lodge with its large gardens, stable and paddock and Robert Hole who owned Alcombe House where William Langdon lived. Several other houses in the Terrace, recently built for John Fownes Luttrell of Dunster Castle, still stood empty although many smaller houses must have been grossly over-crowded since they were inhabited

Alcombe at Worship

Top left: *The first Methodist church in Alcombe was built on the site of a Quaker Burial Ground in 1847.*

Above: *The laying of the foundation stone of the Methodist Church, Hayfield Road, Alcombe in 1930.*

Left: *'Squire George' laying the foundation stone of St Michael the Archangel, Alcombe, 8 June 1902.*

Bottom left: *Entrance to the chapel in Grove Place built by Mr E. Palmer, c.1860.*

Above: *Alcombe Church as it was built originally.*

Left: *Alcombe Church with work progressing on the new chancel and Lady Chapel dedicated in 1937.*

The Britannia Inn, Alcombe, 1930s.

by more than one family. The new houses were destined for a different clientele than the Alcombe cottagers. The Revd Henry Taylor, who lived at Alcombe Cottage (a misnomer), also owned property in the village as did John Fownes Luttrell.

The tanyard near the Britannia Inn was owned by William and Thomas Richards. In 1817, the tanyard, together with Stanley's Meadow, was leased to James Baker of Wootton Courtenay. For this, and the rent of the bark mill and other machinery, he paid £45 a year. It was still a flourishing business then, though by the end of the nineteenth century the property had been split up and the business closed. This had probably happened even by 1851 as there is no mention in the census return for that year of a tanner living in Alcombe although the yard could have been worked by someone living elsewhere. It was the sale of Tanyard Meadow in 1901 by Mr Ridler that made the site for the church available.

In 1841 there was a carpenter's shop in Brook Street where Francis Moore worked and a smithy opposite Nut Tree Field leased by William Criddle. Michael Riddler kept the London Inn and a general shop as well, and in the Tithe Apportionment no other inn is mentioned. Nearby was the toll gate cutting across the main road. It, and the house of the toll-keeper, still in existence but looking rather like a stone shed, belonged to the trustees of the Minehead Turnpike Trust who supervised the roads in the vicinity. There was a malthouse attached to what is now Ferndene which brewed beer for local consumption. The only other trade recorded was that of Mrs Alloway who was a milliner. Most of the other inhabitants of Alcombe would have been working on the land and there would by this time have been a sharp contrast between the way of life of the gentry and the yeoman farmers of Alcombe and the labourers in the small overcrowded cottages.

The census returns for Alcombe for 1851 augment this picture. In addition to the craftsmen mentioned already there were three blacksmiths, three masons and a group of men working as shoemakers and describing themselves by the old term, cordwainer. There were by now two innkeepers and also tailors and dressmakers whose trade would have been increasing with the growing number of retired people and gentry moving to Alcombe and employing servants. A private teacher also lived in the village and perhaps kept the school which quite a number of children up to the age of 14 were now attending. The total population of the village at this time was 241.

Since the Reformation, people wishing to go to church from Alcombe walked regularly to Dunster to the parish church although the medieval chapel may well have been in use for quite a long period after the Dissolution. A note made by George Luttrell about 1600 describes a Rogation Week procession which on Monday of that week in May visited Alcombe from Dunster:

> *The Monday in the Rogacon weke, the parysh going [toward] Alcombe a gospell sayd by Skilaker by the west part of the waye that lieth at the south part of Deneclose were sometyme was a crosse, and from thence to Alcombe Crosse and there was accostomyd to be sayd a gospell, and from thence backwards downe by the water to Yllycombe to Pyne's howse, and theare a gospell and thear the parysh were accostomed to have a drynking, and from thence to Dene Lane and so to Dunster Church.*

We know little else of the church in Alcombe until the nineteenth century. In 1841 two clergymen lived in Alcombe but there is no indication that they worked in the village and no effort was being made to provide an Anglican place of worship in the place. The Nonconformists were more active. Two dissenters, Alexander Prole and Nicholas Blake, are listed as living in Alcombe in 1672. It is possible that they were Quakers and connected with the foundation of the Quaker Burying Ground beside the Dunster road. By the nineteenth century, however, this ground was no longer in use and the Society of Friends were to prove sympathetic to the needs of the

Top: *The site of Betty Cridland's Dame School.*
Above: *Church Street, Alcombe, March 1963.*

Methodists who were looking for a chapel site and could not obtain one in Minehead.

Methodism spread into West Somerset in about 1796 with preachers coming from Taunton. Early in the nineteenth century cottage meetings were started in Alcombe, and by 1825 there was a class of nine members. Two influential members who lived in Alcombe were Robert Moore, a customs officer, and his aunt Priscilla, who lived with their servant Mary Pugsley. Mary was a member of a little Methodist class in Minehead and it was through her that the Moores were converted. When Robert died in 1823 he left money to be invested through Methodist Trustees. Part of the income was used to support a day school in Alcombe. After Robert died a regular meeting was started at the home of Betty Copp.

Part of the £800 left by Robert Moore to help Wesleyan day schools in the area was used to open a little school beside Betty Cridland's cottage near the Great Barn in Combeland Road at Alcombe. Betty Cridland, Betty Copp's daughter, was the schoolmistress, and later on when the school was merged with the larger one at Dunster she continued to run a Dame School on the same site. Many years later an old resident recalled the scene: 'She charged 2d. a week for manners. Often we have seen her in mob cap, white apron, and cane in hand, the children sitting round on low forms.' The barn and the cottage have gone, but the remains of Betty's little school can still be seen on the corner of Combeland and Barton roads.

For many years Alcombe Methodists worshipped at Dunster but they were keen to have a chapel of their own and in 1847 a plot was obtained on lease from the Society of Friends on part of their old burial ground in Combeland Road - a 22ft strip of land for a 'school' for 2s.6d. a year. This first chapel was built of local red sandstone and was used for regular services until the present brick chapel, faced with Portland stone, was opened in Lower Meadow Road in 1930. The old chapel still stands and is now a private house.

During the latter years of the nineteenth century several large houses were built in Alcombe and the population was growing steadily. Round about 1860 Mr Edwin Palmer built a chapel in Grove Place to serve as an Anglican chapel of ease for Alcombe parishioners - who would otherwise have had to travel to Dunster for worship - and it seems to have been used regularly for services. At first music was provided by a harmonium which left much to be desired. In May 1881 it was recorded that:

> *... the behaviour of the harmonium at the Chapel of Ease at Alcombe having become unendurable, the inhabitants collected £40 with which to purchase a pipe organ, and the order was given to Messrs Sparks and Sons of Williton who supplied an instrument of six stops.*

In September 1892 services were discontinued for a while and all the silver and linen was removed to Dunster for safe keeping but within a couple of months Mr George Mildon was licensed as a lay reader and services began again.

The need for a proper church within the community was now becoming apparent and people began to plan for a new church to be built within the parish. Money to pay for it was collected through donations, sales of work and musical and dramatic productions, the latter held in the Victoria Rooms. The movement took so long that it became proverbial - people would say that a bad debt would only be collected 'when Alcombe Church is built'! Nevertheless, the energies of the curate, the Revd J. Utten Todd, led to the start of the building in 1900. The site - at the end of the old Tanyard Meadow - was given by Mr Gatchell; C.H. Samson was the architect and the builders were John Hine and Sons of Dunster. The foundation stone of the church was laid on Wednesday 8 June 1902 by 'Squire George', George Fownes Luttrell. A year later, on 3 May 1903, the nave was opened and dedicated for worship by George Wyndham Kennion, Bishop of Bath and Wells. Besides the subscriptions collected in the parish, many people contributed furnishings which they had made or decorated themselves.

For the first quarter of the twentieth century Alcombe remained a separate, rural community with its life based on agriculture. In 1900 the main road to Minehead was little more than a narrow track. Apart from the small group of houses near the junction with the Porlock Road, there was no building between Alcombe Cross and the Roman Catholic Church in Townsend Road and Glenmore House. The stream ran open through the village, forking at the end of Brook Street. The east stream ran down through the fields where Spring Gardens is now and the west stream turned into Marsh Lane making a watery track towards the sea. Cross Farm and Manor Farm remained centres of employment. Many of the fields belonging to Cross Farm stretched towards the sea and the names of Hayfield Road and Lower Meadow Road mark the agricultural use of the land before the houses were built. Many shire horses were used here and the introduction of the mowing machine was resisted by men who feared that they would soon lose their jobs. An average wage at the turn of the century was twelve shillings a week.

Mr Edmonds at Manor Farm, a descendant of the Giles Edmonds of the 1841 tithe map, eventually sold out to Mr Webber who, until 1932, employed several men full-time. In 1972 Miss Webber talked to me about farming in Alcombe in the 1920s. Besides cattle, sheep and poultry, corn was grown on the slopes above the village. At harvest, as at haymaking, everyone, including women and children, turned out to help stook the corn and, after the last sheaf was cut, a great supper would be given at the farm accompanied by cider made at the cider press in the barn opposite Staunton Lane. Shire horses were used for ploughing and reaping but Mr Case's steam threshing machine was brought regularly from Withycombe to speed the harvest. Wheat for cattle-feed was 'threshed' and broken up with a flail, but for grinding into flour had to be taken to the mills at Dunster or Minehead. The pond, commonly called the mill pond, was used for sheep-dipping. There is a tradition in Alcombe that a mill once stood by the stream just below the 'mill pond' but no definite reference has been found. Manor Farm also provided a milk round for the village and excellent cream could be bought at Cross Farm.

Around 17 January each year the men of the village wassailed the apple trees in the hope of encouraging a good crop. They went from farm to farm, chose a fine tree and made a circle around it. A farm pail was brought, full of warm cider, and toast was dipped in this. Everyone drank and sang:

Old apple tree, old apple tree,
We are come to wassail the tree.
Hoping thou wilt bear well, bear well
'Atfuls,
Capfuls
And a little heap under the stairs.

Then a piece of sodden toast was left in the fork of the tree for the robin.

After 1840, a number of houses, both large and small, were built in Alcombe. These included Dunster Lodge, the home of Attorney Watkins and later of Mr Blofield whose son D'Arcy bred polo ponies and hunters. Another solicitor, Mr Webbe Incledon, built The Dene. At one time a Mrs Hancock lived at Alcombe Lodge and on occasion provided a tea for the village children. Some people remember a sign on the high wall near the stables warning that man-traps and spring guns were set in the garden, surely a necessary deterrent for anyone prepared to climb the very high walls. Alcombe Hall was at one time a guest house surrounded by iron railings with croquet lawns for the guests on the opposite side of the road. Smaller houses had been built in Manor Road and these included, of course, the cottages in Grove Place.

In 1901, the Britannia flourished as a rather dubious public house. On the day of Dunster Fatstock Show it opened very early and at seven in the morning cattle waited in the street outside while their drivers, from Porlock, Luccombe and Bossington, revived themselves inside before setting off again down Pig Street towards Dunster. The Red Lion was then open opposite the church in Church Street and its landlord, 'Pious' John Langdon, was also a wheelwright with a forge in Marsh Road. There was a well-established bakery near the forge, Mrs Jeboult kept a grocery and drapery and Charles Upham ran the Post Office next to the Britannia.

Several schools existed in Alcombe at different times. Once schooling became compulsory, Alcombe children could attend the new National School at Dunster. Many parents, however, preferred to send their children to Mr Hewitt's School in Combeland Road where his wife and daughter taught. Alcombe High School, a boys' private boarding school, was run by Mr Edward Western in the Old School House across the Britannia yard. The boys' ponies were kept in stables opposite. The large upstairs room had a stage for concerts and until quite recently a recipe for making ink was pasted inside a cupboard door in this room.

Although Alcombe was in the ecclesiastical parish of Dunster, in 1916 it came under the

Minehead Hobby Horse outside the Britannia Inn, c.1932.

All hands to the harvest at Ellicombe.

Members of the Hagley and Henson families pose in the gardens of Alcombe Hall Guesthouse during a family reunion. Left to right, back row: Annie and Charlie Hagley (of Combe Farm, Withycombe), Dorcas (d. of Charles), Charles Hagley of Grenada, Daniel Hagley, ? vicar of Raglan, Tom (s. of Charles); seated: Georgiana (d. of Charles), Mary Hagley (sister of Charles and Daniel), Mary Hagley née Henson, Christian Evans née Hagley (sister of Charles and Daniel) holding a young Henson, Dora (d. of Charles), William (son of Daniel), Christiana's daughter; on the ground: Charles (s. of Charles, only partially seen), Willie (s. of Charles) at school in Somerset, Dan (s. of Charles).

VE Day at Alcombe.

The Smithy at the top of Marsh Street (now Marshfield Road), Alcombe, c.1890.

Sheep-dipping in the mill pond at the foot of Staunton Lane, Alcombe.

authority of Minehead Urban District Council. During the 1920s and '30s rows of houses began to be built between Alcombe and Minehead to accommodate the growing population. Many people at this time took in summer visitors who would stay for a week or fortnight, enjoying full board. The passing bed and breakfast trade only developed after 1945 with the popularisation of the motor car enabling people to move on easily to another place.

In 1925, Minehead Urban District Council took over Alcombe Hill Common and Alcombe Marsh under the Commons Act of 1899. These commons dated from at least the medieval period when cottagers would have had the right to graze animals and cut fuel there. By the nineteenth century, people were already questioning claims to common rights in Alcombe, particularly the right to burn (or swale) the common. Some old people in 1972 remembered this practice and also that of collecting the stubs later on for firing. Unfortunately the practice of burning was later abused by local lads and the Council was forced to take the matter to court.

It had been customary for the lord of the manor and other landowners to walk the boundaries of Alcombe each year and this included walking down the centre of the stream which runs through the combe. The lordship of the manor had remained in the Escott family, by now the Sweet-Escotts, but as they no longer lived in Alcombe they used to exchange certain rights with the Luttrells. Then in 1925, the lordship was sold to Mr Blofield of Dunster Lodge who in 1934 sold it to Mr McArthur at Combe End who finally disposed of it in 1952 to the Urban District Council.

As Alcombe grew, so did the movement towards the extension of Alcombe Church. On Tuesday 2 February 1937, in a period of national and international depression and gloom, the Bishop of Bath and Wells, the Rt Revd St John Basil Wynne Willson, dedicated the new chancel and Lady Chapel. Villagers had worked to raise the cost of the chancel, and the Lady Chapel was given by Lt-Col W. Hartley Maud of Periton Mead in memory of his wife. The extension was built of stone from Alcombe Quarry, given by Mr Luttrell, as that for the main part of the church had been. A permanent link with the mother church at Dunster was made by the use of a medieval stone doorway from the parish churchyard and a fragment of carved stonework representing a saint or bishop, both of which were built into the new porch.

Alcombe's population continued to grow and on 27 July 1953 the new ecclesiastical parish of St Michael the Archangel, Alcombe, was established, thus ensuring that the village retained its identity and independence.

FELLING THE BIG TREE IN THE GARDEN OF ALCOMBE HALL AT THE FOOT OF BROOK STREET, 1926

Queen Victoria's Diamond Jubilee

Top: *An unidentified event put on as part of the celebrations for the Diamond Jubilee.*

Above: *Celebrating the Diamond Jubilee of Queen Victoria at Periton, 1897.*

Right: *Queen Victoria's Diamond Jubilee Memorial Fountain designed by W.J. Tamlyn. Unveiled at the bottom of the Avenue in December 1897, this Doulting stone structure was welcomed as 'a decided ornament to that part of the town'. It was removed in about 1935 as part of a road-widening programme.*

Chapter 16
Search for Identity: The Twentieth Century

The twentieth century saw tremendous changes take place in Minehead but these generally followed a pattern similar to those found in many other small seaside towns. Motor transport revolutionised travel bringing Minehead and Exmoor relatively closer to the centres of population that provided the town's summer wealth. Building continued rapidly, only interrupted by the Second World War and its aftermath, and houses soon covered the valley floor, meeting Alcombe creeping towards her from the east. In the 1980s and '90s new estates of houses were built out towards Middlecombe and, in the other direction, towards the marshes and Dunster.

The type of visitor changed. At the beginning of the century Minehead was largely a family holiday centre, catering mainly for the middle-class family who arrived by train, took rooms in one of the many new boarding houses and enjoyed the sea and countryside, making expeditions by carriage or rail. There was, too, an element of the aristocracy and intelligentsia that visited the town regularly, staying in luxury hotels such as the Metropole. Sporting holidays were also popular. Often people brought their horses with them by rail or alternatively hired them at one of several livery stables in the town.

From about 1912 motor charabancs and omnibuses began to replace horse-drawn vehicles and by the 1930s bicycling enjoyed a vogue. Many of the larger properties built as private houses were turned into hotels. Visitors now came to Minehead by rail, lodgings would be taken for a fortnight and the town served as a base for expeditions and exploration. After the Second World War the motor car became cheaper and touring superseded the fixed holiday. Accommodation changed to cater for the passing holiday maker requiring only a night or two's lodging before hurrying on to the next port of call. Gradually Minehead's holiday image altered. In 1962 Butlin's Holiday Camp was built on the marshes. Regarded by some as the saviour of the town, the natural successor of the family boarding house, others saw it as symbolic of a complete reversal of all that Minehead once stood for. Once exclusive, quiet, trading on its natural advantages of coast and moorland,

Plume of Feathers Hotel, c.1910.

Facilities for the Well-Heeled Traveller

HOTEL METROPOLE
MINEHEAD
The most popular CENTRE for HUNTING with the DEVON and SOMERSET STAGHOUNDS and several local Foxhounds and Harriers

GRASS & HARD TENNIS COURTS CROQUET LAWN
18 hole GOLF COURSE WITHIN A FEW MINUTES WALK

Suites facing Sea :: Rooms with Private Bathrooms
Running Water in Bedrooms :: Central Heating
Lift :: Orchestra during Season and at Easter
Dancing :: Garage adjoining for 200 Cars

Special Terms to Visitors during Winter months

Fuller particulars on application to H. HEARSEY WARD, Manager

Telegrams: "METROPOLE, MINEHEAD." Telephone: MINEHEAD 511 (2 lines)

Above: *The Blair Hotel, c.1925, built as a private house in 1884, is now Minehead First School*

Right: *The Brinnington Hotel, c.1950, is now Westerley, a Methodist Retirement Home.*

Bottom right: *The Carlton Private Hotel, c.1925 was built as Greenbank Villa in 1870.*

OUR REPAIR SERVICE
We are skilled Shoe Repairers besides being Shoe Sellers. Carefully repaired, your shoes will give you longer service and sustained comfort. Our prices are reasonable, and every job is attended to with quickness and care.

J. Ridler & Son, Ltd.
14 - 16 Park Street · MINEHEAD
Phone 90

We Stock MASCOTS for Ladies

CARLTON HOTEL

Telephone 60

Proprietor—W. P. GREENMAN

BLENHEIM ROAD, MINEHEAD

CENTRALLY and very pleasantly situated, facing South. Overlooking Winter Gardens. Three minutes from Sea, Station and Tennis Courts. On level. Baths (h. & c.). Sanitation Perfect. Electric Light throughout. Excellent Cuisine. Separate Tables. Every Comfort. Smoking Room. Lounge. Garage. Home Produce.

Note :—Special Winter Terms. Terms Moderate.

Minehead perhaps had to change if she were to become viable as a resort in the last quarter of the twentieth century. Smaller towns and villages have now taken over from Minehead as centres for exploring Exmoor National Park and cater for the walker, rider, and nature lover in a way that Minehead has chosen not to do.

The Urban District Council, first elected in 1894 under the chairmanship of Mr Thomas Ponsford, began rapidly to make improvements and develop the town so that it might be in a better position to compete with other nearby resorts. By 1900 a sea wall and promenade had been built and tennis courts, a band-stand and a stage and seating for summer entertainments were soon provided. One problem met by the Council was that they had no control over the sands of Minehead since their original boundary had been drawn on the high water mark, leaving the land to the seaward side within the parish of Minehead Without and thus the Williton Rural District. This denied them any control over bathing, boating and similar activities and was one of the reasons behind an application to extend the Urban District's boundaries. The application was not opposed and from 1916 land below the high water mark was included in the District together with the village of Alcombe.

The vision of many of the councillors who have served the town of Minehead has never really been fulfilled. Hindered by two wars, by economic depression and by inflation, the development of the town into the ideal holiday paradise envisaged in the early years of the century has been prevented largely by lack of money. In 1950 Thomas Sharp was invited to submit plans to improve Minehead and particularly the sea front in order to attract more visitors. His visionary ideas sunk without trace, the Council preferring to travel forward with Billy Butlin. In 1973, under the new Local Government Act, Minehead and Alcombe were absorbed into the West Somerset District and their identities have to some extent been absorbed as part of this larger unit. Minehead Town Council, restored recently, has views but few teeth. Watchdog organisation, the Minehead Residents' Association, apparently concerned mainly with conservation, has a tendency to be reactive rather than proactive.

Elections for the first Urban District Councils were fought vehemently. Handbills and circulars deluged the town, damning opponents and eulogising favoured candidates. Frequently the publicity was set out in racing idiom with tips to encourage the laggardly backer. Hustings were well attended, no matters minced and the rash or careless word was seized on and chewed and tossed about like a bone. The whole town joined enthusiastically in the fun. A 'programme' from the 1918 election has survived (*see below*). Such cynicism and punning might well be wasted today though the 'pathetic rendering' by the Grand Choir of Ratepayers is surely a perennial theme. To help the uninitiated; in 1918 Alcombe had recently become part of the Urban District; Harry Chidgey kept the Plume of Feathers; Mr Halliday owned a large antiques business, while Mr Kinnersley and Mr Summers were clearly retiring councillors. The rest can be left to the imagination.

The Luttrell family continued to foster the development of Minehead in whatever ways they could. The Urban District Council allowed opportunities to acquire the eastern part of the sea front to pass, and in the 1930s Mr Geoffrey Luttrell, realising its great potential, made plans to develop it. Sadly, most of his schemes did not materialise although a fine swimming pool was built and opened in 1936 for international swimming trials.

The previous year had seen a great furore in the national press concerning bathing at Minehead. Somerset County Council had undertaken a revision of by-laws and had resurrected one made by the Williton Board in the 1890s which stated that, in Minehead, no person over ten years should bathe except from 'a bathing machine, tent or other effectual screen.' Since in the rest of Somerset bathers were only asked to wear a costume, Minehead regarded this as a deliberate slight implying that indecent

MINEHEAD.

A Grand Entertainment

will be held, on MONDAY next, April 7th, in the

EXMOOR HUT 1918

Specially sent over for this purpose by express aeroplane.

The Proceeds will be applied to a Fund for establishing

PALACES FOR POOR PEOPLE.
CUSHY COTTAGES FOR COOPED-UP COMRADES.
WINTER GARDENS FOR SUPERANNUATED COUNCILLORS.
SECONDARY SCHOOL FOR EDUCATING CANDIDATES.
SIDEWALKS FOR SORE-FOOTED SUBURBANITES.
BATH-HOUSES FOR BEAUTIFYING TIRED TOILERS.
ALMSHOUSES FOR RUINED RATEPAYERS.

Opening Chorus ...	Now, are we all here? ...	Yes! All the CANDIDATES
Song ...	There's always room for a girl ...	Miss PARRY
Selections from ...	The Passing Show	RETIRING COUNCILLORS
Song ...	Where my Caravan has rested	... Mr. J. E. VEYSEY
Sacred Solo ...	Come, everyone that thirsteth	... Mr. H CHIDGEY
Song ...	Then you'll remember Me	Mr. JAMES WEBBER
Selection ...	The Old Curiosity Shop	Mr. F. G HALLIDAY
Song ...	Playing the Game in the West ...	Mr. J. NEWTON
Recital ...	If I were King	Mr. JAMES BURGESS
Song ...	The Benches in the Park ...	Mr. W. WILKINS
Sacred Item ...	Entreat me not to leave thee	Mr. G. KINNERSLEY
Concerted Item	Boys of the Old Brigade	Messrs. DERRICK, HILL & JOHN BURGESS
Song ...	Drink to me only	...Mr. J. F. ETHERDEN
Solo ...	The Sewer went forth Sewing	...Mr. G. DAVEY
Song ...	Let the Great Big World keep Moving	Mr. A. H. ANDREW
Quartette ...	Let 'em Alcombe	Messrs. HITCHCOCK, HINE, MASON & QUANTICK
Song ...	Good-bye. Summer, Good-bye. Good-by-ee	Mr. W. S. SUMMERS
Pianoforte Solo	Melody in "A" Flat	Mr C. W. RICHARDSON
Song ...	I dreamt I dwelt in Marble 'alls	Mr J. H. PIDGEON
Recitation ...	If you don't want the goods, don't muck 'em abaht	Mr. W. H. CHANIN
Song ...	Keep a little Corner in your Heart for Me	Mr. T. YANDLE
Song ...	The Jolly Waggoner ...	Mr. T. LOVELL
Disconcerted Piece	All dressed up and no-where to go	UNSUCCESSFUL CANDIDATES

The Programme will conclude with a pathetic rendering by a Grand Choir of Ratepayers of the Sacred Chant, "Lord, how are they increased that trouble me."

Man, thy name is Dust: Along comes the sprinkling cart of Fate
And, lo, thy name is M.U.D.C.

The Sea Front

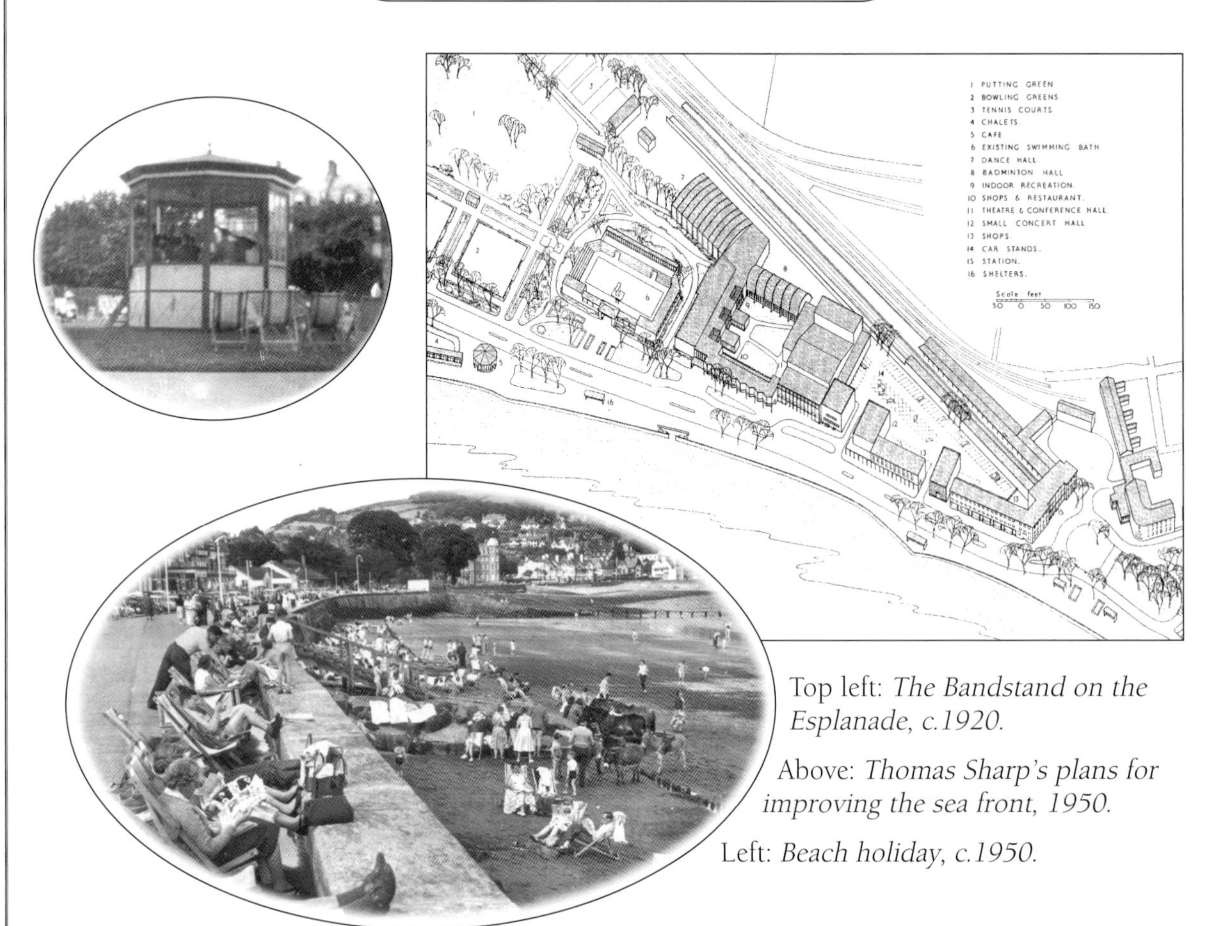

Top left: *The Bandstand on the Esplanade, c.1920.*

Above: *Thomas Sharp's plans for improving the sea front, 1950.*

Left: *Beach holiday, c.1950.*

Right: *Until the 1950s the eastern end of the harbour belonged to the Luttrell family who made a charge for parking. Payment was collected at this toll-gate.*

Below: *An advertisement for the new swimming pool from Minehead Publicity Association's Official Guide.*

Left and above: *The new pool was used for international competitions. Water was pumped from the sea to fill the pool. Bob Light (right) and Arthur Bull in the filter room.*

bathing was the practice in the town. National papers charged Minehead with the title 'Home of Mrs Grundy' and the town feared the damaging effect that this might have on holiday-makers seeking freedom at a modern resort. Fortunately an appeal to the Home Office led to the quashing of this particular by-law, and the magnificent new swimming pool must have helped undo any damage. It was later taken over and run by a group of local businessmen until eventually purchased by Butlin's and demolished.

Long before this the western end of the sea front towards the harbour had been opened up. The storms of 1910 had damaged the properties near Lamb Cottage and later houses in Quay Street which had to be pulled down because of road widening. After 1918 the sea wall and promenade was continued to meet the harbour. Another scheme that added to the amenities of the town was the laying-out of Blenheim Gardens which were opened in 1925. Until the 1970s the huge elms on their bank marked the old field boundaries of the North Field and the breath-taking flower beds still contribute to Minehead's continuing success in the 'Britain in Bloom' contests. The Parks Walk laid out at the end of the 1920s was one of the areas planned specifically to provide 'health, quietness and rest' for the intending resident. These projects are typical of the attitude of the Town Council in the twenties which could see, if it were not careful, the essence of Minehead disappearing with the noise and traffic which came with the town's growth.

We have already seen how improved means of transport helped the town by bringing greater numbers of visitors to Minehead. The railway continued to be the most popular means of reaching the area until the 1950s when it was overtaken by motor buses and, a little later, motor cars. It was forty or so years earlier in 1908 that the first motor bus appeared on the roads near Minehead, causing so much anger and consternation that a petition was drawn up by many of the leading residents of Alcombe and Minehead. The coach was making excursions to 'Dunkery Hill Gate, Winsford, Cloutsham, the Doone Valley and Lynton,' and must have had an intrepid driver and valiant passengers since the narrow roads to these places can have been little more than stony tracks at the time. The petitioners complained that the coach bore 'a striking resemblance to a Hay Elevator' and was likely to cause accidents such as had already occurred. They went on to state that the neighbourhood was well supplied with horses and carriages and that a large number of people earned their livelihood from them, so that the coach was neither necessary nor suitable. What became of the petition we do not know but it is hard not to think that some petitioners, at least, were conscious of the threat the motor vehicle posed to the old order. The charabanc was to become a popular form of holiday transport and by 1920 the long-established four-horse coach service between Lynmouth and Minehead (*see page 110*) had been finally ousted by the motor coach.

By 1910 most carriage works were offering garage services in addition and several new garages had sprung up, Capron and Sons' Motor and Cycle Depot being the pioneer in 1908. The first private motor car to appear in Minehead is said to have been a 10hp Gobron Brille belonging to a gentleman, Mr Clarence Gregson, who was staying at the Plume of Feathers. It caused intense excitement, particularly when the chauffeur was allowed to give rides up and down the length of the Parade. Earlier in October 1897 Mr Carver, agent for the Horseless Carriage Co. Ltd of London, demonstrated a petrol-driven motor tricycle in the town which, at 150 guineas, caused much interest.

Top: *A fancy-dress parade in Blenheim Gardens, c.1936.*
Centre: *John Burgess speaking at opening of the Gardens (Minehead Winter Gardens), April 1925*
Bottom: *Publicity picture for Western National Buses in the early 1950s.*

Minehead Harbour showing the working tackle, sea-legs and rail track used for unloading cargoes. On the right is the Perriton *built in Minehead for Thomas Kent Ridler and on the left are the Ridlers'* John and William *and the* Argo (see also page 56).

Ketches in Minehead Harbour, c.1900. Such vessels continued to bring in coal to local ports until 1950. Visible in the background are the harbour warehouses and storage cellars.

Little has been said of the harbour at Minehead since 1800 and, regretfully, this reflects its declining influence in the town. James Savage, writing in the *Hundred of Carhampton* in 1830, noted that the port's former trade had been lost:

> *... there are at present only Five or six vessels belonging to the port, two of which are employed in the Bristol Channel trade, to which place they carry grain, malt, bark, timber, flour and some leather, landing back with groceries, iron etc; the others trade to Wales and carry thither flour, malt and timber; their return cargoes being coals, culm or limestones. Herrings are still Fished but erratically.*

This rapid decline led in 1834 to the diminution of the status of Minehead, the limits of the Port of Bridgwater being extended to cover Minehead's former jurisdiction. Eight or ten smacks continued to ply the Bristol Channel until the early 1900s when these, too, began to disappear. The largest vessel of this period was the French-built schooner, *Flying Foam*, belonging to Edward Perkins of Porlock. Thomas Kent Ridler, the grandson of John Ridler who developed a trading business in the town, owned the *Perriton*, the last working ship to be built in Minehead, together with the *Looe*, built in Cornwall in 1787, the *John and William*, built in *Porlock*, the *Susannah* and the *Orestes* which continued to bring coal to Minehead until 1935 when Ridler's business was given up. The *Perriton*, named after the hamlet where the Ridlers lived from 1844, was built, not on the yard to the west of the harbour where earlier ships like the *Endeavour* had taken shape, but at the head of the beach near Blenheim Road by Benjamin Williams of Watchet in 1881. After the Second World War only Captain Philip Rawle's 56-ton ketch, the *Emma Louise*, was left running as a collier and manoeuvering a new hazard, a large shingle bank which was gradually accumulating at the mouth of the harbour. This became so dangerous to shipping that in 1947 the harbour was officially closed, but in 1951 the shingle was removed and on 2 June of that year the harbour was handed over to the Urban District Council by Mr Luttrell in return for a peppercorn rent. From that time the harbour has been used fully, particularly during the holiday season. Steamers call occasionally but they are again limited by the tide since the pier from which passengers used to embark was taken down at the beginning of the Second World War for military reasons. Now the harbour is filled with small sailing boats and like the rest of the town is geared to the promotion of recreation. Fishing has been carried on erratically in this century since herring (in particular) no longer appear regularly in local waters, and it is now largely an amateur activity.

A lifeboat station was opened in Minehead in 1901 to provide for the gap in services shown up by the epic Forrest Hall incident when the Lynmouth lifeboat was manhandled to Porlock Weir because the weather prevented it being launched from its own beach. A motor boat succeeded sailing and pulling boats in 1939 and - to cope with the new situation of pleasure boat and bathing incidents - two inshore rescue boats have now replaced the conventional boat.

Main picture: *The Lifeboat being brought up through Blenheim Road on Lifeboat Day.*
Inset: *The launch of the lifeboat by tractor. In the background are the Gas Works.*

Minehead Hospital

Above: *Minehead Hospital was built between 1889 and 1892 as the Town Hall where exhibitions and concerts were held. It later became known as Bank House, part of the premises being occupied by Lloyd's Bank. In 1914 the building became the Minehead Auxiliary Red Cross Hospital where VADs, trained locally since 1908, nursed convalescent soldiers. They were helped by the 1st Minehead troop of Boy Scouts.*

Above right: *VADs training at Porlock.*

Above: *Patients being taken on stretchers to the train from the improvised hospital at Blue Anchor, c.1919.*

Left: *When war broke out mules were sent to be trained on North Hill by detachments of the West Somerset Light Infantry who held regular camps in the area (see* The Book of Porlock*). Injuries to soldiers led to the establishment of a nursing centre in Blenheim Road.*

Right: *Red Cross VADs at the beginning of the First World War. Left to right, back row: Miss Dorothea Shaw, Miss Hawkins, Mrs Palfield, ? Chard, Miss Southey, ?, Miss Stoate, Miss Everard, Miss Audrey, Miss Dorothea Rogers; front: Sister Hull, ?, Sister Alice Smith, Mrs B.D. Dawson Thomas (commandant), Dr Hamilton Ollerenshaw, Miss Forbes, Miss Laura Brameld.*

The Minehead and West Somerset Hospital (Luttrell Memorial) was opened in 1920 in the building which had been erected as a Town Hall in 1889 by Thomas Ponsford. Until 1920 Minehead had been served by the Dunster and Minehead Village Hospital which had been opened in Dunster in 1867. The Town Hall was used as a Red Cross Hospital from 1914 to 1918 and, with the rapid growth of Minehead, it was clearly wise to continue this use in the larger and more central building. The Police Station at the rear was purchased later and, together with extensions and the provision of modern equipment, the hospital has largely overcome the natural disadvantages of the building. The Friends of Minehead Hospital have been invaluable in fund-raising for improvements to the hospital.

The new Police Station and Court in Townsend Road were opened in 1936 to replace the former outdated buildings at Dunster. The Fire Station at the beginning of the century was in Market House Lane. For a long time the obsolete horse-drawn, pump-handled engine stood behind the Tanyard railings at the top of the Avenue. It had been replaced by a horse-drawn engine that was used until after the First World War. The horses were kept nearby in the stables of the Plume of Feathers yet harnessing up the machine could be a lengthy business. Two cottages in Staunton were burnt to the ground because it took so long for the engine to arrive, and when the scenery at the Queen's Hall caught fire one night, the first fire-fighting equipment to arrive was the hand-truck and hose-pipe pushed by Archie Burgess! In 1925 when the Hopcott House Hotel (*below*) caught fire the hose-cart was hurried to the scene while the engine itself was delayed for a while since it proved difficult to start up the motor that was to tow it. The hotel was burnt to the ground.

Many older people look back nostalgically to events such as the Minehead Carnival that took place annually on 5 November and became notorious for the wild and unruly behaviour that often occurred. For years before 1889 the mob had run riot through

An alternative St George's Day during the First World War.

the streets, accompanying effigies for burning and frequently rolling blazing tar barrels. Surprisingly, the magistrates were generally very tolerant with the offenders brought before them and it was the police who bore the brunt of the crowd's opposition. In 1888 the effigy of an unpopular police sergeant was carried through the town followed by a coffin for the ceremonial burial. The next year police reinforcements were brought in and in the confusion one man was killed by a blow from a truncheon. This had a relatively sobering effect and future carnivals were kept under stricter control. In 1894 a committee arranged for a bonfire to be lit in Ball Park (a field lent by George Thristle, the landlord of the Plume of Feathers and now under the new houses at the top of West Street) after the carnival procession had passed through the streets. Householders en route were invited to illuminate their windows and the Parade was described as a blaze of light. Sadly, this carnival was marred by the refusal of the Minehead Town Band to play as they had in previous years unless they were paid £1. This was refused and so musicians from Exton accompanied the proceedings. Apparently on an earlier occasion the Town Band had been promised free refreshments which had all been consumed by the time they reached the spot and although they managed to obtain a drink they were later sent a bill for it for 1s.3d. The teetotal members of the band had done better than the others because there was more mineral water left at the end than beer! Quite naturally the band demanded their rights and for 1894, at any rate, withdrew their services.

There was entertainment to suit all tastes during the 1920s and '30s - drama, ballet, concerts, pierrots and even elephants!

Only in 1909 does there seem to have been a return to the wild days of the 1800s. In that year the carnival was marked by fireworks battle in Wellington Square. A Bilbrook carpenter, Thomas Besley, lost the sight of an eye and was later awarded £600 damages. In evidence, the jury was told of decorated cars being set alight, the band being silenced because of the damage to their instruments and the carnival secretary being so badly burned on the leg that he was on the sick list for a fortnight. Fortunately that night was exceptional and Minehead carnivals continued in a more orderly manner for many years, eventually amalgamating with the Alcombe carnival.

Another regular event was - and still is - the appearance of the hobby horse on May morning (*see page 11*). Savage in the *Hundred of Carhampton* described the horse and its antics and spoke of the custom as having 'prevailed for ages'. Yet this is the earliest reference to the horse so far discovered, and so we can only accept the traditional view that the custom is ancient. As this is the case, the origin of the hobby horse can only be guessed at. Almost certainly it is a genuine survival of ancient fertility rites, its appearance on May morning in conjunction with maypole dancers in earlier years making this the most probable explanation. The horse may also have been used in some form of beating the bounds, perhaps a later development to which the customary visits to Whitecross, Cher and Periton give some credence. Yet a third possibility is that the horse dates from the time of the Danish invasions and symbolises local resistance. Whatever its origin, the hobby horse with its brightly-decorated hessian wrapped over a wooden frame, its central head under a high, be-ribboned conical hat and grotesque mask, has danced throughout the last 200 years. About 1905 a second horse was introduced and became known as the Town Horse, as opposed to the older Sailors' Horse stabled at the quay. Today there are at least two horses and a certain element of competition is a regular part of the proceedings. The horse continues to fascinate, drawing crowds of spectators, particularly children who follow the monotonous music of drum and accordion as if it were the piping of the Pied Piper, yet admitting always to deep-rooted fear of the beast.

Seaside entertainments in the 1930s provided many memorable occasions. Evelyn Hardy and her Ladies' Band played regularly in the old Bandstand sited where the Jubilee Tea Rooms are now. The Pierrots had a permanent position on the site of the Gaiety Theatre (*above*), with a covered stage and open seating facing towards the railway. The Races that had been such a feature towards the end of the century had been abandoned by 1898. Begun in 1865, they soon drew crowds who came by steamer and later rail for the six-race meeting including the Hunters' Stakes of twenty sovereigns, over hurdles. There was a Ladies' Plate and also a pony race. All along the Promenade eastward from the railway station were booths and amusements. Boxing bouts, roulette and shooting galleries were popular and there were plenty of bookies and 'wide boys', including two men who sold lucky number tickets at one penny each and had a monkey to pull the lucky number from a box. In 1914 the Queen's Hall and the Strand Hotel were built. The Queen's Hall, used regularly after the war, provided a high standard of entertainment and was popular and well-attended. Repertory companies, sometimes from London theatres, would play in Minehead for three days at a time so that there was a constant change of programme. Stars of their day who performed at Minehead included Anna Pavlova, the Russian ballerina, Gladys Cooper in Somerset Maugham's *The Letter* and Sir Johnston Forbes-Robertson and Lady Patrick Campbell in the comedy, *At Mrs Beam's*.

The first cinema was a wooden building on the site of the Model Village but the Cosy Cinema in Bancks Street soon replaced it. The end of the old projection room could, until recently, be seen protruding from Henry Wood's Second-hand Emporium. The Regal Cinema was built in 1934 on the site of the Tanyard. After it closed in the 1980s local people worked hard to revitalise the cinema which is now a well-presented venue for plays, concerts - both professional and amateur - as well as films.

Not all entertainment was laid on. By 1910 there was an abundance of clubs and societies, many long-established and catering for every interest. Musically, besides the Town Band, there was an Orchestral Society, a Choral Society and the Minehead Apollo Male Voice Choir. Sports featured largely: golf, cricket, hockey, tennis, football, athletics and, of course, polo, all being provided for. The Minehead and West Somerset Golf Club was founded when golf was still young in England, in 1882. The course was first laid out as a nine-hole course, but by the end of the century it had been extended to eighteen holes. Flooding has always been a hazard to the course and in 1910 it was estimated that 6000 tons of shingle were deposited by the sea at the last hole. An early writer described the course as 'thoroughly delightful and entertaining... the holes call for interesting and accurate shots' and the Spring Meeting, begun in 1891, soon became a popular annual event.

Minehead Cricket Club was founded in 1867 and enjoyed its heyday in the 1890s when it employed a professional and was able to call on many skilled players, both local and those visiting the town. The Football Club, on the other hand, founded in 1889, began the most impressive part of its history when it signed its first professional, player-manager Steve Walker, in 1949. It then progressed through the Western League to the First Division of the Southern League and won decisively in 1976. The Recreation Ground that accommodated many clubs in the early part of the century was founded by a private

Pony races on the beach at Minehead.

Minehead and West Somerset Golf Club

Right: *Members at the formal opening of the first purpose-built clubhouse in 1894.*

Left: *The Minehead and West Somerset Golf Club was a boon to local business. These advertisements come from an edition of the Club's Official Handbook of January 1956.*

Above: *Watercolour by Harry Frier, a Taunton artist. The cottage in the foreground was demolished in 1978.*

Right: *Another painting by the same artist. The club building had been extended by this time (1909) but North Hill remained virtually undeveloped.*

West Somerset Polo Club

Right: *Practice in February on the beach.*

Below: *International and ex-international players moving at full gallop.* (Photos by R. Kingsley Taylor)

Below right: *Advertisement from an early West Somerset Polo Club brochure.*

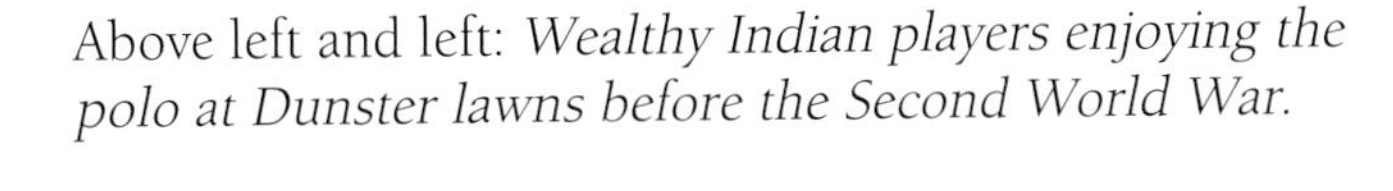

Above left and left: *Wealthy Indian players enjoying the polo at Dunster lawns before the Second World War.*

Right: *North Road before the Metropole Garage was built and the polo ponies out for exercise.*

Minehead Football Club, 1900–07. Left to right, back: P.J. Staddon, E.W. Parker, A. Willis, W. Thresher; centre: P.C. Morris, S.J. Floyd, T.W. Lovelace, N. Upham, A. Burgess; front: F.W. Chidgey, F.N. Webber.

Runners-up in the Western League, May 1967.
Left to right, back row: J. Castle (Hon. Treas.), L. K. Axon (Hon. Sec.), A. Venn-Fielden (President), M. Clausen, M. May, T. Holehouse, T. Clausen, M. Madge, F. J. Jacobs, A. C. Milton, D. Holecombe (Chairman), J. Artus (Trainer); front: A. Stone, C. Jacobs, T. Smith, A. Williams, R. Smale, J. Morgan.

company and later bought by the Council. Later sports clubs included the Bowling Club founded soon after the First World War - a game with a tradition in Minehead dating back to the seventeenth century when there was a green under Culver Cliff.

The most spectacular and vivid memories have perhaps been left by the West Somerset Polo Club, founded in 1898 through the encouragement of Dr T. H. Ollerhead. The club played first on the sands at Minehead, moving to New Bridge in 1904 and eventually to Dunster Lawns in 1910. At first there were several local players but by the 1930s the number had diminished and only the co-operation of Mr Luttrell in forming a proprietary club ensured the game's continuance until the war.

Then the Lawns were put under the plough and the club's equipment auctioned in front of the pavilion presented by the Maharajah of Jodhpur in 1925. Players from the United States, the Argentine and, indeed, crack players from this country, all competed at Dunster, but it was the colourful Indian teams that caught the imagination. The Indian princes stayed at the Castle whilst lesser mortals and grooms were accommodated at the Metropole Hotel, where ample stabling was available for strings of sleek polo ponies exercised each morning on the beach by turbaned Sikhs. This was the zenith of Minehead's career as a holiday resort.

THE WEST SOMERSET FREE PRESS

MINEHEAD TOWN BAND OVER 40 YEARS AGO

This photograph of the Minehead Town Band in the early 1920's was taken in a field adjoining Burford's Bakery at Alcombe, and all but one have been identified to us as the following, reading from left to right:—

Back row—Walt. Knight, Billy House, Ern. David, Sid. Webber.

Middle row—Jack Vinnicombe, Douglas Bryant, Ted Higgins, Harry Snell, Ivor Dyer, ——, Len. Hunt, Martin Axon.

Front row—Bob Upham, Harry Dyer, Fred Hurford, Ralph Prole, Jack Pugsley (Bandmaster), Harry Coles, Bill Parsons, and W. Potter.

The bass drum shown in the front is still in use by the Town Silver Band.

Top: *From the* West Somerset Free Press, *June 1967.*

Centre: *In the background is Bampton Street's own Regal Cinema. The projectionist at the town cinema, Mr Francis Purnell, organised films at the weekend in his back garden. Seats were primitive but prices were low - 1d. or 2d. Both children and adults enjoyed the shows.*

Left to right: Violet Land, Iris Down, Valerie Milton, Brenda Fry, Joyce Bindon, Francis Orr.

Above: *Cricket during the war. On the left is Roy Chenappa who accompanied pupils from West Ham to Minehead. Second from right, middle row, is Tom Bryant.*

Chapter 17
After the Millennium

During May 2002 the rotunda on Minehead sea front was transformed into an analemmatic sundial which had been commissioned by the West Somerset District Council's Jubilee Committee, headed by Steven Pugsley, to mark the occasion of Queen Elizabeth II's Golden Jubilee. The dial was opened on Tuesday 28 May by the Chairman of the Council, Geoff Day, in the presence of the Mayor of Minehead, Meigan Lyons, councillors and children from Townsend Road School.

An analemmatic sundial is laid out on the ground and a person stands in the centre and casts a shadow which tells the time by the hour points around the edge of the circle. David Brown, once Head of Physics at Minehead School, designed the dial which features the Jubilee logo, a facsimile of part of the Queen's message on the 50th anniversary of her accession as well as the emblems of West Somerset's four towns and, encircling the central quadrant, the names of all 42 parishes in the District. David carved the dial in hard-wearing York stone and Rod Shoulders of the West Somerset Garden Centre helped him to install it. Rod did most of the paving while David cut stones to fit and, in true Jubilee fashion, it rained most of the time!

The sundial was one of the features of the rebuilt wider promenade. The coastal areas of Minehead have always suffered from flooding at exceptionally high tides and in the late 1990s a scheme to improve the town's sea defences was put in hand. The Environment Agency, the West Somerset District Council, Butlins and Somerset County Council were all involved and by 2001 new, higher sea walls, rock armouring and a replenished sandy beach had been completed at a cost of around £14.5 million. Unfortunately, over the years, the sand has shifted around with the passage of the tides and the littoral drift, to make neighbouring beaches sandier! The promenade was landscaped with new street lighting, seating and 'bucket and spade' bollard features as well as the sundial. A stone sculpture designed by College student, Sarah Ward, and constructed by Owen Cunningham (an associate of public artist, Gordon Young) marks the start of the South West Coast Path which attracts many walkers to the town.

Marker at the start of the 630-mile long South West Coast Path. (Jonathan Greenhow)

Since the Millennium, Minehead has done much to redefine itself both as a town and a holiday resort with an emphasis on community. The town has grown and population has risen to around 11,500 with, according to figures released by the Office for National Statistics in 2009 for West Somerset, the highest average age in the UK at 52, with almost three in 10 people aged over 65. This is visible in the town, with many new housing developments containing bungalows and age-friendly houses. Many people are employed in providing services for the elderly, whether it be in the numerous care homes, often adapted from the town' older properties, or visiting the elderly in their homes. Those of retirement age, perhaps with more time to spare, contribute a great deal to the numerous community enterprises which thrive in the town.

Life for young people also improves, with schools which perform well and send increasing numbers

Mariners Court on the seafront at Minehead built on the site of the Art Deco swimming pool (see p 144) *and completed in 2004.* (Elizabeth Jessup)

into higher education. In September 2008 the West Somerset Community College opened its new Skills and Enterprise Centre and College Farm which together are revolutionising vocational learning in the Exmoor area, offering courses which were formerly only available in Taunton and Bridgwater. Today post-16 students are able to study not only for traditional A levels but for qualifications in subjects such as Hospitality, Beauty Therapy, Construction and Land Based Studies.

Left: *West Somerset Community College Farm.* (Jonathan Greenhow)
Below: *Megham White, Georgina Rayson and Oliver Hill, students at the College, at Dunster Show 2011.* (Steve Guscott)

It was a sad day when the Aquasplash swimming pool closed in 2008 but there are many thriving Sports Clubs in the town - the Rugby Club and the Cricket Club, for example - which offer excellent coaching opportunities to youngsters.

Minehead Eye, a new youth and community centre was opened in August 2010 not far from the seafront. The facilities include a multi-purpose hall with skate park, a café with viewing balcony, IT suite

High in the air at Minehead Eye. (Josephine Collingwood)

for internet and WIFI access, pool table and table football. Regular music events, courses and activities take place all year round and it has become a great place for young people to hang out, get active, join in, learn and have fun!

Minehead - the Gateway to Exmoor - has been attracting holiday visitors for over 200 years and continues to do so. Walking and riding, exploring Exmoor and enjoying the seaside are timeless activities as popular as ever and many people stay in family-run accommodation, small hotels or on nearby camping and caravan sites. Butlins, with its traditional holiday camp activities and a new focus on outdoor pursuits - a dedicated archery range is being opened this year - can accommodate some 6000 people at a time. Over the last few years the town has organised a Summer Festival with air displays featuring the Red Arrows being organised by Butlins as a thank you to the people of the town for their continued support.

The West Somerset Railway continues to go from strength to strength. Run by numerous dedicated volunteers, it provides a regular steam or diesel service on the 22-mile heritage line between Minehead and Bishop's Lydeard throughout the year. Special events include steam weekends for enthusiasts and themed train journeys which range from the Hestercombe Gardens Express, the Art Train and Summer Evenings by the Seaside to Murder Mystery Specials and Carol Trains. All this has helped to increase the number of passengers carried on the line. In 2002 there were 172,457 passengers but over the last seven years more than 200,000 passengers have travelled each year with the record being 2009 when there were 226,737.

One thing that has helped to ease the running of the railway has been the installation of a turntable which was rescued from Pwllheli in North Wales and sat for many years in a siding at Minehead waiting the right opportunity for restoration. It was eventually lowered into place on 10 February 2008 and put into use later in the year.

Right: *The turntable is tested for the first time, 2008.* (Martin Snell).

Minehead Station 2012. The Friends of Minehead Station contributed to the renewal of the canopy over the platform in the background.
(Jonathan Greenhow)

Minehead Farmers' Market 2007.

The Friends of Minehead Station are another group of volunteers who raise money towards the upkeep of the station buildings and over the last ten years have contributed in the region of £200,000 towards projects which include re-roofing the canopy over the two platforms, repairs to the chimneys on the station site and replacing the gate into the locomotive yard. Funds are also used for providing flowers and maintaining the grass and wildflower areas from the seafront to the level crossing at Seaward Way.

During the last decade, Minehead, like the rest of the country, has suffered from the economic downturn and for a while closed shops and struggling businesses gave an air of seediness to the town centre. The development of supermarkets on the outskirts drew shoppers away from the centre – Somerfield had been taken over by Tesco before the millennium, but in Vulcan Road Macdonalds was lately joined by Morrisons following a public consultation which showed that people wanted more variety and competition in that area. Today in the town centre there are numerous charity shops and although the town lost its much loved ironmongers, Tarr & Foy, a farmers' market now takes place every Friday in the Parade, the independent greengrocer, Jones, thrives as does Toucan Wholefoods who in 2012 are celebrating 30 years of trading. Old established stores are being refurbished and a number of vibrant new independent shops and businesses have been opened up by a new generation of local people, often younger, with adventure in their hearts. Taking the town all in all you can obtain practically everything that you need, whether you choose to use the supermarkets or the locally-run small specialist shops and businesses.

Several local pubs have also been revamped (and, in some cases, re-named), the most significant being, perhaps, the regenerated Hobby Horse Inn, located in part of the old Metropole Hotel. The Metropole was built originally in 1893 as the Esplanade Hotel but was soon sold on and refurbished becoming the most fashionable and exclusive hotel in the town during the 1920s and '30s. Times changed and in 1953 the hotel was given up, the property divided and sold and the main part converted to flats. The bar and ballroom became the heart of the Hobby Horse Inn, a popular and glamorous venue for prestigious social events but after a number of changes of ownership was eventually closed and boarded up. When Derek Merson, a local businessman, bought the property he wasn't sure what he was going to do with it but peo-

Tea Dance, the Hobby Horse Inn, 2012.

Minehead Community Hospital opened in 2011.
(Jonathan Greenhow)

Art work by College students enhanced the hoardings while the hospital was being built.

ple's memories of happy times and their enthusiasm to see the Hobby Horse Inn brought back to life led to the decision to restore it to its former glory: the elegant ballroom, with its magnificent ceiling dome and Victorian cornices, as well as the bars and Oak Room, where Balls and Dinners, Tea Dances and Wedding receptions are being held once again.

The greatest care was taken with this restoration in exactly the way that is encouraged by The Minehead Conservation Society. This Society was founded in 2003 in succession to a Conservation Group formed the year before in response to the first villa demolition on North Hill and general public concern at the threat of continuing unsympathetic development. A number of carefully researched exhibitions drew attention to the Victorian and Edwardian architecture of the town including 'The Villas of North Hill', 'Minehead between the Wars', 'Minehead Seafront' and in 2011 the traditional dancing hobby horse! There is a fine line between conservation of the environment and resisting progress but the Conservation Society has done much to promote awareness of Minehead's architectural heritage, limit unsuitable development in the town and ensure that new building blends in with the old.

One property causing concern at the moment is the former Minehead and West Somerset (Luttrell Memorial) Hospital, built between 1889 and 1892 as the Town Hall. As the buildings became increasingly inadequate for a modern hospital it was decided by the NHS that a new purpose-built community hospital was needed and this was opened in Luttrell Way, Alcombe on 14 February 2011. This brand-new hospital with its 19 inpatient and eight day surgery beds, minor injuries unit and facilities for out-patient surgeries is welcoming and spacious. Noteworthy is the art work on many of the interior walls which is the result of a project in 2009 by West Somerset Community College students led by Andy Davey, then artist-in-residence. Originally intended for the hoardings protecting the hospital building work, the paintings were so appreciated that they were adapted for permanent display inside.

Meanwhile the old redundant Hospital needs a new use. Situated at the heart of the town, this site and its listed buildings offers a unique focal point for the economic and social regeneration of the town. Community consultation has suggested strong support for saving the building as a community asset and for including the library, Visitor Information Point and a museum within the complex. Restoration of the old Assembly Rooms upstairs could provide an open space for arts events and meetings of all kinds while a café and shops might be part of an undercover venue which would be welcomed by visitors particularly in bad weather. The whole project is being led by the Minehead Development Trust, founded in June 2010, which is representative of many key organisations in the town. At the time of writing, search for funding and support is on-going.

This is a project which is community-led for the benefit of the community and there is no doubt that Minehead is a town with a strong sense of community. This year Minehead Methodist Church will hold its tenth Christmas Tree Festival in aid of Save the Children. Last year, 2011, the church was decorated with some 40 trees provided by charities and other local organisations working to help and support others. Minehead is twinned with St Berthevin in France and another anniversary took place in 2011 when the towns celebrated the twentieth anniversary of the signing of their charter which pledges 'to main-

French and English twinners on a trip to Dunster 2012. (Martin Evans)

tain permanent bonds between Minehead and St Berthevin ... with the aim of fostering, through greater mutual understanding, the true spirit of European brotherhood ... peace and prosperity.'

For the last 10 years the Regal Theatre has been striving to find the funding and planning permissions to build a lift to enable access for the whole community. In 2012 these plans are finally coming to fruition, and the theatre will close in September for building to start. When it re-opens early in 2013 there will be a modern access lift on the front of the building, reached from the new enlarged box office at street level.

Like the West Somerset Railway, the Regal Theatre has become an outstanding example of community effort and remains sustainable without any means of public funding through the efforts of over 200 volunteers. During the long struggle to improve the facilities, volunteers and local businesses have created a new bar, new accessible toilets, re-covered the 400 seats in the auditorium and improved many of the technical aspects of the theatre. It is still a work in progress, and the occasional splash on the forehead signals a roof which bears witness to its long history!

Just a few weeks ago the country marked the Queen's Diamond Jubilee. In Minehead and Alcombe and the villages round about, numerous celebratory events were held but the largest locally was surely the Street Party organised by Churches Together in Minehead. It was to be held in Blenheim Gardens but the Jubilee rain meant a move to the Methodist Church complex in the Avenue where 2000 or so people packed together in a joyful atmosphere - young and old, babes in arms and people in wheelchairs - to enjoy local entertainment and cream teas with excellent scones made by the local churches from scone mix provided by Foxes Academy, Minehead's wonderful training hotel and catering college for young people with learning disabilities. They did all the ordering for the event and also provided lunches for all the volunteers. It was a truly happy community event.

A permanent memorial of the Diamond Jubilee will be a Clock Tower which it is hoped will be in position by the end of 2012. Purposely designed by Peter Ferguson, a conservation architect born in Minehead, to complement its maritime position - it is based on the design of a Screwpile lighthouse - the tower will be located on the promenade opposite the West Somerset Railway station and will carry a four-sided display, three sides telling the time and the fourth the current tide times.

Artist's sketch of the proposed Diamond Jubilee Clock Tower by kind permission of Peter Ferguson.

So, when you visit Minehead, if the sun is out you can consult the Golden Jubilee sundial, or, if it is raining, the Diamond Jubilee clock, while remembering that 'Time and Tide wait for no man' and that the town of Minehead continues to redefine itself and to flourish.

The Jubilee Street party was enjoyed by old and young with entertainment and cream teas. Some people even utilised the hedges as makeshift tables. (Phil Sanderson)